Longford Castle

The Treasures and the Collectors

Longford Castle

The Treasures and the Collectors

Amelia Smith

with a Foreword by Sir Nicholas Penny

UNICORN

Published in 2017 by

Unicorn, an imprint of Unicorn Publishing Group LLP

101 Wardour Street

London

WIF OUG

www.unicornpublishing.org

ISBN 978-1-910787-68-7

10 9 8 7 6 5 4 3 2 1

Designed by Libanus Press, Marlborough

Edited by Elisabeth Ingles

Printed in Slovenia for Latitude Press Ltd

Note: the archaic spelling of original documents has been retained throughout.

Page 1: *Neptune in his Boat*, carving above the front door of Longford Castle, 2016

Frontispiece: Hans Holbein the Younger (1497–1543), *Erasmus*, 1523 (detail of fig. 38)

Contents

Foreword

SIR NICHOLAS PENNY
Director of the National Gallery 2008–2015

During the first half-century of the National Gallery's existence, following its foundation in 1824, its trustees and directors sought to increase the range and improve the quality of its holdings largely by acquiring Old Master paintings from Continental Europe. The Gallery showed, by contrast, little regard for what was available in Britain, whether in the palatial London houses of the nobility or in country seats. Then, suddenly, from the 1880s buying major works abroad became more difficult and, simultaneously, the contents of Hamilton Palace, a large portion of the collection at Blenheim and a group of masterpieces from Longford Castle came on the market or were offered for sale by private treaty. Thereafter, for over a century, the Gallery's officials regarded the contents of great family collections with a sort of embarrassed rapacity, whilst also hoping that the sales abroad and the demolition of great houses would cease.

The partnership between the National Gallery and Longford Castle forged six years ago marks a change of attitude and represents a broadening of vision and responsibility. The Gallery undertook to help organise and promote the public access that is a precondition for the enlightened legislation enabling Longford to retain its fine collection. Great paintings from Longford – acquisitions made over more than a century including Holbein's *The Ambassadors* bought in 1890 and Poussin's *The Adoration of the Golden Calf* purchased in 1945, along with loans agreed more recently – may be seen on the Gallery's walls at Trafalgar Square, but still more great paintings also remain *in situ* at Longford itself. There they continue to be displayed in the company of splendid furniture and sculpture, and against rich textiles, near Chinese lacquer and porcelain, in a family house with a formal garden and extensive parkland visible through the windows – which is of course how the Earls of Radnor, who built this collection, hoped that the paintings would be admired.

Longford Castle has for more than two hundred and fifty years been home to one of the nation's greatest collections but its history had never been fully studied before Amelia Smith applied herself to doing so. That her research should be so speedily converted into a book is greatly to her credit and that of Lord and Lady Radnor, who have encouraged her work from the start. They have also made possible the conservation and the public consultation of their family papers, through transferring the Longford archives into the care of the Wiltshire and Swindon History Centre.

At the same moment the libraries and archives of the National Gallery, which had previously been considered primarily as an internal resource, became a centre for international scholarship in art history. One facet of this new emphasis on research has been the welcoming of post-graduate students – some of whom are co-supervised from within the Gallery. Research into the history of collections and the art market has been especially encouraged. And so it has come about that, at the same time as more members of the public have visited Longford, more has been discovered about the collection housed there.

A retired Director is able to disregard the conventions discouraging the naming of colleagues. The partnership with Longford and the research into the history of its collections owes much to the remarkable energy, efficiency and enthusiasm of Kate Howe and Susanna Avery-Quash. But they would agree that this preface must conclude by congratulating Lord and Lady Radnor on their determination and imagination, divided equally between care for the past and concern for the future.

Introduction

This is a book about a house and a home and about those who have lived in it for over four centuries; a book about how the house has been beautified, filled with the most exceptional furniture and objects, with a collection of paintings of supreme importance, several of which need little introduction.

The origin of Longford Castle, in the reign of Elizabeth I, would be hard to invent: it was built with the proceeds from the contents of one of the Duke of Medina-Sidonia's galleons which sank in the wake of the Spanish Armada, the rights to which treasure were granted by the Queen herself. There is good reason why Neptune in his boat is carved in stone above the front door of Longford.

Longford Castle is no ordinary house; it is an extraordinary building. It may not be as familiar as some of this country's great houses, but it has fascinated many over the centuries. It was meant to be the inspiration for 'the Castle of Amphialus' when Philip Sidney was writing *Arcadia* at Wilton House nearby. It has also been cited as one of the influences for the triangular design of Catherine the Great's Chesme Palace just outside St Petersburg, originally called the Frog Palace as it was built on a marsh full of frogs. Longford appears on an item of the famous frog service made for Catherine the Great by Wedgwood. In more recent times Longford was converted into the Royal Palace of Genovia in Disney's *The Princess Diaries*, much to the occupants' surprise as it was filmed from the air for the closing scenes.

Over those four centuries Longford has survived siege, intended demolition, abandonment and fire. In the First World War it was a hospital and in the Second it was taken over by the army. All these events have left their mark and have contributed to the building's mutation into the complex, magnificent structure it is today.

Three families have lived in Longford in just over four centuries: the Gorges, the Coleraines, and for three of them my family, the Bouveries. I will not steal the author's thunder by illuminating the occupants in too much detail here or revisiting the work of other publications that outline our early family history.

My father's book *A Huguenot Family* outlines the family history from when Laurens des Bouverie (1536–1610) landed in this country to escape religious persecution, to the purchase of Longford Castle by Edward des Bouverie from Lord Coleraine in 1717. It ends with the death of the 4th Earl of Radnor in 1889.

Helen Matilda Radnor, the wife of the 5th Earl, not only catalogued the pictures in two volumes with William Barclay Squire, but in later life also published her memoirs, *From a Great Grandmother's Armchair*. She had her own all-female chamber orchestra and the composer Hubert Parry wrote the *Radnor Suite* for her. It is fitting that the present volume's author finishes her book with this formidable woman, leaving me to summarise the history from the twentieth century onwards.

Longford's greatest acquisitions in terms of pictures include Holbein's *Ambassadors*, his portrait of *Erasmus*, the portrait of *Aegidius* by Quentin Matsys, *Juan de Pareja* by Diego Velázquez, *Sea Coast with the Landing of Aeneas in Latium* (*Morning*) and *Pastoral Landscape with the Arch of Titus* (*Evening*) by Claude Lorraine, Poussin's *Adoration of the Golden Calf* and *Crossing of the Red Sea*, Sebastiano del Piombo's *Portrait of a Lady*, and Jan de Beer's *Virgin and Child with Saints*, some of which have departed, and some of which remain. The observant will notice that five of these pictures are in the National Gallery, two by acquisition (*The Ambassadors* and *The Adoration of the Golden Calf*), and three on loan from the Longford Collection (*Erasmus*, the Sebastiano del Piombo and the Jan de Beer). The details of the disposals can be gleaned from *The National Gallery, a Short History* by Charles Saumarez Smith.

Following the death of my father, the 8th Earl of Radnor, Longford entered into a unique arrangement with the National Gallery whereby the house is opened to art lovers on selected days during the spring, summer and autumn. It also seems fitting that *Erasmus* is now reunited with *The Ambassadors*, so that they sit comfortably with each other once again. Visitors to

Longford on National Gallery tours each receive a copy of Sir Nicholas Penny's excellent pocket *Guide to Longford Castle,* which encapsulates the house and its collections in a nutshell.

The pictures mentioned above appear in publications too numerous to mention, but other artists at Longford include Frans Hals, Avercamp, Jan Brueghel, Van Dyck and Rubens, and there are sixteen family portraits by Gainsborough and Reynolds, which makes comparison between these two great rivals almost inevitable.

The furniture in Longford is almost as notable as the pictures. It is mostly English, of the eighteenth century, with a number of the great cabinet-makers represented. A glance through *The Dictionary of English Furniture* by MacQuoid and Edwards, or *The History of English Furniture* by MacQuoid, will yield many examples of the pieces at Longford.

The collection is bound together by many other beautiful objects: sculpture, tapestries and porcelain in profusion. Now that National Gallery tours are well established it seemed an opportune time to bring out a book that will encompass Longford, its history, its collections and collectors, which have all made it the home it is today.

In addition, following the death of my father all family archives remaining at Longford were moved to the Wiltshire and Swindon History Centre in Chippenham, where they have been painstakingly catalogued, making detailed research very much easier. Previously these archives sat in a hundred or so metal boxes in the Muniment Room in Longford, making any significant publication a daunting prospect.

I hope that this book will provide an intriguing insight into the house, my family, and the treasures they accumulated over several generations, while at the same time marking the tercentenary of Bouverie residence.

WILLIAM PLEYDELL-BOUVERIE, 9TH EARL OF RADNOR

INTRODUCTION

CHAPTER I

Early History of Longford Castle and the Bouverie Family

> Therefore keep yoe Mansion=House as if itt were Garrison'd . . . see that the Coast
> bee cleare about itt: that ye Enemy seize nott on the Outworks of your Lands while
> you are busy within doors contriveing to Line yoe Walls with gold or Tapistry . . .[1]

Longford Castle is an unusual and beautiful country house, home to a multitude of historic treasures in the form of fine furnishings and works of art, and it is also a remarkable survival. Just after the Civil War, the first history of Longford was written. The author, the Reverend H. Pelate (dates unknown), chaplain to the Coleraine family who occupied the castle at the time, gave those words of advice. They hint at Longford's dramatic early history, to be explored in this chapter, and are prescient in advocating that the owners of this 'Mansion=House' defend and conserve, as well as adorn it.

As this book will show, Longford has changed significantly over the course of its four-hundred-year history. The interior and exterior architecture that we see today bears traces of changes made in the Georgian and Victorian ages, yet the preservation of the castle's quint-essentially Elizabethan character and spirit is testament to its successive owners' abilities to look both outward and inward, to the past and to the future, and to simultaneously preserve and improve this greatest of heirlooms for posterity.

Longford Castle has been owned by three families: first, the Gorges, from the time of its creation until 1641; secondly, the Coleraines, until 1717; and thirdly, the Bouveries (ennobled during the eighteenth century to become the Earls of Radnor), in whose ownership it remains to this day. Longford Castle was built by Sir Thomas Gorges (1536–1610) to replace an earlier manor house on a site previously occupied by a variety of 'Lords of Longford or Langford', from families including the de Langfords and the Cervingtons.[2] It is located close to the River Avon, on an estate three miles from the historic city of Salisbury, and represents one of many 'new' houses constructed in the Elizabethan era of prosperity, along with its Wiltshire neighbours Wilton House and Longleat House.[3] It is believed to have been completed in 1591, as this date appears in the fabric of the building.

What immediately set Longford apart from its contemporaries, however, was its distinctive and unusual triangular shape. The castle originally comprised three circular towers, connected by three long apartments enclosing a central triangular courtyard. Although it was not uncommon for Elizabethan houses to be built as devices, their form imbued with symbolic significance, triangular houses were rarely seen at the time. The Gorges also built a three-sided hunting lodge, New House at Redlynch, again in Wiltshire, but this was Y-shaped; and the only other Elizabethan house built to the same triangular configuration as Longford was Rushton Lodge, Northamptonshire, for Sir Thomas Tresham (1543–1605).[4] Rushton was not a grand house, however, but a small folly, built for Tresham's warrener between 1593 and 1597.[5] As it postdates Longford's completion, and because Tresham may himself have been aware of Longford's design, through a family connection with the Gorges,[6] Longford may therefore have been the first triangular house built in the country.

Because of their shape, both Longford Castle and Rushton Lodge have been interpreted as symbols of the Holy Trinity. The earliest evidence we have for this takes the form of a series of architectural drawings, associated with the builder John Thorpe (*fl.* 1570–1610) and said to represent Longford. The drawings label the three round towers respectively as *Pater*, *Filius* and *Spiritus* ('Father', 'Son' and 'Holy Spirit'), and the centre point as *Deus* ('God').[7] Rushton also contains numerous references to the number '3', as a playful take on Tresham's name, and evincing his interest in symbolism: he also built the cross-shaped Lyveden New Bield in Northamptonshire.[8]

The inspiration for Longford's design has been variously linked to German, Flemish and Scandinavian precedents, some of which may have been known to Sir Thomas and his wife, Helena Snakenberg, Marchioness of Northampton (1548/9–1635), who was of Swedish descent.[9] For instance, Longford has been linked to Gripsholm Castle in Sweden, a structure that likewise bears circular towers at its corners.[10] Longford has also been associated with Wewelsburg Castle in Germany, and two eighteenth-century engravings of this building are to be found within the Longford archive.[11] Further, scholars have debated whether the castle of Uraniborg in Denmark, established by the nobleman Tycho Brahe (1546–1601) as an astronomical observatory, acted as architectural inspiration for Sir Thomas's project.[12]

If some continental influences were at play in Longford's design, they were, however, tempered by the retention of a distinctly English and local flavour. A glance at the fabric of the building reveals hints as to its Wiltshire location. It is formed of Chilmark stone, a form of limestone quarried in the county. The round towers comprise alternating pieces of Chilmark stone and flint, a design typical of the region.[13] We can gain an insight into the late sixteenth-century appearance of the north-west entrance front of the castle from an early drawing made of Longford (fig. 7). The artist appears to have begun to draw in the alternating pattern of stone and flint on the right-hand round tower, but has left this depiction incomplete. Today, one can appreciate the building's slightly weathered fabric, the patina of age heightening the charm of its historic associations (fig. 8).

This stylistic melange of the continental and the local is matched by the way in which the castle's design incorporates references to both the classical past and the chivalric medieval

Longford House near Sarum
Built by the Lord Gorges

Fig. 7 English school, *Longford Castle*, late sixteenth century, pen and brown ink on paper, 31.1 x 39.4 cm, Longford Castle

Overleaf: Fig. 8 Entrance Front of Longford Castle, 2016

tradition: as Nicholas Penny has noted, the double loggia on the entrance front, a style reminiscent of Renaissance Italian architecture, may be one of the first seen in England.[14] Neoclassicism in architecture was, of course, to grow immensely in popularity in Britain over the course of the following two centuries. The amalgamation of styles visible on Longford's entrance front at the time of its creation thus speaks of a pattern that – as we will see – recurs throughout its history: the successful negotiation of tradition and fashion.

Longford's unique architectural origins are not the only interesting aspect of its early history. It apparently played host to some of the most important historical figures of the sixteenth and seventeenth centuries, including Queen Elizabeth I (1533–1603), to whom the Gorges were courtiers. In a late seventeenth-century poem about the castle, its then occupant,

EARLY HISTORY OF LONGFORD CASTLE AND THE BOUVERIE FAMILY

Henry Hare, 2nd Baron Coleraine (1636–1708), described the 'best' bedchambers, 'where the two happiest Queens, wch ere did reign, The first & second Elizabeth have lay'n'.[15] The other queen referred to here is Queen Elizabeth of Bohemia (1596–1662), daughter of King James I and VI (1566–1625).

These illustrious historical links have helped in the construction of a romantic history of Longford. For instance, eighteenth- and nineteenth-century accounts of Longford and guide-books to the region capitalised particularly upon the connection with Queen Elizabeth I when promoting the castle to their readership. In 1809, the antiquarian John Britton (1771–1857) relayed in the second volume of his publication *The Architectural Antiquities of Great Britain* how 'it is traditionally said that the Queen occasionally resided here [at Longford] ... one apartment is still called the *Queen's Bed-chamber*'.[16] Royal and historical links were known for helping to draw visitors to castles,[17] and the thought that such an important figure in British history was once entertained at the castle continues to contribute to its romantic appeal.

A portrait at Longford of Queen Elizabeth I by the circle of Marcus Gheeraerts the Younger (*c.* 1561/2–1636) provides a visual reminder of this important historical association (fig. 9). When Helen Matilda Chaplin, Countess of Radnor (1846–1928), catalogued the painting in the early twentieth century, it was described as having been 'painted late in life'.[18] Queen Elizabeth famously exercised a large degree of control over her likenesses, relying upon the repetition of sanctioned face patterns to ensure she was depicted in a flattering light.[19] Although the artist has included some indications of the passage of time, such as lines surrounding the sitter's eyes, this painting nonetheless chimes stylistically with many other portraits of the Queen. The pearls hung around her neck and ornamenting her hair, dress and ears, and the contrasting use of black and white in the dress and ruff, were motifs frequently seen in her portraits, and understood as symbols of the Queen's virginity.[20] Although it is uncertain when this painting arrived at Longford, or who acquired it, it is known to have been at the castle since at least 1814, when an inventory of the pictures was made.[21] Today, it hangs, most appropriately, in the Green Velvet Drawing Room, the room once known as the 'Queen's Parlour',[22] along-side other works of art and furnishings that speak to this important period in Longford's history, and which will be explored later in this book.

To return to its moment of inception, however, it is important to recognise how, in its plan, Longford Castle also contained some elements that were conventional for English country houses of the time. For instance, it featured a first-floor long gallery, running the length of one of the sides of the triangular structure. This type of room commonly featured in Elizabethan houses, and can be seen at houses such as Hardwick Hall in Derbyshire, Montacute House in Somerset and Parham House in Sussex. Long galleries were originally intended to house portraits of family members and royal and aristocratic connections, to advertise their owners' status, and thus the proportions of these rooms were usually such that a single row of full-length portraits could easily be accommodated; long galleries were also used

recreationally, their length enabling occupants to use them for taking exercise during bad weather.[23]

Although the long gallery at Longford has since been extensively refurbished – a topic to be explored in the following chapter – an insight into the appearance and use of this room in the late seventeenth century can be gained from the aforementioned poem written by the 2nd Lord Coleraine. He described 'a wainscoted <u>long Gallery</u>' containing 'Some noble Ancestors; Relations; ffriends In Picture: frustrating Death's Envious Ends'. This whimsical account shows how this room was decorated in line with the long gallery tradition, containing portraits displayed for posterity, which would have reminded the occupants of their ancestors and past connections. Moreover, the poem also reveals to us how the room functioned as a space for leisurely pursuits: the 2nd Lord Coleraine described how games of 'Billiard, Bowles, or Shittle-cock' were played 'Even in worst seasons'.

The written accounts of Longford that survive from the late seventeenth century, such

EARLY HISTORY OF LONGFORD CASTLE AND THE BOUVERIE FAMILY

as this poem and the aforementioned history by Reverend Pelate, record the state of the castle after one of the most challenging periods in its history. Sir Thomas's grandson, Richard, 2nd Baron Gorges (c. 1619–1712), had been obliged to sell the estate in 1641 to pay debts: it then passed into the hands of Hugh Hare, 1st Baron Coleraine (1606–1667), who was a friend of King Charles I (1600–1649).[24] Shortly thereafter, during the Civil War, the building was garrisoned.[25] However, on 17 October 1645, Oliver Cromwell (1599–1658) wrote a letter from Salisbury to the Speaker of the House of Commons, wherein it was ordered that 'the said Commanders in chief of the said Garrison shall surrender the said House and Garrison to the said Lieut. General *Cromwell*'.[26]

Longford might have borne witness to a pivotal moment in history, had an assassination attempt upon Cromwell from one of the first-floor windows of the castle been successful. According to the story passed down by Longford's occupants, the fatal shot hit the person standing next to Cromwell, rather than its intended target. A portrait of Cromwell hangs at Longford Castle today near the window from which this shot was supposedly fired, in the first-floor Chapel Lobby, reminding all who visit the castle of this important moment in its history (fig. 10). This small three-quarter-length portrait, showing Cromwell dressed in armour, was acquired in 1793 for £7 7s,[27] and is most likely to have been purchased for its historical significance for Longford's owners. Eventually, and most fortunately, the house was not sacked, as a friend of the 1st Lord Coleraine, who happened to be a Cromwellian, intervened to prevent it.[28]

It appears that Longford's fabric still suffered a great deal during the strife of the Civil War, however. Reverend Pelate described 'the rage of a civill war wherein shee was twice garrisond & ransackt & layd open to ye weather, without a glass window left', and flattered his patron, the 2nd Lord Coleraine, by recounting with high praise the extent to which the latter had restored the building. The picture we can construct of Longford at this date is enhanced by the fact that Reverend Pelate's laudatory written account of it is matched by a series of drawings of its exterior and its grounds and gardens, which were executed contemporaneously.

The topographical artist Robert Thacker (dates unknown) created these drawings, of which there are eleven in total. When Reverend Pelate wrote a dedication for his history, he noted that he hoped his 'designe will bee answerd & comended by the Care & art of the Ingraver & Delineator', with the name 'Mr Thacker' appearing alongside others in the margin. This suggests that the two projects were undertaken at the same time, most probably at the behest of the Coleraines, to provide a comprehensive visual and written record of Longford following its restoration.

Within the drawings, the castle's surroundings are carefully delineated, showing a formal arrangement of paths, walls and beds, and their great detail rewards close scrutiny. They reveal how Longford was at this time surrounded by formal gardens and a moat, and one of the illustrations, an engraving of which is reproduced here, shows a rectangular 'Stewpond neare the close-Arbour Walk, by the River-side' (fig. 11). Geometric expanses of water were popular

garden features at the time, thanks to French influences upon garden design following the Restoration.[29] Longford's gardens would, therefore, have been considered highly fashionable at this period.

Reverend Pelate described how the 2nd Lord Coleraine had 'rebuilt most of the garden walls'; 'new modelled' the parterre; and 'with greate Cost first chalkd & then gravelled the walks', in order to improve Longford for the future: 'as the profit thereof will advance to the next age by his Lordshipps indefatigable care'. However, these designs were not long maintained: during the eighteenth century, as we will see, the Bouverie family instead pursued a simplified and more informal aesthetic in the gardens, in line with later gardening trends.

An engraving of the drawing of *A View of Longford Castle att an Angle* (fig. 12) enables us to appreciate the triangular form of the castle at this point in its history. The pattern of

Fig. 11 Nicholas Yeates
(*fl.* 1669–1686) after Robert
Thacker (dates unknown),
*A View about Longford Stewpond
neare the close-Arbour Walk, by
the River-side*, late seventeenth
century, engraving,
sheet 40.0 x 58.4 cm,
Longford Castle

Chilmark stone and flint is clearly visible in the depictions of the round towers. This drawing is also notable for the fact that it is populated with two small figures: one approaching the entrance front of the castle apparently followed by a dog, the other standing in the formal garden. Fascinatingly, the artist has 'cut away' the brick walls that divide these sections of the garden, to enable the viewer adequately to comprehend the entirety of the garden design, and also to discern these figures within the composition.[30]

This, and other images in the series also featuring various small figures occupying the grounds surrounding the castle, suggest a degree of openness towards a wider community on the part of the Coleraine family. Anne Laurence has noted that many late seventeenth-century and early eighteenth-century topographical paintings portrayed 'people riding by on the road, approaching and leaving the house and passing traffic, showing how the world of the country house was not enclosed'.[31] Thacker's drawings echo that trend, by representing Longford's gardens as a space in active use by a range of people. This insight is corroborated by Reverend Pelate, who stated in his dedication to the 2nd Lord Coleraine: 'I perceive yor Honr is nott so jealous of [Longford] as to shutt her up from the salutes of stranger On ye other hand you are so nobly free as to let all honest personages have leave to see her when they desire itt, & they as frequently admire as visit her.'

This passage suggests that the Coleraines' pride in Longford was manifested in a gracious sense of hospitality, and that Reverend Pelate deemed this an appropriate way to flatter his patron. These visual and textual descriptions suggest that Longford's owners wished to convey

Fig. 12 Nicholas Yeates
(*fl.* 1669–1686) after Robert
Thacker (dates unknown), *A View
of Longford House att an Angle*, late
seventeenth century, engraving,
sheet 38.1 x 58.4 cm,
Longford Castle

Prospectus angularis Ædium duo Latera comprehendens; una cum Viridariis, Longo-Vadensium.   *A View of Longford House att an Angle.*   8

to the wider world an image of the castle and its grounds as receptive to visitors and the wider community, in line with the tradition of rural hospitality at the country house. These precedents may have set in train a culture of country-house visiting that encouraged Longford's later owners to continue to open it up later in the eighteenth century. As we will see, the castle was to receive a number of tourists and visitors in the centuries that followed, a trend that continues to the present day.

Thacker's drawings were engraved and published around 1680 jointly by the printmakers Nicholas Yeates (*fl.* 1669–1686) and James Collins (*fl.* 1675–1717). According to the architectural historian John Harris, they are notable for possibly being one of the first engraved 'suite of views' made of a British country house, along with a series by Henry Winstanley (1644–1703) depicting Audley End House, a Jacobean building in Essex.[32] Although they would have been created only for limited circulation, the existence of these engravings might have served to heighten awareness of Longford among a select audience. Copies of the engravings appear, for example, in the collection of geographical and topographical maps, prints and drawings amassed by King George III (1738–1820), held at the British Library.[33]

The writer Daniel Defoe (1660–1731) was one early visitor to '*Langbro*' a fine seat of my Lord *Colerain*, which is very well kept'.[34] He visited as part of a tour of Britain, remarking of Wiltshire that it was a county 'full of memorable Branches of Antiquity',[35] of which Longford must have been one. Among other visitors during this period was Celia Fiennes (1662–1741), who travelled extensively around England in the late seventeenth and early eighteenth centuries. She took a particular interest in industrial innovations and modern architecture, but also visited a number of older country houses, including Burghley House in Lincolnshire and Longford's neighbour, Wilton House.[36]

Fiennes visited Longford when it was owned by the Coleraines, and remarked that it 'looks like a good Building of stone but its just so upon the great River [the Avon] that it looks like a little Castle or Shipp'.[37] Many early descriptions of Longford contained remarks upon its situation close to the River Avon, reflecting a general preoccupation among contemporaries regarding the position of great houses. For instance, Fiennes noted of Burghley House how 'the Scituation is the finest I ever saw on the side of a hill and severall rows of trees of severall acres above it quite to the Road, it stands in a very fine park'.[38]

Notably, Reverend Pelate also described Longford's position in naval terms, writing how 'in a flood [it] looks like a Ship att anchor in some good Harbour'. That both individuals remarked upon its ship-like quality next to the river attests to the particularly striking impression left by the castle's situation upon these early tourists. One can postulate that perhaps the relief carving depicting a boat on the entrance front of the castle inspired them. Alternatively, it may have been the case that Fiennes had access to Reverend Pelate's manuscript history on her visit, and was able to borrow the simile.

The castle's situation did not always meet with approbation in seventeenth-century accounts, however. Pelate attempted to 'obviate an Objection (if raised) why this Pile was stuck so farr into the River; & placed on the very brink of the Chanell . . . When (as about ye middle of ye High Crtyard pasture) there might have bin a farr more beautyfull & convenient Station for the Residence in respect of Aire, health, prospect & Ornament'. He concluded, however, that as 'the House is now up', it was necessary that 'the Fabrick bee maintaind & defended' where it was. He went on to discuss at length the saying 'Status Non Situs' – taken to mean the superiority of the castle's condition relative to its situation – which was at the time carved 'in golden Capitalls' above the entrance. In the eighteenth century, as we will see, Longford's riverside position was considered worthy of greater exposure and celebration, and today, the sight of the River Avon flowing past the restored formal gardens is particularly scenic. Yet, in the seventeenth century, Longford's owners and occupants clearly felt the need to forestall criticism of its position.

It is notable that, unlike many tourists who visited Longford in the eighteenth century, neither Defoe nor Fiennes described its interiors or contents at length. This may reflect the fact that, at this stage, Longford was not furnished and filled with important works of art to nearly the same extent as it would later be under Bouverie ownership, when the collection was continuously growing. Moreover, Defoe's account revealingly noted that the Coleraine family 'it seems is not much in this Country, having another Estate, and Dwelling at *Tottenam-High-Cross* near *London*'.[39] This refers to the family's other residence, Bruce Castle, in Totteridge, Hertfordshire, and provides a reminder that aristocrats would often divide their time

between different houses and estates, some of which may have been more important to them than others.

The final member of the Coleraine family to own Longford was Henry Hare, 3rd Baron Coleraine (1693–1749). As Helen Matilda recounted, his preference for Bruce Castle, and his need to release money, led him to attain 'an Act of Parliament to allow him to break the entail and sell Longford'.[40] It was in 1717 that the estate was sold, coming into the possession of Sir Edward des Bouverie (*c.* 1690–1736). Three hundred years later, his descendants occupy the castle today.

The Bouveries' history saw a family of descendants of a Huguenot refugee, Laurens des Bouverie (1536–1610) (fig. 13), active in business and overseas trade, become aristocratic land-owners, politicians and philanthropists over the course of a century. In the late sixteenth century, Laurens, like many other Huguenots (members of the French Protestant church), fled Catholic persecution in what was then the Spanish Netherlands. He arrived in Frankfurt, where he learnt silk-making, before eventually bringing his trade to England, settling in Kent and, later, the City of London.[41] His descendants made a considerable fortune in the seventeenth

century working for the Levant Company, capitalising upon its most profitable period of trade with Turkey, before turning to landownership and residency in England.[42]

In 1707 the family's estate was valued at £122,667 1s 6d; in 1713 Sir William des Bouverie (1656–1717) was knighted by Queen Anne (1665–1714) and, a year later, made a baronet.[43] The patent of baronetcy is preserved in the Longford archive.[44] Sir Edward (fig. 14) was the last of the family to live and work abroad, and was granted a licence by Queen Anne – also kept in the Longford archive – to return through France to England in 1713,[45] after which he settled in what was to become the family's permanent country of residence.

The Bouverie family's transition to noble status in England is exemplified not only by these royal favours, but also by the way in which, from 1680 onwards, they began to invest in property, as opposed to relying upon overseas trade for income. Land was, of course, not only valued for being a secure form of income,[46] but as a visible and traditional status symbol. The Bouveries acquired land through purchase, lease and inheritance, predominantly in the south-west of England, and often for farming purposes.[47] Sir Edward's purchase of Longford Castle, however, was arguably the most significant property acquisition, as it was to become the main family seat for the Bouveries over the following three centuries. The somewhat unlikely yet romantic story passed down by the family over generations is that he arrived at Longford on horseback, carrying in his saddlebags the coins with which he paid for the castle.[48]

The eighteenth century was a particularly important period in the establishment of the Bouveries' aristocratic status. It saw their name anglicised from des Bouverie to Bouverie, and two ennoblements elevating the heads of the family first to the status of viscount, in 1747, and subsequently to that of earl, in 1765. As well as integrating themselves into English aristocratic society, the family continued to nurture links with the Huguenot community over the following centuries.

It is worth considering how far the family's trajectory during this period should be deemed one of 'assimilation' into the English aristocracy. One could argue that, to an extent, the Bouverie family's business acumen placed them in a strong position from which to gain social prominence in the ever-changing social arena of eighteenth-century Britain. During this time, established landed families themselves had to adapt to the country's new commercial character, demonstrating that 'assimilation' was a two-way process.[49] For instance, many adopted the practice of keeping accounts, previously associated with the middling classes, particularly as their estates had themselves to be run as trading enterprises and required 'good stewardship'.[50] Given the preservation of meticulous accounts relating to eighteenth-century expenditure at Longford Castle, one might argue that the Bouverie family – either intentionally or subconsciously – used their commercial background to advantage in this respect, appropriating the customs they had learnt through trade to ensure their continued success in this new landed context.

Given the family's mercantile background, Sir Edward's decision to purchase Longford Castle, an established Elizabethan country house ninety miles from London, is intriguing. The merchant elites of the eighteenth century often inhabited villas near the capital and their place of work, which were seen as 'welcome retreats and worthwhile investments', as opposed to 'far-flung country estates of the aristocratic type'.[51] Although they also owned a number of other properties throughout this period, as will be alluded to later in this book, Longford was generally considered the family's main seat. This demonstrates the Bouveries' commitment to aristocratic, rather than mercantile, patterns of property ownership.

In addition, it is notable that many individuals who had made their money in trade chose to build anew or completely remodel an older house, empowered by their financial and social circumstances to make a decisive break with the past, and a great many new country houses were built in the neo-Palladian style during the Georgian period.[52] For example, the Whig Prime Minister Sir Robert Walpole (1676–1745), who was made 1st Earl of Orford towards the end of his life, remodelled the red brick house he had inherited at Houghton, Norfolk, in that style.[53] Similarly, in the early eighteenth century, Richard Child, 1st Earl Tylney (1680–1750), built a grand neo-Palladian house at Wanstead, Essex, just a few miles from the City of London:

a building that was to become an architectural blueprint for much eighteenth-century house-building.[54] Child, whose wealth stemmed from the East India trade, was ennobled twice during his lifetime, and thus provides a parallel with the Bouverie family's transition from mercantile to aristocratic status. His decision to build a new house from scratch, in the most fashionable architectural style of the day, contrasts with the Bouveries' acquisition of an unusual sixteenth-century castle.

Attitudes towards Elizabethan and Jacobean architecture in the early eighteenth century were not entirely favourable. It appears that buildings of this period were generally eschewed in favour of newly built houses in the neoclassical style. The architectural writer and country-house historian Mark Girouard argued that, despite interest on the part of some individuals later in the eighteenth century, older houses did not generally attract 'much enthusiasm'.[55] Manor houses, for example, were not seen to be in line with the increasing sophistication of Georgian tastes.[56] Moreover, this lack of interest may be accounted for by the somewhat chequered history of certain older buildings, which had sadly endured the destructive effects of the Civil War: the historian Peter Mandler has accounted for the 'desertion' of ancestral castles during the early eighteenth century as the result of the damage they had incurred during seventeenth-century 'domestic strife'.[57] As we have seen, Longford's fabric and surroundings underwent a certain amount of damage during the Civil War, but had subsequently been amply and ably restored by the 2nd Lord Coleraine. Yet, in the years immediately preceding Sir Edward's purchase of the castle, it had been left uninhabited, while the 3rd Lord Coleraine resided instead at Bruce Castle, and it has been suggested that Longford was 'in a rather derelict condition' by 1717.[58]

How, then, to account for Sir Edward's decision to purchase Longford Castle, rather than to build anew in an up-to-date style? The choice may have been motivated by personal whim, and the castle's unique form and romantic history may have exerted a pull upon him, as they have done for many subsequent visitors. The castle may have held a personal resonance for him, as it was built at the same time as his ancestor, Laurens, had migrated to England. Living in a house with an Elizabethan heritage could have helped to communicate and consolidate the family's own sense of lineage and Englishness, which dated back to this time. The choice to reside in a late sixteenth-century castle enabled Sir Edward to associate himself and his family with the Elizabethan era, with the result that they appeared established and engrained members of the English nobility. Longford, which evoked an English golden age, but which was nevertheless a melange of various continental and vernacular styles, arguably acted as a vehicle through which the Bouveries could express their own sense of identity.

It is notable that Sir Edward's two successors – Sir Jacob Bouverie, 1st Viscount Folkestone (1694–1761), and William Bouverie, 1st Earl of Radnor (1725–1776) – more or less retained Longford's architectural fabric in the state in which they inherited it, undertaking some improvements but not altering its basic structure, triangular form or Elizabethan character. It therefore seems that Longford's heritage was always a part of its appeal for generations of the Bouveries. The family nonetheless simultaneously subscribed to fashionable contemporary taste, but predominantly through their redecoration of the castle's interiors, and their patronage of the best artists of the day, as the following chapters will show.

Sir Edward did make some changes at Longford upon his acquisition of the castle, however, perhaps in response to the neglect it had lately received, or to stamp his own mark upon his new home. A plan of the castle made in 1766, and later included in the fifth volume of the architectural publication *Vitruvius Britannicus*, stated that the castle had been 'repaired and altered' in 1718.[59] One of the changes was the removal of the motto 'Status non Situs', discussed earlier (page 26), from the castle's exterior: perhaps Sir Edward did not share the Coleraines' compulsion to justify or excuse the castle's riverside position. Alternatively, he may have wished to strip away signs of its previous period of ownership, which were not, after all, original to the building.

Sir Edward also made some amendments to the interior architecture of the castle, suggesting a desire to modernise his new home, and to make it a more easily habitable and comfortable space. For example, the chapel had previously been located on the ground floor, and Sir Edward decided instead to turn this ground-floor space into a parlour, and use one of the first-floor round tower rooms for religious observance.[60] Today, this tower room is still known as the Chapel Room. It is a particularly fascinating space because of its unusual ceiling (fig. 15). It features a large hanging pendant, believed to date from 1591, which Girouard has described as 'much the most striking Elizabethan vault to survive'.[61] The 2nd Lord Coleraine mentioned this room in his poem about Longford, noting how the 'ten polish't columns hold up Rooff & all' and the 'pendant centre . . . Which for this hundred years uncrack't hangs down'.

One important change made to Longford's interior architecture during the early to mid-eighteenth century was the transformation of the entrance hall into a two-storey space. Although the space has since been reconfigured, the evidence for this arrangement comes from plans of the ground and first floors of the castle drawn up in 1766. Helen Matilda stated that it was Sir Edward who was responsible for this alteration, which she deemed 'quite out of keeping with the style of the building'.[62] The one-time existence of a two-storey entrance hall at Longford is interesting, however, as it suggests a desire on the part of its early Bouverie owners to experiment with the accommodation of the architectural fashions of the day within the boundaries of the Elizabethan structure – even if the result was judged by later generations to have been an unsuccessful blend of styles.

The design may indicate the influence of nearby Wilton House, with its famous Double Cube Room. Double-height spaces were fashionable within neo-Palladian interiors, and John Cornforth has noted the particular prevalence of double-height entrance halls in country-house architecture during the 1720s and 1730s.[63] He saw this trend as a response to the Italian architectural theory held in high esteem at the time, but as also bound up with the traditional English

notion of the great hall, symbolic of a landed family's hospitality.[64] In this light, the decision to create a new two-storey entrance hall at Longford may be seen as an attempt to unify new stylistic fashions with older country-house traditions.

It was not until Sir Jacob inherited Longford from his brother in 1737 that the majority of the redecoration and refurbishment of its interiors was undertaken, and the family began to collect art on a large scale. However, the Longford archive does reveal some insights into works of art and furniture acquired by Sir Edward. Fascinatingly, it appears that some highly significant paintings were bought along with the castle itself, in 1717. Documents pertaining to the purchase of the castle from the 3rd Lord Coleraine and Elizabeth, Dowager Baroness Coleraine (dates unknown), indicate that some pictures, among other contents, formed part of the sale:

> The said Elizabeth Baroness Dowager of Colerane Hath bargained & sold & by those presents Doth fully & absolutely bargain & sell assign transfer and set over unto the sd. Sir Edward Des Bouverie all and singular the Goods Chattells Household Stuff Pictures Utensils Implements . . . & Things which do belong & appertain unto & which are now remaining and being in or about the sd. Capitall mess or Tenemt. Of Langford . . .

This account suggests that parts of the Longford art collection were, to an extent, 'ready-made'. This acquisition method was arguably more akin to inheritance, evoking the passing on of a house with its art collection intact that would ideally occur when an incumbent died. We cannot be certain of the precise identity of the pictures included in the sale, as they are not detailed, but it has been suggested that portraits by the seventeenth-century master Sir Anthony Van Dyck (1599–1641) and the leading portrait painter Sir Godfrey Kneller (1646–1723) were among them.

In the early twentieth-century catalogue to the art collection, Helen Matilda suggested that Kneller's portrait of the Honourable Hugh Hare (1668–1707) was acquired in this way (fig. 16).[65] Hugh Hare was the son of the 2nd Lord Colcraine, but died before his father, which meant that it was Hugh's son who became the 3rd Lord Coleraine.[66] It is uncertain why the 3rd Lord Coleraine would have wished to part with a portrait of his father when he sold Longford, but he may, of course, have owned further likenesses.

Kneller's painting is a full-length portrait, executed in 1685, according to an inscription on the lower left-hand side of the canvas. It shows the sitter wearing a grey coat with lace cuffs and a brown mantle, leaning against a piece of sculpture with a view to a landscape beyond, accompanied by drapery. J. Douglas Stewart discussed the painting in his 1983 book *Sir Godfrey Kneller and the English Baroque Portrait*, when it was on loan to the Ministry of Works (now the Government Art Collection) and displayed at Lancaster House, London.[67] The author described how, within the portrait, the artist had achieved a 'total effect . . . of quiet, unassuming

Fig. 16 Sir Godfrey Kneller
(1646–1723), *The Honourable Hugh
Hare*, c. 1685, oil on canvas,
241.3 x 152.4 cm, Longford Castle

grandeur', prefiguring Kneller's portraits of the late 1680s wherein 'power and slightly aggressive swagger tend to be replaced by grace and ease'.[68] A small oil painting on paper by Kneller of Hugh Hare, in the Scottish National Portrait Gallery, corresponds almost exactly with the Longford portrait,[69] and may have been made as a preparatory sketch by the artist before he began work on the final canvas. As this portrait recalls a period in Longford's own history, it helped to lend a sense of continuity to the art collection during the early days of Bouverie ownership.

It has been suggested that three other paintings were included in the 1717 sale of the castle and its contents. They are portraits of King Charles I and his Queen Consort, Henrietta Maria (1609–1669) (fig. 17), and of Gaston, Duke of Orléans (1608–1660) (fig. 18), all by Van Dyck.[70] Although the former is no longer at Longford, the latter two are among a number of examples of Van Dyck's work at the castle today. The portraits of Charles I and Henrietta Maria may have been given personally to the 1st Lord Coleraine, as he was a friend of the King.[71] They were painted around 1632, and in 1633 the artist received an Exchequer warrant for payment for these and a number of other portraits of the royal couple.[72]

The painting of Queen Henrietta Maria shows the sitter against a relatively plain background, with some drapery to the left and a crown resting upon a table. The three-quarter-length depiction shows the Queen slightly inclined towards the viewer, cradling her right hand on top of her left, holding a rose. The rose may have been included to represent her third pregnancy.[73] The portrait is one of the first that Van Dyck painted of the Queen, and is considered less formal than many other representations the artist made of her: the pose has been deemed 'spontaneous', and the portrait is considered to have been painted for 'private consumption rather than an official and formal occasion'.[74]

If it was indeed the case that Sir Edward acquired the portraits of the royal couple along with the castle and the portrait of Hugh Hare, they would have helped to smooth the transition in ownership that took place when the castle was sold. Owning these historical portraits of royal and noble sitters would have evoked a sense of longstanding membership of the aristocratic classes, through the associations conferred by the paintings' subject matter and provenance. As discussed earlier (page 20), the long galleries of Elizabethan country houses were often decorated with portraits of illustrious connections. Although no evidence remains to suggest exactly where these portraits might have hung at Longford in the early eighteenth century, their presence at the castle would nonetheless have meant that its sale did not provide too visible a rupture in its history, and, significantly, would have provided the foundations for the art collection that was to be amassed over the following decades.

One of the first bespoke items of furniture commissioned in the eighteenth century for the Bouverie family was a bureau or study-table made by Robert Hodson (*fl.* 1712–1725) in 1724 for Sir Edward. Hodson was a cabinetmaker based in Soho, London, who worked for a number of aristocratic patrons in the early eighteenth century.[75] Although its intended location within

EARLY HISTORY OF LONGFORD CASTLE AND THE BOUVERIE FAMILY

the castle is unknown, we can gain an insight into the commission from a letter that survives in the archive, written by Hodson to Sir Edward:

> [The bureau] has been seen by several Curious Gentlemen that came to my Shop accidently and was always approvd of Extreamly well. I have made it pretty full of drawers because I thought your Honour would have Occasion for a great many Sorts of papers or Writings, and have made Extraordinary Locks also on that Account, with two Keys, one being a Master Key to go through all, and the other only to open fifteen drawers, which all lye on one side of the work, in Case you shoud have a mind, any one beside your self shou'd come at part of the Writings . . .[76]

As this letter shows, Hodson was concerned with his patron's privacy, and such a preoccupation was common amongst cabinetmakers of the time: for instance, many took pride in creating concealed drawers, or ensuring that compartments were lockable.[77] Many more pieces of bespoke furniture were later bought and commissioned for Longford, as we will see, and indeed the furnishings and decorative arts are on a par with the paintings and sculptures at the castle in terms of quality and significance.

Sir Edward's tenure at Longford ended in 1737. As he died childless, his brother, Sir Jacob, inherited the castle. On 8 February 1737, Sir Jacob recorded his 'Expences in a journey to Longford' in his account book,[78] signalling the beginning of a new era at the castle: one which would see the acquisition of many important contemporary and old master paintings, and the redecoration of a number of the interiors. The foundations laid by the castle's previous owners – the Gorges, the Coleraines and Sir Edward – were to be further embellished and ornamented, but signs of their heritage and history retained, respected and celebrated.

Sir Jacob had previously resided in rented houses, moving between London and Kent, and a pastoral ode written upon his and his wife's departure from Kent demonstrates the esteem in which they had been held there.[79] It also suggests Sir Jacob's landowning credentials, and prefigures the success of his tenure as incumbent and *paterfamilias* at Longford, the subject of the next chapter:

> Go tell Amyntas – All the Sheep
> Will soon be Scatter'd o'er the Down,
> None will the flocks So wary keep,
> Nor lead So steady, now He's gone . . . .
> Shepherd & Shepherdess, farewell;
> Know You no Grief, nor Shed one tear:
> You'll happy be, where-e'er you dwell,
> And make Arcadia ev'ry where.[80]

Fig. 19 View of Longford
Castle, entrance front, 2016

EARLY HISTORY OF LONGFORD CASTLE AND THE BOUVERIE FAMILY

CHAPTER 2

Jacob Bouverie, 1st Viscount Folkestone

> When any Body sees a fine House, admirably well contrived, wth. Sumptuous
> Apartments, & all manner of Conveniencys; He immediately admires the Beauty
> & Usefullness of the Building; but the first Question is, who built it, as
> He knows very well, there must have been some contriver of it.[1]

Sir Jacob Bouverie (1694–1761) was perhaps the most important patron and collector of art to reside at Longford Castle. Between 1737 and 1761, the period of his tenure, he remodelled the grounds and gardens, redecorated and furnished many of the castle's interiors, and bought a great many important and interesting works of art, firmly establishing the collection that his successors would add to. Some of Longford's greatest treasures were acquired by Sir Jacob, including two suites of fine eighteenth-century gilded and upholstered furniture, two important landscape paintings by the seventeenth-century French master Claude Lorraine or Lorrain (1600–1682) and three marble portrait busts of members of the Bouverie family by the famed eighteenth-century sculptor John Michael Rysbrack (1694–1770). The results of the works undertaken at the behest of Sir Jacob remain visible today, and have been enjoyed and appreciated by generations of the Bouverie family and visitors to Longford. His activities demonstrate how he – like many other eighteenth-century patrons – simultaneously improved the surroundings, interiors and decoration of his country seat in line with the trends of the day.

Although he can be credited with doing much to bring Longford up to date, Sir Jacob's approach to the refurbishment of the castle, and to the formation of the art collection, also showed a great respect for the traditions of the past. His words from around 1755, quoted above, formed an analogy within a 'short sketch of religion for my children', wherein he made the case that 'when any Body looks upon the wonderfull Frame & Order of the World, He surveys it with Delight & Astonishment; but at the same time is convinced, that there must have been an All=Powerfull All=Wise & All=Good Maker of it: & that Maker is God'.[2] His reminder to look to the origins of a 'fine House', however, is especially telling, as it sums up Sir Jacob's attitude to Longford Castle. The way he approached the decoration of the castle during the mid-eighteenth century demonstrated a clear interest in its heritage, and an appreciation of the castle's original Elizabethan aesthetic. This chapter will show how he achieved in his patronage

Fig. 20 Michael Dahl (1659–1743), *Sir Jacob Bouverie, 1st Viscount Folkestone*, 1724–5 (detail of fig. 22)

41

Fig. 21 Michael Dahl (1659–1743), *Mary Clarke*, 1724–5, oil on canvas, 123.2 x 99.1 cm, Longford Castle

and acquisitions a decorous balance appropriate to his ascending social status, by looking simultaneously to the past, present and future, combining longstanding traditions with fashionable innovations, in order to establish Longford as the repository of a multitude of treasures for posterity.

Sir Jacob was the first member of the Bouverie family to reside permanently in England, and the first to engage significantly with the aristocratic lifestyle. Even before he had inherited Longford, he was actively involved in commissioning family portraits from artists who worked for a range of high-status patrons. One of the first acquisitions he noted in his accounts was a 'picture in enamail', bought from Christian Friedrich Zincke (*c.* 1684–1767), miniaturist to royalty and the aristocracy, in 1727.[3] In the early 1730s, he paid 'Mr. Philips the Painter' – presumably Charles Philips (1708–1747), a successful and esteemed portraitist with aristocratic clientele – 'for the picture of my family' and 'for mine & my Wife's picture'.[4] These commissions indicate the importance that he ascribed, even at this early date, to documenting his family for posterity, and to amassing a portrait collection in line with those of other noble patrons of the day.

One of Sir Jacob's most significant early commissions was a pair of three-quarter-length portraits depicting himself and his first wife, Mary Clarke (*d.* 1739), from the painter Michael Dahl (1659–1743) (figs 21, 22). They cost £63, and were acquired during the winter of 1724–5, shortly after the pair were married.[5] Along with the birth of a child, coming of age and inheritance, marriage was a life event that was often commemorated by means of a new portrait commission in the eighteenth century.[6] The acquisition of pendant portraits of husband and wife, in particular, was typically precipitated by the desire to celebrate a recent union and the promised beginning of a new dynasty. It is notable that some time shortly after the pair married, Sir Jacob received from his new father-in-law, Bartholomew Clarke (dates unknown),[7] two paintings by Claude: *Moses and the Burning Bush* and *Ezekiel Weeping on the Ruins of Tyre*. This transfer may well have been intended as a means of materially entrenching good relations between the two recently conjoined families, commemorating the union in tandem with the new portraits. Although the Claudes were later sold,[8] the gift may have contributed to Sir Jacob's taste for the works of the seventeenth-century French old masters, and may have spurred him on to seek out other art by Claude.

To return to the portrait commissions, it is interesting to consider Sir Jacob's choice of artist for these important paintings. In the mid-1720s Dahl was an established portraitist, and arguably a sensible choice for someone who, like Sir Jacob, was just beginning to amass his family portrait collection. Dahl had emigrated to England from Sweden in 1689; he is thought to have worked with Sir Godfrey Kneller (1646–1723) and was patronised by Queen Anne.[9] The latter association may have made him particularly attractive to Sir Jacob, because the Bouverie family, as we have seen (page 28), owed their baronetcy to the Queen. Dahl's links with seventeenth-century portraitists, in addition, would have helped to root Sir Jacob's image within the esteemed English Baroque portrait tradition, making him appear established and engrained as a member of the English nobility.

By looking closely at Dahl's portrait of Sir Jacob (fig. 22), and contrasting it with the same artist's depiction of Sir Edward (see page 28 and fig. 14 in previous chapter), we can also gain an insight into how Longford's new owner wished to be portrayed: as in touch with both tradition *and* contemporary fashions. Although Sir Jacob's accounts do not explicitly refer to a payment for Sir Edward's portrait, one might reasonably conjecture that the paintings were commissioned in tandem, because of the similarity between the sitters' poses and

Fig. 22 Michael Dahl (1659–1743), *Sir Jacob Bouverie, 1st Viscount Folkestone*, 1724–5, oil on canvas, 124.5 x 99.1 cm, Longford Castle

costumes. This affinity suggests to us that the family wished to project a coherent image of themselves as confident and wealthy patrons. However, Sir Jacob's likeness can be construed as more forward-looking, stylistically, than that of Sir Edward.[10] The landscape background and less staid expression set his portrait apart from the more old-fashioned depiction of his brother. Moreover, Sir Jacob was painted with one hand tucked inside his unbuttoned jacket, a fashionable motif frequently used in portraits of gentlemen during the eighteenth century.[11] Therefore, although the choice of artist for this early commission created links with the past, the end result still looked to the future stylistically.

As was noted in the previous chapter (page 38), before he inherited Longford Sir Jacob lived in both Kent and London, in houses that were rented and therefore not permanent homes. The portraits of Sir Jacob and his wife, therefore, were most probably not intended for ongoing display in any one space within a particular interior. In that case, the choice of a three-quarter-length format was probably not conditioned by practical factors such as availability of space in a designated room, but perhaps by a desire to tie in with the portrait of Sir Edward, or by a sense of social decorum. The size and format of portraits of the time, along with the pose in which a sitter was depicted, were often governed by their status.[12] The three-quarter-length format was more expensive than a head-and-shoulders or a half-length depiction, but was of course not as costly and grand as a full-length. Sir Jacob's choice may therefore speak of his ascending social status at the time.

Sir Jacob's actions generally – both in the realm of the arts, and more widely in terms of his political and philanthropic activities – put him at the forefront of new eighteenth-century trends but at the same time demonstrated a subscription to some of the aristocratic traditions of the past, and, importantly, a desire to celebrate his family's own heritage. In the 1720s, before he inherited Longford, he travelled to continental Europe, visiting northern France and the Netherlands, from where the Bouverie family originated. Their forebear, Laurens des Bouverie, had been born near Cambrai and Lille, in the small town of St-Jean du Melantois.[13] A letter written to Sir Edward from Angers suggests that the family were keen at this time to trace their Huguenot origins:

> You wrote me yt the place where I am to make some enquiry about our Family, lays between Cambray & Lisle. . . . There are some People here in this Town of our name . . . about two hundred years agoe one of our name here married ye. daughter of a Lawyer. . . . I have seen his arms in ye Cathedrall=Church, wch are not at all like ours.[14]

This investigation may also have been driven by a desire to ascertain whether there was any property in the area they could lay claim to (thanks to Alison Yarrington for this suggestion). In any case, the family's interest in their Huguenot heritage continued to be nurtured throughout the eighteenth century and beyond, even when they had become established members of the English aristocracy. For example, Sir Jacob's son, William Bouverie, 1st Earl of Radnor, was the first of many heads of the family to become involved with the French Hospital, 'La Providence', a charity set up in London to provide care for impoverished, elderly or infirm Huguenot refugees arriving in England in the eighteenth century.[15] The family still keep the portrait of their ancestor Laurens (fig. 13) on display at Longford Castle, alongside new acquisitions and commissions. In addition, they have owned two small-scale paintings depicting John Calvin (1509–1564), the sixteenth-century theologian whose writings first inspired the French Protestants, and his disciple, Theodore Beza (1519–1605), since the mid-eighteenth century, when the pictures were recorded as present within inventories of the Longford collection.[16]

After Sir Jacob inherited Longford he appears to have felt a need to demonstrate his commitment to an English identity, as well as to his continental ancestry. An Act of Parliament of 1737 allowed the family to anglicise their surname, so that it became simply *Bouverie* rather than *des Bouverie*.[17] The preposition 'de' can indicate French or Norman ancestry,[18] so the change was a significant public declaration of the family's sense of Englishness, at the moment when Sir Jacob inherited his country seat.

The name change may not have been his decision alone, however: its formalisation may also have been the result of longstanding practical concerns and customs on the part of the family. A nineteenth-century copy of the Act of Parliament for the name change reveals that three deceased members of the family 'for several years before their respective deaths did write themselves by the Sirname of Bouverie and not Des Bouverie',[19] suggesting that the practice had been taken up informally by others, aside from Sir Jacob, before it was made official. Furthermore, the 'bill of charges about an Act of Parliament for writing my name Bouverie only', noted in Sir Jacob's account book, was shared between himself and a relative, 'my cousin, Bouverie being to pay the other half'.[20]

Sir Jacob's role in formalising the change, however, takes on further currency when considered alongside his other actions. He adopted many of the traditional customs of the landed aristocracy, fulfilling the role of local landowner. For instance, during the 1740s he was a Member of Parliament and Recorder (judicial officer) for Salisbury, and was made Deputy Lieutenant of Wiltshire in 1750.[21] By taking on political responsibilities in the locality near his new Wiltshire seat, he demonstrated his commitment to his new home. His activities evoke a traditional and paternalistic approach to the

Fig. 23 Thomas Hudson (1701–1779), *Jacob Bouverie, 1st Viscount Folkestone*, 1749, oil on canvas, 124.5 x 99.1 cm, Longford Castle

local community, in line with the historian Nigel Everett's 'Tory view of landscape', wherein landowners subscribed to an outlook 'in which wealth was supposed to be accompanied by obligations and rank by duties'.[22] This viewpoint, according to Everett, was 'opposed to a narrowly commercial conception of life',[23] suggesting a polarity that had to be reconciled, between landowning traditions and the increasing commercialism of eighteenth-century society. As the Bouveries had previously been involved in trade, it was arguably important for Sir Jacob to involve himself in his local community and to thereby integrate himself within English traditions, to consolidate his new social status.

The way in which Sir Jacob presented and conducted himself during these early years, through patronage and political work, may have been instrumental in his advancement within the ranks of the nobility. In 1747 he was made 1st Viscount Folkestone, a title that reflects the Bouverie family's landholdings in Kent (fig. 23). (To avoid confusion, he is referred to as 'Sir Jacob' throughout this chapter.) He had done much to transform Longford Castle before this date, turning it into 'a truly English Country Gentleman's Establishment'[24] to match his rising social position, and it is to those extensive refurbishment works that we now turn.

Sir Jacob began redecorating at Longford almost as soon as he came to live there, and used

　　　　　　　　JACOB BOUVERIE, 1ST VISCOUNT FOLKESTONE

Fig. 24 Round Parlour, Longford Castle, 2016

the castle's interiors as a vehicle through which to express his new identity as a landowner. It is striking that his successors retained the key Longford interiors more or less as he left them, with the result that many of the improvements he undertook can still be seen and appreciated today. The high cost of the renovations, and the fact that some of the best furnishers of the day were contracted, may have deterred later incumbents from making changes, or rendered such changes unnecessary.

One of the first and most significant rooms to receive Sir Jacob's attention was the Round Parlour. One of the ground-floor tower rooms, it connects the entrance and garden fronts of the castle (fig. 24). The Round Parlour continues to be one of the first rooms experienced on a tour of the castle for today's visitors, as it was for eighteenth-century tourists. The room's circular form provides an unequivocal reminder of the castle's unique architecture. Its treatment during the eighteenth century offers a rich example of how Sir Jacob was able to unite Longford's unusual and whimsical form with eighteenth-century fashions.

In November 1737, Sir Jacob wrote a letter to his brother-in-law, from which we can gain an insight into his ambitions for the room:

> The sixth Week is now entred into since the Parlour was begun upon, & I believe it will take up ten days longer before it will be finished; I have added a good deal more guilding than We talked of & in my Opinion not a bit too much; I was advised to guild the mouldings of the Pannells, but I think it best as it is.[25]

This letter reveals how Sir Jacob was responsible for painting and re-gilding the room's wall panelling, and how he was careful to ensure that just the right amount of gilding was undertaken. In his accounts for this month, Sir Jacob made a payment of £38 to 'Mr. Kent for painting & guilding ye. Parlour', and added a note stating 'NB [Mr. Kent] says new painting ye. Parlour now might come to £4 or £5-, if it was quite plain, it would not come to above £1:10:0, or £1:15:0'.[26] The fairly extensive re-gilding that took place under Sir Jacob's instruction suggests his aspiration to the heights of contemporary fashion, as gilding was considered a 'great extravagance' within the eighteenth-century interior.[27]

In June 1738, another payment was made to 'Mr. Kent for additionall guilding & painting the Parlour', and further payments to this craftsman appear throughout Sir Jacob's account book.[28] It is possible that they refer to William

Kent (*c.* 1685–1748), the renowned eighteenth-century architect and furniture designer who created decorative schemes for other important country houses such as Wanstead House in Essex and Holkham Hall in Norfolk. The architectural historian Christopher Hussey rejected this idea on the grounds that the name 'Mr. Kent' continues to appear in the Longford accounts after William Kent's death in 1748, sometimes for services unrelated to interior decoration.[29] However, these later payments may refer to a different individual, simply described in the account books, as most contractors were, by title and surname only. It is still conceivable that William Kent was indeed responsible for the gilding in the Round Parlour, given his work in this vein at Houghton Hall, Norfolk, described by John Cornforth as 'the most extensive and … skilfully planned example of gilding to survive'.[30]

In the absence of definitive evidence, we can only conjecture as to William Kent's possible involvement at Longford. What is of undoubted significance, however, is that, regardless of the identity of the craftsman responsible, Sir Jacob was clearly thinking in line with fashions of the time when gilding the Round Parlour to such a degree, bearing in mind the work being undertaken concurrently by other country-house owners such as Sir Robert Walpole at Houghton.

Despite this, the works did not represent a complete overhaul of the appearance of the room, which contemporaries might have deemed excessive. For instance, the sixteenth-century chimneypiece was kept in place, and its sculptural relief depicting Mars and Venus can still be appreciated today. During the eighteenth century, designers such as Kent and sculptors such as Rysbrack produced stone overmantel reliefs with classical subjects for country-house interiors,[31] so this Elizabethan survival would not have seemed outmoded at the time. Sir Jacob also chose to refurbish, rather than replace, the room's existing wainscoting, which features classical patterns such as Ionic columns and fans, and which is believed to date from 1591.[32] It had originally been gilded but not painted, as the description by Henry Hare, 2nd Baron Coleraine, of the room in his late seventeenth-century poem about Longford attests: 'Through a fair entry, doth ye <u>Parlour </u>shine Gilt round (as Ovid did Sol's house designe)'.[33]

Sir Jacob may have wished to respect the castle's original interior fabric; he might also have been influenced by the room's function, when making decisions as to what to retain. The neo-Palladian architect Isaac Ware (1704–1766), who wrote an architectural treatise in the mid-eighteenth century, described how wainscot was considered at the time to be the 'properest' form of interior decoration for a parlour, and also the 'neatest' type of decoration generally (with stucco being the 'grandest', and hangings 'the most gaudy').[34] Sir Jacob's decision to retain 'neat' wainscot, considered appropriate to the context of the Round Parlour, spoke of his well-informed attitude to interior decoration. As the historian Amanda Vickery has observed, 'neatness' was seen to encapsulate 'the opposite of showy excess' in the eighteenth century, and was therefore adopted by patrons for rooms 'that made claims to taste, but not ostentatious grandeur'.[35]

While gilding was more commonplace within eighteenth-century country-house interiors, the use of white paint at this date was less conventional. The museum curator and historian of interiors Peter Thornton has noted that white and gold colour schemes were more commonly seen in France, and that it was not until after 1750 that the style took off in England.[36] Other examples can be seen at Petworth House in Sussex and in the Music Room of Norfolk House, London, now preserved in the Victoria and Albert Museum.[37] The Round Parlour at Longford, decorated during the late 1730s, is therefore a notably early example of a white and gold interior.

In the late 1730s, the French architect Jacques-François Blondel (1705–1774) had written that carved wall-panelling ought not to be painted in colour but covered in plain varnish: if white *was* to be used, he suggested it was best suited to rooms used during the daytime or during the summer months.[38] One can imagine that the Round Parlour was indeed used in this way, as it has a number of exposed exterior walls, indicating that it may have been colder, and thus less frequently used, in the winter. Additionally, the room's circular form allows light to enter during the day from multiple aspects, which serves to highlight the gilding. Elizabeth Somerset, Duchess of Beaufort (*c.* 1713–1799), who visited Longford in 1753, described how the room 'looks very agreably to the Garden',[39] suggesting that its daytime views were part of the room's appeal. The decision not to decorate the room with, for instance, tapestry or damask wall hangings may also have been influenced by its intended function. The room was described by eighteenth-century visitors as an 'eating' room,[40] and patrons of the time tended to favour wood panelling for such spaces, rather than soft fabrics, which would 'retain food smells'.[41]

This room provides just one example of Sir Jacob's decorous taste and desire to work sympathetically with the architectural legacy he had inherited. This is also apparent in a furniture commission he made for the Round Parlour. He acquired a marble-topped side table, along with other items of furniture, from the cabinetmaker Benjamin Goodison (*c.* 1700–1767), one of the foremost furniture-makers of the day. Goodison's clientele also included Thomas Coke, 1st Earl of Leicester (1697–1759), of Holkham Hall, and the Royal Family.[42] The side table is notable for having a curved back to fit the unusual shape of the Round Parlour (fig. 25). Although fitting the table to the curvature of the room may have arisen from practical concerns, it also suggests a desire to unite new fashions with the castle's idiosyncratic heritage.

Another almost identical side table, this time featuring a straight back, may have been commissioned at the same time. This latter table is now at the Victoria and Albert Museum,[43] having once been on display at Coleshill House in Berkshire, a country house that came into the Bouverie family's ownership through the 1st Earl of Radnor's marriage to Coleshill's heiress, Harriot Pleydell (1723–1750). The Bouverie family sold this house in the mid-twentieth century, and today it no longer survives, having been destroyed by fire in 1952. Although the precise provenance of the Coleshill table has caused some scholarly uncertainty, the stylistic similarity of the two tables suggests that they may well have been commissioned together by Sir Jacob.[44] The side tables are likely to have been acquired in 1740 for the sum of £413, although, as a number of payments to Goodison appear in Sir Jacob's account books, indicating that he

Fig. 25 Attributed to Benjamin
Goodison (c. 1700–1767),
Pier Table, c. 1730–40, white
enamelled pine surmounted by
a slab of *verde antico* marble,
208.3 x 86.4 x 92.7 cm,
Longford Castle

produced a range of items for the Longford interiors, it is not certain which entry relates precisely to this commission.[45]

The straight-backed side table may have been intended for display in the new neo-Palladian entrance hall at Longford, discussed in Chapter 1, as side tables were often seen in country-house halls in the early eighteenth century, for instance at Ditchley Park, Oxfordshire, and Houghton Hall.[46] The classical style of the table would also have complemented its surroundings in the newly designed Longford entrance hall. It is likely that the table was transferred to Coleshill when the house was in Bouverie ownership, and perhaps when the neo-Palladian entrance hall at Longford was remodelled.

Happily, the side table in the Round Parlour remains today in the interior for which it was created. The table's iconography is particularly significant, when considered as an expression of Sir Jacob's social status at the time. Here, it is possible to claim an indirect link with William Kent, as Goodison worked to Kent's designs.[47] Side tables attributed to Kent often featured Italianate motifs, such as acanthus leaves, putti and sphinxes.[48] The carvings on the Longford table, however, combine such references to the classical world with some distinctly English features. For example, the female head in the centre of the carving represents Diana, the Roman goddess of hunting, and at either end two foxes stand guard. These symbols work together to evoke the aristocratic pastime of hunting. Moreover, the carving features oak leaves and acorns, suggestive of patriotism and Englishness: oaks, 'like the ideal landed family', were understood to be 'venerable, patriarchal, stately and guardian'.[49]

In this bespoke commission, Sir Jacob therefore brought together a range of symbols to express his new identity visually as both traditional landowner and fashionable connoisseur. Similarly, one can see foxes and oak leaves on furnishings and the interior architecture at Houghton Hall, alongside armorial motifs,[50] suggesting that Sir Robert Walpole – who was elevated to the position of Prime Minister – also wished to express a sense of patriotism through the country-house interior. Considering that Sir Jacob had recently officiated over the anglicisation of his family name, the use of such iconography in an important furniture commission may have been bound up with a wish to express a sense of English aristocratic identity: one that was also felt by others experiencing social escalation.

This Anglo-Italian hybrid iconography can be seen elsewhere in the interiors at Longford. In what is known today as the Long Parlour but which in the eighteenth century was divided into two separate rooms – a Parlour and a Drawing Room – there are two eighteenth-century marble chimneypieces decorated with oak leaves and acorns, repeating and consolidating the message conveyed by the side table in the Round Parlour. Many important eighteenth-century sculptors, including Rysbrack and Sir Henry Cheere (1703–1781), were commissioned to produce new and costly chimneypieces for Longford, perhaps to replace earlier examples not considered as worthy of saving as the sixteenth-century chimneypiece retained in the Round Parlour. For instance, in April 1743, Sir Jacob paid the remainder of a bill of £805 10s to 'Mr. Chere … for chimney-pieces & tops &c'.[51] Oak and acorn motifs also appear on other items of furniture throughout the castle, including console tables, pedestals and mirror surrounds: their frequent recurrence within the most important and lavishly furnished rooms at Longford indicates that the resultant image of the Bouverie family as established English landowners – as well as fashionable and wealthy patrons – was one consciously and consistently promoted.

References to trees in the iconography of items of furniture helped create a sense of cohesion between the castle's interiors and its surroundings. In the mid-eighteenth century, Sir Jacob had begun planting new trees in the Longford grounds, as payments in his accounts for 3,000 seedling beeches, 'garden seeds & Trees for planting' and 'Planes & Chestnut Trees' attest.[52] The landscape historian Tom Williamson has noted how the longevity of trees on an estate created a sense of 'continuity', and was connected to the 'stability and security' of the family who owned it.[53] Tree planting was therefore a symbolic exercise, enabling individuals to confirm their role as landowner, particularly as 'the scale of property' could also be defined through the careful placing of clumps of trees on one's estate.[54] The fashion for populating the country estate with trees was also linked to aristocratic country pursuits, such as pheasant shooting, since pheasants prefer living under tree cover and around the margins of woodland.[55]

In planting trees at Longford, Sir Jacob literally and symbolically laid his roots at his new family seat, expressing and consolidating his aristocratic status and securing it into the future. Jonas Hanway (1712–1786), a visitor to the castle in the middle of the eighteenth century, remarked that the trees were 'thinly planted, and not affording any shelter from the sun',[56]

Fig. 26 Picture Gallery, Longford Castle, 2016

evincing their infancy at this period. His observation provides a reminder that tree-planting schemes were not about immediate gratification, for either the family or those who visited Longford as tourists. Instead, the endeavour was part of a long-term investment for the benefit of future generations, who would experience the trees in maturity.

Tree planting was an activity that a number of eighteenth-century country-house owners engaged in for patriotic reasons, as it helped to rebalance the country's supplies of wood.[57] It was therefore an endeavour encouraged by the Society for the Encouragement of Arts, Manufactures and Commerce (now the Royal Society of Arts), with which Sir Jacob was closely involved, as one of its founders and its first president. The Society was established in 1754, with the aim of encouraging the contemporary arts in Britain, and Sir Jacob's involvement in it can be deemed one of his principal philanthropic commitments, as well as a key way in which he engaged with one of the new prerequisites for noble status in eighteenth-century England: leadership of clubs and societies, and charitable activity on a national scale.[58]

Sir Jacob's presidency of the Society reflects his pre-eminence within the eighteenth-century art world. He had commissioned works from some of the artists who were also involved in the Society. These included the sculptor Sir Henry Cheere, who, as we have seen, provided new chimneypieces for Longford Castle, and the painter and art dealer Arthur Pond (c. 1705–1758).[59] Pond was known for producing quality copies of old master paintings for clients wishing to fit out their new homes.[60] In 1737, Sir Jacob had paid Pond for a copy after a painting of 'Ld. Strafford & his Secretary' – Thomas Wentworth, 1st Earl of Strafford (1593–1641), and Sir Philip Mainwaring (1589–1661) – by Sir Anthony Van Dyck (fig. 27).[61] This is described as a 'Copy from the Celebrated Vandyke at Blenheim' in eighteenth-century inventories of the Longford collection, and is faithful to the original, showing the two men seated, engaged in correspondence.[62] This commission is interesting, as it shows that Sir Jacob did not only contract artists to produce original works of art for display at the castle.

One can understand why, in 1737, a relatively early point in Sir Jacob's art-collecting career, when he had only just come into possession of Longford Castle, he might have enlisted such an artist to produce a copy of an important and famous historical portrait from an equally important and famous country house. It would not only have helped to fill Longford's walls but also to associate Sir Jacob and the castle with the original painting, the master, and the collection at Blenheim Palace, Oxfordshire, enhancing his and his castle's status. Although contemporary commentators debated the merits of copies, collectors often felt it was preferable to obtain copies of great pictures, rather than originals that were considered lesser works.[63]

After the first phase of refurbishment at Longford, which focused upon the redecoration of the Round Parlour in the late 1730s, Sir Jacob turned his attention to one of the castle's most important rooms: its first-floor Gallery (fig. 26). It appears that a great deal of work was carried out in this space, which, as we saw in Chapter 1 (pages 20–21), had previously been used in line with the Elizabethan Long Gallery tradition, before the Bouveries owned the castle. Here, the transformation that took place under Sir Jacob's direction eclipsed the room's original aesthetic to a greater degree than is the case in the Round Parlour. He did not retain the wall panelling but instead rehung the room with green silk damask, creating the ideal background for the collection of fine art he was concurrently amassing.

Fig. 27 Arthur Pond (*c.* 1705–1758), after Sir Anthony Van Dyck (1599–1641), *Thomas Wentworth, Earl of Strafford, and his Secretary, Sir Philip Mainwaring,* *c.* 1737, oil on canvas, 142.2 x 134.6 cm, Longford Castle

In 1745, Sir Jacob summarised the outgoings that had been 'Layed out on the Gallery at Longford' in his account book. His consolidation of his expenditure on the room's decoration in another set of accounts reveals its magnitude – a total of £1,296 – highlighting the importance he accorded to interior decoration, and also shows how he saw it as a separate and significant undertaking.[64] He noted his expenditure for various works, including 'plaining the Gallery Architrave round the doors ornaments to the Chimney &c'; 'Painting the Gallery'; 'The stucco of the Ceiling'; 'cleaning mending & binding' of a carpet; 'Mr. Kilpin the Upholsterer's bill' of £125; 'Mr. Goodison the Cabinet-Maker's bill' of £400; various sculptural decorations and a total of 283 yards of green damask.[65]

This complete overhaul demonstrates Sir Jacob's eagerness to concentrate money and effort on bringing Longford's principal room into line with the fashions of the day. He commissioned Goodison to produce an extensive suite of furniture, comprising two day-beds (fig. 28), two long stools and eight lesser stools, featuring gilt mahogany frames carved with scallops and acanthus leaves and upholstered in green damask to match the walls. Eighteenth-century country-house owners often used the same fabric to cover walls and furnishings, in order to achieve an effect of unity within an interior: similar schemes can be seen at Houghton Hall, for example.[66] Many patrons commissioned full suites of furniture for their galleries at this time: at Temple Newsam House in Yorkshire, for instance, Henry Ingram, 7th Viscount Irwin

(1691–1761), acquired chairs, settees and a couch for his Long Gallery from the craftsman James Pascall (*c*. 1697–*c*. 1746) during the 1740s.[67]

Sir Jacob's furniture commissions were therefore in line with contemporary trends. However, Goodison's suite of furniture in the Gallery at Longford was not only at the apex of style but was of the highest quality, and has been described as one of the finest of its type.[68] Furniture historians have paid tribute to the quality of design of the pieces in the Gallery: Peter Macquoid, for instance, has stated that the 'suite of fine mahogany and gilt furniture' at Longford is 'contemporary with specimens at Houghton, but altogether superior in style'.[69]

Tourists who visited Longford during the eighteenth century shared a sense of approbation at the programme of redecoration undertaken by Sir Jacob. In the mid-1750s, when most of the refurbishment had been completed, Richard Pococke (1704–1765), a prelate and anthropologist best known for his travel writings, observed that Longford 'is esteemed as one of the best finish'd and furnished houses in England', adding that 'the apartments below are exceeding neat and handsom, as those above are very fine and grand'.[70] Another visitor, whose travel accounts were published anonymously in 1762, remarked that 'the Apartments are very elegant, and the Furniture and Decorations shew an excellent Taste'.[71] Although, as we saw earlier, Sir Jacob had retained a 'neat' appearance on the ground floor in his decoration of rooms such as the Round Parlour, one can gain the sense from these contemporary descriptions that the new decoration of the first-floor Gallery was intended to impress visitors, and to allow the room to stake its claim as the most important within the castle.

The extensive refurbishment works in the Gallery may have been undertaken with a view to what was to come. As the room was primarily intended for the display of works of art, it was clearly important that it be decorated to the fullest extent in what was considered the appropriate manner for an eighteenth-century picture gallery. Damask was frequently used in rooms destined for the display of pictures, and red and green were considered particularly apposite backdrops for the works of Italian old masters, as they complemented the paintings' red-ground gesso bases.[72]

By this time Sir Jacob had established the foundations of his art collection by purchasing some prestigious paintings. In 1737 he had bought two paintings by Claude, entitled *Sea Coast Scene with the Landing of Aeneas in Latium* and *Pastoral Landscape with the Arch of Titus*, some-

Fig. 29 Claude Gellée, called Claude Lorraine or Lorrain (1600–1682), *Sea Coast with the Landing of Aeneas in Latium (Morning – the Rise of the Roman Empire)*, 1650, oil on canvas in an early eighteenth-century French carved and gilded frame, 101.6 x 134.6 cm, Longford Castle

Fig. 30 Claude Gellée, called
Claude Lorraine or Lorrain (1600–
1682), *Pastoral Landscape with the
Arch of Titus (Evening - the Decline
of the Roman Empire)*, 1644, oil
on canvas in an early eighteenth-
century French carved and gilded
frame, 101.6 x 134.6 cm,
Longford Castle

times known as *Morning* and *Evening*, and understood as representations of the rise and fall of
the Roman Empire (figs 29 and 30). These paintings had an illustrious provenance, having
previously resided in the art collection of Jeanne Baptiste d'Albert du Luynes, comtesse de
Verrue (1670–1736), in Paris.[73] Sir Jacob imported them from France, and a transaction is listed
in his accounts for November 1739 for 'Mr. Hoare's bill for two Landskips of Claude Loraine's
£417:00:0, charges in France £4:17:9 charges at ye Custom-house here £5:19:0'.[74] The price
paid for the paintings is about equal to that spent on Goodison's suite of furniture, showing
how Sir Jacob was keen to spend large amounts on both the fine and the decorative arts at
this time.

The paintings suited their new decorative surroundings, particularly given the frames in

JACOB BOUVERIE, 1ST VISCOUNT FOLKESTONE

which they were housed when they were brought over from France, and which still encase them today. These early eighteenth-century French carved and gilded frames would have chimed stylistically with the gilded day-beds and stools, lending a sense of continuity to the room's decoration. The fact that the paintings were hung in some of the finest frames then available also speaks of Sir Jacob's desire to recall their French provenance, and to celebrate their calibre.

Inventories of the Longford collection from later in the eighteenth century show that the two Claudes were hung facing one another, at opposite ends of the Gallery, bookending the space. It is notable that this is where they still hang today. Although they were actually painted six years apart,[75] it seems that the paintings have always been considered a pair, and displayed accordingly: opposite one another, and in almost matching frames. In the Gallery at Longford, the pairing of the Claudes does not simply make for a neat arrangement, structuring the hang and organising the room, but is particularly suitable considering their subject matter. As viewers enter the room, they encounter a representation of sunrise, and, as they leave, they see an image of sunset, lending a sense of decorum to the picture hang, and symbolising the beginning and end of their tour around the room. As an introduction and finishing note to the works of art housed within the Gallery, the paintings act to reinforce to visitors the prestige of the Bouveries' collection.

Tourists' accounts of visits to Longford, dating back to the eighteenth and nineteenth centuries, reveal how the Claudes were some of the most admired paintings within the collection. Mrs Caroline Lybbe Powys (1738–1817), who travelled extensively around England during the eighteenth century, staying with friends and family, recorded her experiences of the architecture, interiors and way of life at a number of country houses, including Longford Castle.[76] She visited in 1776, and wrote in her journal that she 'went on purpose to see' the two paintings by Claude.[77] She was pleasantly surprised by the other works of art she encountered at the castle, noting that she was 'quite pleased the Claude Lorraine had tempted us these three miles out of our first propos'd excursion'.[78] The Claudes seem, therefore, to have been something of a draw for visitors considering paying Longford a visit. Even in 1794, when the art collection was much bigger, Joseph Farington (1747–1821) recorded in his diary that the patron and amateur painter Sir George Beaumont (1753–1827) had likewise been to Longford expressly 'to see the Claudes'.[79]

The Claudes are the works of art most frequently mentioned in visitors' written descriptions of Longford. One of the earliest visitors to the castle after it came into Bouverie ownership was the antiquary George Vertue (1683–1756). He commented on the cost of the Claudes,[80] but it must be remembered that at the time of his visit, in 1740, Sir Jacob had not yet acquired many other paintings upon which the visitor *could* comment. Vertue also described how Longford was 'by the present possesor much adorn'd within', and how Sir Jacob was at the time 'furnishing a room purposely for pictures',[81] alluding to how the refurbishment works in the Gallery were planned with the art collection in mind. Other visitors throughout the eighteenth and

Fig. 31 Nicolas Poussin (1594–1665), *The Adoration of the Golden Calf*, 1633–4, oil on canvas, 153.4 x 211.8 cm, National Gallery, London

nineteenth centuries variously described the Claudes as 'most distinguished'; 'two of the best Pieces of *Claude Lorrain*'; 'the two celebrated pictures of Claude Lorraine ... amazing fine landscapes indeed'; 'the two most admired pictures in this collection' and 'of the greatest beauty'.[82]

Taste for the acknowledged masters of the French school was widespread among English collectors of the time, which may have contributed to this praise. Works of art by the seventeenth-century painter Nicolas Poussin (1594–1665) were similarly much sought after.[83] Thomas Coke, 1st Earl of Leicester, displayed a total of seven works by Claude in the Landscape Room at Holkham Hall, and Henry Hoare II (1705–1785) of Stourhead, not far from Longford, owned an important Poussin.[84] Sir Jacob purchased a pair of paintings by Poussin for Longford in 1741, entitled *The Adoration of the Golden Calf* and *The Crossing of the Red Sea* (figs 31 and 32), for £481 5s and related costs.[85] Now at the National Gallery in London and the National Gallery of Victoria in Melbourne, Australia, respectively, the pair once hung near the Claudes in the

Fig. 32 Nicolas Poussin (1594–1665), *The Crossing of the Red Sea*, 1632–4, oil on canvas, 155.6 x 215.3 cm, National Gallery of Victoria, Melbourne

Gallery at Longford, and again drew the attention of many visitors to the castle. These paintings, with their dynamic compositions and rich use of colour, depict biblical, rather than classical subjects. Like the Claudes, they were housed in fine French gilded frames, which would have added further to the sense of harmony and cohesion upon the Gallery's walls.

Sir Jacob's interest in Poussin's work is also evinced by the fact that he bought two volumes of 'Poussin's prints' from 'Mr. Pond' – presumably Arthur Pond, with whom, as we have seen, he had had earlier dealings – in 1744.[86] Sir Jacob demonstrated the acumen of a connoisseur and his fashionable taste through his interest in Poussin, and also through the purchase of paintings from the academically esteemed Italian school. He did not amass his art collection on a Grand Tour of continental Europe, as was the case with many eighteenth-century members of the English aristocracy. This may account for why the Longford art collection does not contain a large amount of antique sculpture, an interest in which 'lay at the very centre of Grand Tour taste'.[87] However, he took advantage of alternative mechanisms of acquisition that were available to him to purchase Italian art. As well as buying paintings at auction in London – such

Fig. 33 English school, *John Bouverie*, early eighteenth century, oil on canvas, 73.7 x 61.0 cm, Longford Castle

as a 'Picture of the holy family done by the School of Andrea del Sarto after a Picture of his at Florence', which he purchased from 'Norton's sale' in 1740[88] – he also imported works of art from abroad.

For example, he paid a bill of £146 12s 'being money remitted to Rome for a Guercino' in 1741, perhaps influenced by his cousin, John Bouverie (*c.* 1723–1750), who was at the time travelling on the continent gathering a collection of drawings by the Italian Baroque painter Guercino (1591–1666).[89] At Longford Castle there is a portrait of John, by an unknown eighteenth-century English artist, showing him contemplating an album of drawings that may well be representations of his 'celebrated Guercino series' (fig. 33).[90] John's Grand Tour shows that the extended Bouverie family, as well as those members of the family based at Longford, were also engaging in art collecting at this time. Another instance of Sir Jacob's importing art from abroad was in 1742, when he paid a bill 'from Leghorn for ye. bustos': this perhaps refers to some classical sculptures described in later eighteenth-century inventories of the Longford art collection.[91]

Fig. 34 Italian school, *River Tiber*, late seventeenth century, bronze with lacquered brass and mahogany, 47.0 cm wide, Longford Castle

Fig. 35 Italian school, *River Nile*, late seventeenth century, bronze with lacquered brass and mahogany, 47.0 cm wide, Longford Castle

Many Grand Tourists bought small-scale bronze copies of antique sculptures on their travels for display in their country houses.[92] Sir Jacob, rather than buying such pieces on the continent, instead acquired a number of bronze statuettes at auction in London in the late 1730s and the 1740s. A particularly notable example is a pair of bronze representations of the River Tiber and River Nile (figs 34 and 35), which he bought in 1740 alongside a range of other items at a sale of works of art and curiosities previously belonging to Charles Montagu, 1st Earl of Halifax (1661–1715).[93] These were included in Sir Jacob's aforementioned list of items 'Layed out on the Gallery at Longford'. Intriguingly, this list dealt mainly with furnishings, and does not mention any of the paintings displayed in the Gallery. This suggests that Sir Jacob considered these bronze statuettes as, above all, part of the interior decoration scheme. The sculpture historian Malcolm Baker has argued in relation to other purchases made by Sir Jacob that his interest in bronze statuettes lay primarily in their decorative potential, rather than their value in terms of connoisseurship.[94]

Closer inspection reveals, however, that Sir Jacob collected and appreciated bronzes for a range of reasons. Other notes he made about his purchases do demonstrate an interest in connoisseurship, and show that he consulted the opinions of others regarding the attribution of certain works of art. For example, he noted down how he had purchased, along with some paintings, 'a Bronze of a Bacchus by M. Angelo, & of Antinous its Companion' from Robert Bragge's (*fl.* 1741–1780) sale in 1744.[95] At this time, art dealers such as Bragge would visit the continent and bring back art to sell to English buyers,[96] and Sir Jacob took advantage of the opportunities presented by these middlemen to acquire esteemed pieces. He noted next to the record of his purchase of these bronzes that 'Sr. Andrew Fontaine reckons them done by Soldani'.[97]

Copies of antique sculptures by the Italian sculptor and medallist Massimiliano Soldani (1656–1740) were much sought after by English Grand Tourists,[98] and it is interesting to note that Sir Jacob clearly shared an interest in the attribution of the bronzes on this occasion, and wished to buy works associated with the most fashionable artists. Moreover, he also took into account the judgements of other connoisseurs. Sir Andrew Fountaine (1676–1753) was a famed art collector who undertook a number of Grand Tours, sometimes collecting on behalf of others such as the Pembroke family of Wilton, and was considered 'the equal of any Italian dealer'.[99] He was, therefore, a venerable figure in the eighteenth-century art world whose opinion would have been well worth listening to.

Sir Jacob's interaction with other individuals active within the eighteenth-century art world suggests to us that he was keen to increase his knowledge as well as his collection. He bought works of art from abroad with the help of agents and dealers working on the continent. For instance, in 1745, he paid a bill 'for ye. Prime cost of a Landskip of Zucarelli's' to 'Mr. Smith of Venice' – most probably Joseph Smith (c. 1673/4?–1770), art collector and British consul at Venice, who was a patron of the Italian artist Francesco Zuccarelli (1702–1788).[100] Enlisting the help of others to procure works of art from abroad demonstrates Sir Jacob's eagerness to acquire pieces from the highly regarded Italian school, which were especially admired at the time, thanks to the influence of recently translated continental art-theoretical texts.[101]

Although Italian art was equated with good taste, and was ranked more highly than Dutch and Flemish art by the academic theories of the time, Sir Jacob is notable for having nonetheless acquired a fairly high number of works of art from the Northern schools.[102] In fact, the Longford collection is characterised by a wealth of Northern works. Of the paintings bought by Sir Jacob and his two successors, the 1st and 2nd Earls of Radnor, on the secondary market, and which can be identified in the accounts, it appears that approximately two thirds were from the Northern schools, with the remainder from the French and Italian schools. It is important to remember that individual preferences and predilections were important factors in the amassing of an art collection: the Bouverie collectors may have acquired pieces that spoke to their personal tastes and interests, as well as wider fashions and conventions among collectors. Moreover, despite the articulation of academic ideals in the eighteenth century, there was in fact a broad discrepancy between theory and practice. This was sometimes the result of practical factors, such as a lack of availability on the market of paintings held most desirable, but many also rebelled against the dictates of received art theory, which placed Italian art over Dutch.[103]

Sir Jacob was the most prolific collector of the Northern schools at Longford. His taste might have been influenced by his travels to the Netherlands and northern France in the 1720s, and by his interest in his family's origins. Moreover, during the 1740s, when he was beginning to put together his collection, Dutch art was more readily available for purchase than works of art from other schools, possibly as war had disrupted trade from Italy and France.[104] Sir Jacob often acquired several pieces at once via auction in London during this decade. For instance, in 1744, he bought a range of paintings attributed to Dutch artists at a sale conducted by the auctioneer Christopher Cock (fl. 1717–1748), including one work of art that he described as 'Figures Scating by Old Brueghell' in his account book.[105] This painting is still at Longford

Fig. 36 Hendrick Avercamp
(1585–1634), *A Frozen River Scene
with Numerous Figures on the Ice
and Buildings on the Left*, early
seventeenth century, oil on
panel, 68.6 x 109.2 cm,
Longford Castle

today (fig. 36), although it has since been reattributed to Hendrick Avercamp (1585–1634). Avercamp was influenced by the work of Pieter Brueghel the Elder (*c*. 1525–1569), which accounts for the earlier misattribution.[106] Both artists painted a number of winter landscape scenes, populated with figures engaged in a range of leisure and everyday activities.[107]

The painting Sir Jacob acquired for Longford shows a great many people gathered around and on the ice, in pairs or small groups, skating and enjoying one another's company. Other skating scenes by Avercamp, showing people going about their everyday life on the ice, can be seen in the collections of the National Gallery in London and the Rijksmuseum in Amsterdam.[108] When the art dealer John Smith (1781–1855) catalogued the Longford picture collection in 1829 he described the painting – which was then displayed in a Dressing Room – as a 'Winter scene representing a view on a river with numerous figures skating & variously amusing themselves'.[109] The painting hangs today in the Round Parlour at Longford, where the white hues of the ice and sky are perfectly complemented by the white wall panelling that forms its backdrop.

Sir Jacob kept a copy of the auction catalogue for the sale at which he bought this painting, and it has been preserved in the Longford archive ever since. He – or perhaps an agent working on his behalf – added ink crosses next to the entries for certain pictures, and pencil and ink annotations recording prices.[110] This intriguing glimpse into his art-collecting procedure suggests that he may have gone to the sale informed, having decided in advance which works of art he wished to bid for. The annotations may also indicate that he wished to record the prices fetched by certain paintings, as a guide to future collecting. Acquiring works of art at auction was a good way for someone relatively early in their collecting career to purchase a number of pieces at once, as Sir Jacob did. His priority at this time may have been to gather a group of paintings to help establish his art collection and status as a collector. This contrasts with the habits of his successors, the 1st and 2nd Earls of Radnor, who did not collect art on quite such a large scale – but who had the benefit of having inherited the ample foundations that Sir Jacob had laid. The 1st and 2nd Earls instead focused on acquiring key pieces on separate occasions, as we will see later in this book.

Other important works of art acquired by Sir Jacob included a charming flower piece painted on copper by the Flemish artist Jan Brueghel the Elder (1568–1625) (fig. 37). He bought it from the second-generation picture dealer and restorer Isaac Collivoe (c. 1702–1769) in 1744, paying £3 13s 6d to acquire the painting, and a further £4 4s to Collivoe 'for cleaning' it.[111] It is striking that the cost of restoring the painting exceeded its purchase price, and this provides an important reminder that, while he was happy to spend hundreds of pounds on paintings by artists such as Claude and Poussin, Sir Jacob also purchased less costly works of art, and items that might have been appreciated and viewed in different ways. The flower piece is a much smaller painting, and is highly detailed. Furthermore, its copper base imbues it with a certain technical brilliance. These qualities mean that it is best appreciated from close up.

Dutch still life paintings, such as this representation of flowers, often acted as a *memento mori* (a reminder of the transience of life).[112] Works of art in this *vanitas* tradition were often seen in seventeenth-century cabinets of curiosities, or *Kunstkammern*,[113] and indeed many works of art acquired by the Bouverie family for Longford would not have been out of place in such a cabinet. Small-scale works of art, such as groups of bronze statuettes like the representations of the River Nile and River Tiber discussed earlier, were collected for seventeenth-century *Kunstkammern*, where they were admired for their 'aura of preciousness' and were observed and handled up close.[114] Scholars have previously seen the eighteenth century as a moment of transition, which saw a change from virtuosic traditions of collecting to those of connoisseurship. Connoisseurship is seen to be based on the central tenets of knowledge, attribution and aesthetics, rather than the values of impulse, 'wonder' and 'delight', which supposedly characterised Renaissance virtuosi's approach to fine art.[115]

However, recent reassessments of this transition have suggested that the perceived boundary between the two types of collecting was actually less clearly defined than previously supposed.[116] Sir Jacob's acquisitions indicate that, while he had tendencies towards connoisseurship in his methods, he also took an interest in curiosities, defined in a broad sense to encompass works of technical brilliance, of unusual or rare subject matter, or on a small

Fig. 37 Jan Brueghel the Elder
(1568–1625), *Flowers in a Glass Vase
on a Ledge*, late sixteenth to early
seventeenth century, oil on copper,
29.2 x 19.1 cm, Longford Castle

scale,[117] supporting this new proposition that virtuosic traditions of collecting continued to guide patrons in the eighteenth century.

One eighteenth-century art collector who continued the virtuosic tradition of art collecting, and who placed value on 'objects of curiosity', was the physician, philanthropist and polymath Dr Richard Mead (1673–1754).[118] When Mead's art collection was put up for sale at auction in 1754 following his death, Sir Jacob bought two important paintings from it: portraits of *Erasmus* and *Aegidius* (figs 38 and 39), both then attributed to the sixteenth-century German painter Hans Holbein the Younger (1497–1543).[119] These paintings were then understood to be a pair but in fact had been painted by different artists. The portrait of the Dutch Renaissance humanist Erasmus (1466–1536) is still attributed to Holbein; however, we now know that the one of Aegidius – the Latinised name by which Erasmus's friend and fellow humanist Peter Gilles (1486–1533) was known – is the work of the Flemish painter Quentin Matsys (1466–1530).[120] It had been enlarged on all sides at some point in its history to match *Erasmus* in size.[121]

Holbein and his followers painted a number of portraits of Erasmus, of which the Longford example was the first.[122] It shows the sitter with both hands resting on a book, and in the background can be seen a column, a curtain and a shelf laden with more books. It has been argued that this painting represents the moment at which Holbein pioneered the technique of painting a sitter surrounded 'with objects . . . that explain [their] profession and interests': a convention that reached its 'fullest elaboration' in one of the artist's most celebrated paintings, the double portrait known today as *The Ambassadors*.[123] Significantly, as we will see later in this book, *The Ambassadors* (fig. 100; now in the National Gallery) once hung at Longford Castle. The Bouverie family's appreciation for the best works of this important artist, which endured across generations, demonstrates their calibre as art collectors.

In comparison to many of the other works of art Sir Jacob purchased at auction, the *Erasmus* and *Aegidius* portraits were relatively expensive, costing £100 apiece, and the acquisition is particularly interesting as Holbein's work represented a somewhat eccentric taste for the time. The early eighteenth century had seen appreciation for this artist waning, with his work sparking the interest of only 'a handful of antiquaries',[124] very unlike the appetite for painters such as Claude and Poussin. This prompts the question: why did Sir Jacob wish to spend a fairly large sum on acquiring these two paintings?

He may have felt that they complemented the Elizabethan architecture of Longford Castle, and the other historical portraits he owned, such as those of Calvin and Laurens des Bouverie. They might have created a sense of connection with the past, which might have been valued for lending a degree of historical continuity to the Bouveries' art collection, functioning in much the same way as the Van Dyck paintings acquired with the castle, discussed in Chapter 1 (page 33). In a similar manner, Queen Caroline (1683–1737), wife of King George II (1683–1760), had taken an interest in works by Holbein in order to forge material connections between the new Hanoverian regime and the revered Tudor dynasty for which the artist had worked.[125]

Fig. 38 Hans Holbein the Younger (1497–1543), *Erasmus*, 1523, oil on panel, 76.2 x 51.4 cm, on loan from Longford Castle to the National Gallery, London

Sir Jacob may also have been interested in the sitters, as well as the artist: it is revealing, for instance, to find that a few years later he purchased a *Life of Erasmus*, suggesting that he was interested in discovering more about the history of this outstanding individual.[126]

Here, it is important to consider the question of provenance, which often added both financial value and cultural cachet to a work of art, thereby making it more attractive to potential buyers. The fact that Mead had owned these paintings might have helped legitimate Sir Jacob's interest in the Holbeins. The artist had been revered in his own time, and later attracted the attention of one of the first great English art collectors, the 'Collector Earl', Thomas Howard, 21st Earl of Arundel (1585–1646), who himself had once owned the painting of *Erasmus*.[127] It is known that Mead wished to emphasise the links between himself, Arundel and other 'seventeenth-century virtuosi',[128] and arguably Sir Jacob felt the same desire to associate himself with these unique and pioneering art collectors.

In addition, he may have wished to follow in Mead's footsteps, not only as a collector guided by virtuosic traditions but as a philanthropist within the art world. During his lifetime, Mead had opened up his collection to artists, and also worked to promote the Foundling Hospital, a charity for orphans that held art exhibitions.[129] Sir Jacob was a governor of the Hospital and, as we have seen, in the same year as Mead's sale had been instrumental in the establishment of the Society of Arts. In purchasing the paintings from his collection, Sir Jacob thus revealed a range of ambitions and associations.

Fig. 40 John Michael Rysbrack (1694–1770), *Jacob Bouverie, 1st Viscount Folkestone*, early to mid-eighteenth century, white marble, 64.8 x 53.3 cm, Longford Castle

As well as collecting historical works of art on the secondary market, Sir Jacob continued to acquire pieces by contemporary artists for Longford Castle throughout his tenure there. These fine-art commissions were predominantly representations of members of the family. Although the majority were painted portraits, one of the most important examples of patronage undertaken by Sir Jacob was a commission for three marble portrait busts depicting family members, including himself (fig. 40) and his young son, William (later the 1st Earl of Radnor; fig. 42). These busts were made by the sculptor John Michael Rysbrack, and it is likely that payments totalling £350 made to Rysbrack on account in November and December 1739 related to the purchase.[130] Compared to the cost of the two oil paintings (£63) portraying Sir Jacob and his wife, commissioned from Michael Dahl fifteen years earlier, this sum highlights the relative values of the two media, and also highlights the extent to which Sir Jacob deemed it important to be depicted in marble.

This commission, taking place shortly after Sir Jacob's inheritance of the castle, and concurrently with his improvements to its interiors, is significant, and may have been bound up with his new identity as landowner. The busts alluded to the castle's present and future

Fig. 41 John Michael Rysbrack (1694–1770), *Edward Bouverie*, early to mid-eighteenth century, white marble, 61.6 x 57.2 cm, Longford Castle

incumbents, and the materiality of the marble entrenched a sense of permanence in this representation of the family dynasty. The art historian Matthew Craske has suggested that families who made the transition from trade to land might often celebrate the first man of noble title in marble.[131] Although Sir Jacob had not yet received his viscountcy at the time of this commission, the bust nonetheless fitted with this patronage trend, celebrating him, shortly after his inheritance, as *paterfamilias* (head of the family).

Eighteenth-century sitters, and especially politicians, were often represented wearing classical dress in marble busts, as such representations created links with antique statuary and the 'Roman Republican tradition of civic virtue', thereby enabling the busts to gain 'authority as [images]'.[132] However, Sir Jacob was instead shown dressed in a loose, creased cap, and an unbuttoned shirt and jacket. One might wonder why he did not choose to be portrayed in classical dress to link himself with the august Roman past, like other patrons of the time. It must be remembered, however, that this commission was still made relatively early on in his collecting career: at a time before he had entered political life as Member of Parliament for Salisbury. Although he may have held ambitions to enter Parliament at this time, he might not have wished to have himself represented as a born political leader quite yet. His decision to patronise Rysbrack, who was known for depicting men of trade in simplified contemporary dress and a soft cloth cap, a style known as *en négligé*,[133] instead speaks of a desire to express his multifaceted sense of identity, and not actively to dissociate himself from the Bouverie family's mercantile origins following his inheritance of Longford.

We can gain a sense of how Sir Jacob was negotiating a range of associations – his family heritage and his new status as landowner – through his patronage, by considering other early commissions he made from contemporary artists. He acquired an estate portrait of Longford Castle from the artist George Lambert (1700–1765) in 1743 (now in the Government Art Collection), reinforcing his ownership of the castle and estate. It was common for patrons of the time to commission estate views: for example, Lambert had also worked on a set of views of Chiswick House, London, for Richard Boyle, 3rd Earl of Burlington (1694–1753).[134] Again, it seems that Sir Jacob patronised one of the choicest and most fashionable artists for the job.

As well as acquiring a painting depicting Longford's grounds, Sir Jacob bought a number of works of art specifically intended for display out of doors. He acquired a range of garden sculptures from a 'Mr. Cheere' – most likely John Cheere (1709–1787) of Hyde Park Corner, the brother of Sir Henry Cheere. John Cheere, as distinct from his brother, worked in lead and plaster rather than marble, producing a great quantity of figures, statuettes and busts in a range of sizes during the 1740s and 1750s for display in patrons' gardens.[135] For instance, he supplied a statue of a *River God* costing £98 for Stourhead, Wiltshire, in 1751, and nineteen lead statues for Blair Castle, Perthshire, in 1754.[136] Again, it seems that Sir Jacob was at the forefront of contemporary taste when making these acquisitions.

In 1743 he paid £3 10s 6d to 'Cheere at Hyde-Park-Corner for 3 plaister Bustos bronz'd & cases'.[137] In 1759, he bought statues depicting the Roman deities *Flora* and *Augusta* from the sculptor, which came to '£8:8:0 each' with 'oyling, painting, & packing cases', and also paid a supplier for 'six stone Terms at £8:8:0 each' and 'Mr. Devall for the Portland stone for d[itt]o'.[138] The decision to purchase these decorative items for the garden may have been precipitated by the works that had recently been undertaken to redesign the Longford grounds in line with the new trend for informality in country-house gardens. In 1737, Sir Jacob wrote to his brother-in-law describing these works. The letter reveals that the designer and Royal Gardener Charles Bridgeman (1690–1738) had been involved, and gives an insight into the type of changes that were made:

Fig. 42 Attributed to John Michael Rysbrack (1694–1770), *William Bouverie* [later 1st Earl of Radnor], early to mid-eighteenth century, white marble, 49.5 x 38.1 cm, Longford Castle

> I have been a good deal at a loss for want of Bridgemans Company; however I have not been idle, what I have ordered as to Pollards &c & here & there a tree absolutely necessary to come down, will take up three or four men I am informed as many months: I have been making interest with my Neighbours & have let severall pretty views into my Garden, & the bushes on the other side ye. river are cut down which makes the Gardens exceedingly pleasant & ye. river look half as broad again.[139]

This excerpt provides evidence that Sir Jacob was keen to conform to various eighteenth-century gardening fashions: for instance, he appears to have been keen to open up views and vistas within the Longford gardens. Bridgeman, who worked on the gardens at Wimpole Hall in Cambridgeshire and Stowe in Buckinghamshire, among others, was particularly interested in working on a large scale and opening up views, for instance through the use of ha-has.[140] Contemporary gardening manuals also promoted such principles. The landscape designer and writer Batty Langley (1696–1751) decreed 'that Views in Gardens be as extensive as possible' in his 1728 book *New Principles of Gardening*.[141] Fashion also endorsed the enlargement of rivers and lakes, as happened in the early eighteenth century at Boughton in Northamptonshire, for example.[142] Sir Jacob's note that the River Avon at Longford appeared 'half as broad again' implies that he was aware of this trend, and wished to follow it.

The gardens were further transformed during this period by the addition of various other ornaments, including stone vases from Bath, a summerhouse, a balustrade and an obelisk.[143] The latter was created by William Privett of Chilmark (dates unknown), for a cost of £29 13s 10d.[144] This was very much in line with the fashion for decorating country-house gardens with classical features, such as temples and sculptures.[145] The gardens at Longford have since undergone numerous further changes, and not many of these features still survive. A lead statue of *Flora*, however, still stands in pride of place in the recently restored formal gardens outside the garden front of the castle (fig. 43).

This *Flora* may be the statue bought from Cheere in 1759, although her companion, *Augusta*, no longer remains at the castle.[146] *Flora* is today housed in a 'columned canopy surmounted by an urn and raised on steps'.[147] The columns were made by Privett for the 1st Earl of Radnor in 1769 to house a statue of *Fame* by Rysbrack. Although country-house gardens are by their very nature evolving entities, for those who today stroll through

Fig. 43 Possibly John Cheere (1709–1787), *Flora*, possibly 1759, lead, Longford Castle

the gardens or gaze out from the windows of the Long Parlour or the Picture Gallery *Flora* provides an indication of how the Longford gardens would have appeared during the mid-eighteenth century, when they were remodelled in line with the new fashions of the time.

The renovations undertaken at this point in Longford's history meant that the seventeenth-century formal gardens, as featured in Robert Thacker's views of the castle and its surroundings (discussed in Chapter 1, pages 22–5), were swept away. A sketch plan of the grounds made in 1770 shows that, by this time, these garden features had almost completely disappeared. They had instead been replaced by open meadows, some shrubs and plants, a 'rock with arcade' and gravel walks in place of the old formal gardens.[148] Visitors' accounts from the middle of the eighteenth century concur with this picture of the gardens. Richard Pococke, who came to Longford in 1754, described how 'the river is on two sides of the fine lawn and plantations', and how 'in the part near the house are knots of flowering shrubs', evincing a much more simplified aesthetic than is shown by our seventeenth-century sources.[149] This raises the question: why did Sir Jacob wish to overhaul the formal gardens? As we have seen, the Coleraine family had carefully restored them after the destruction of the Civil War.

The decision may be attributed to a range of factors. First, the works may have been motivated, like Sir Edward's removal of the golden motto 'Status non Situs' from the castle's exterior, by a desire to sweep away signs of the Coleraine family, which were not, after all, part of the original Longford. Moreover, orderly, controlled, formal gardens were considered very outdated in the mid-eighteenth century. The fashion, instead, was for informality, while older gardening styles attracted derision. For example, the anonymous poem *The Rise and Progress of the Present Taste in Planting Parks, Pleasure Grounds, Gardens, Etc* somewhat contemptuously described 'The false magnificence of Tudor's day' and 'Trees clipt to statues, monsters, cats and dogs, And hollies metamorphos'd into hogs' at Nonsuch in Surrey, a Tudor palace.[150] Owners of other Elizabethan houses adopted eighteenth-century gardening styles. For example, at Burghley House in Lincolnshire, the renowned garden designer Lancelot 'Capability' Brown (1716–1783) remodelled the landscape against a sixteenth-century architectural backdrop.[151] To follow this course was not, therefore, uncommon.

The pursuit of these new trends in garden design went hand in hand with Sir Jacob's modernisation of the Longford interiors, and was perhaps consciously and deliberately planned to create a harmonious effect between inside and out. Contemporaries appreciated a sense of fluidity between the interior and exterior of a country house. Mrs Lybbe Powys, who visited Longford as a tourist in 1776, approved of the fact that the castle 'stands in the middle of the garden, only one step from the ground, so that you may instantly be out of doors'.[152] Conversely, the arrangement of nearby Fonthill House did not meet her approbation. She said reprovingly that, unlike at Longford, 'which we had that morning admir'd for being so near the garden, the ground apartments at Fonthill by a most tremendous flight of steps are, I believe, more distant from the terrace on which the house stands than the attic storey of Longford Castle'.[153]

Country-house owners purposely tried to achieve a sense of harmony between interior and exterior by ensuring that the views from their windows complemented the scenes depicted in the paintings on display on their walls. At Holkham Hall, for instance, a dedicated Landscape Room was hung with paintings by Claude, Poussin and Salvator Rosa (1615–1673), believed to embody the notion of the picturesque, so as to complement 'the Arcadian landscape of serpentine woods and lakes outside the windows'.[154] A similar imperative seems to have been felt at Longford. As viewers walk through the Gallery, they not only take in the old master landscape paintings by the likes of Claude but are also able to appreciate the views through the windows to the River Avon and the grounds beyond. The combination of water and trees depicted in the Claudes would have been mirrored by the gardens outside, adding to the sense of fluidity between inside and out.

Today, another important landscape painting hangs in the Gallery at Longford, adding to this sense of unity. Although it was displayed elsewhere in the castle during the eighteenth century, it was purchased by Sir Jacob in 1741, and is another fascinating acquisition worth our attention for what it says about his taste, and about the continued significance of the

Fig. 44 Jean-Baptiste I Martin, called Martin des Batailles (1659–1735), *An Extensive View of the Palace of Fontainebleau with a Boar Hunt in the Foreground*, late seventeenth to early eighteenth century, oil on canvas in a contemporary French carved and gilded frame with the initials of King Louis XIV, 116.8 x 162.6 cm, Longford Castle

provenance of paintings in the Longford collection. The painting is an aerial depiction of the Palace of Fontainebleau and its grounds by the painter and designer Jean-Baptiste Martin (1659–1735) (fig. 44).

It is a highly detailed representation of the buildings, gardens, water features and surrounding landscape of the palace, and its foreground is animated by the inclusion of figures engaged in a hunt. Today's visitors to Longford can admire the French scene while taking in the view of the River Avon, the castle's newly restored formal gardens and the extensive surrounding landscape through the adjacent windows. The frame in which the painting is displayed merits close inspection, as it bears relief carvings depicting the royal monogram of King Louis XIV (1638–1715), and thus is likely to be the frame in which the painting was originally housed.[155] An inventory of works of art at Longford made later in the eighteenth century mentioned that this painting 'has been in some of the French King's collections, as may be seen by the Frame'.[156] Although the inventory's author did not provide details of many of the other frames on display at Longford at the time, he clearly felt that this royal association was worth recording.

In the light of the extensive modernisation of the Longford grounds and interiors during his tenure, it is interesting to consider Sir Jacob's disinclination to make fundamental changes to the Elizabethan appearance and fabric of the castle's architecture. As we saw in Chapter 1 (page 30), his predecessor, Sir Edward, had made the untypical decision to purchase an unusual Elizabethan country house, rather than build anew, or remodel the castle in the neo-Palladian style. Sir Jacob's attitude mirrored that of his brother: although he was happy to bring key interiors up to date, showcasing his fashionable taste, he did not make any substantial changes to the castle's exterior appearance. Certain entries in his account books do suggest that he was interested in exploring various options regarding architectural works at Longford; however, what is most significant is his decision to retain the castle ultimately more or less as it was.

For instance, in November 1750, he made a payment to 'Mr. Wood the Architect for coming over from Bath to Longford, (a day) when He gave his opinion only, but gave no design, as nothing was agreed on'.[157] This may have been either John Wood the Elder (1704–1754) or John Wood the Younger (1728–1782), the architects responsible for many of the neo-Palladian buildings erected in the fashionable spa town of Bath throughout the eighteenth century.[158] This implies that Sir Jacob was keen to solicit the advice of fashionable architects, even if he did not ultimately follow up this consultation.

In 1757 he undertook some works to the loggia on the entrance front of the castle, listing payments in his accounts relating to 'the logio roof' and 'for carving capitals'.[159] Christopher Hussey described these works as 'repairs', suggesting that they took the form of maintenance, but also noted how the 'carved features of the lower loggia . . . are curiously rococo in feeling',[160] implying some deviation from the original style. Yet the fact that many original features of the castle's front were left – such as the Dutch gables, and a relief carving of a boat – indicates a fundamental desire on Sir Jacob's part to retain Longford's distinctive exterior much in its original state. His conservative approach, making small amendments to the castle, reflects a sense of decorum, and a desire not to be seen to be ostentatious in his patronage. He was sympathetic to Longford's heritage and individuality, yet simultaneously ensured that it was suitably maintained and improved. Mrs Lybbe Powys notably remarked in 1776 that the castle 'neither looks modern or ancient but between both':[161] a unique condition that Sir Jacob admirably conserved.

It appears that his priority was, above all, to keep Longford Castle in good repair, to maintain and look after the family seat, as part of a secure legacy to be handed down the generations. This was enshrined in his will, which treated Longford as both the inheritance of the first son – precluding any potential split in the estate – and as a home that was not allowed to undergo neglect or decay but which should be maintained and improved. He willed that a trust be set up to provide an annuity of £600 for 'repairing or adorning my said House and Gardens at Longford', and hoped that his heirs would settle the same conditions upon their inheritors.[162] Here, it is important to remember that Longford Castle's primary role has always been that of a home, even in the eighteenth century when the culture of country-house tourism began to expand.

A national pastime today, country-house visiting took off in the Georgian period, through a range of factors. First, the building boom meant that there were many more houses to visit, and the codes of polite society advocated that they should be open to genteel visitors.[163] Secondly, improvements in carriage design and the turnpike road system quite literally smoothed the way for tourists, meaning that travel itself did not entail the same degree of trouble and discomfort as previously.[164] Longford's neighbour, Wilton House, was the first to publish a catalogue to its art collection,[165] and, along with other local attractions such as Salisbury Cathedral and Stonehenge, may have acted as a draw for tourists. It was not until the middle of the nineteenth century that a guidebook dedicated to Longford Castle was published, and there is no evidence to suggest it had regular opening hours for visitors during the eighteenth century, as at Woburn Abbey in Bedfordshire and Blenheim Palace in Oxfordshire, for instance.[166]

However, tourists were accommodated at Longford during the eighteenth century on a less formal and more *ad hoc* basis. One visitor wrote of the warm welcome he received, noting in his travel account: 'I think we were at no place treated with more politeness than here, and we must not forget the obliging manner in which you was invited to drink chocolate by the house-keeper.'[167] Sir Jacob may have been motivated to open up his home and art collection to tourists because of his commitment to the improvement of the arts in Britain. John Cornforth has linked Sir Jacob's readiness to share his art collection with his involvement in the Society of Arts.[168]

In 1753 Sir Jacob conducted a tour of Norfolk, recording in his account book 'Expences on the Norfolk Expedition'.[169] This county was another popular eighteenth-century destination for seeing country houses: a tour encompassing visits to Houghton, Holkham, Blickling, Felbrigg and Raynham Halls had become 'almost as obligatory as the Grand Tour itself' by the 1770s.[170] It is very likely that Sir Jacob's excursion included a visit to Houghton, as he had purchased the *Aedes Walpolianae*, a catalogue of its collection of pictures, and 'two books about Ld. Orford's [Sir Robert Walpole's] house' the previous year,[171] possibly in preparation for the visit. Seeing and learning about the art collections at other important houses may have influenced his artistic tastes.

We have already heard throughout this chapter the voices of some of the Georgian visitors Longford received, and seen how much they admired and esteemed the treasures it contained. Yet it is particularly interesting to note how, despite the public role that Longford – like many other country houses – took on during this period, what many most appreciated about the castle was its domestic nature. A number of visitors remarked upon the suitability of the Long-ford interiors to their role as inhabited spaces. For instance, Jonas Hanway wrote that 'convenience with grandeur seem to be so admirably mixed, that one is rather tempted to envy the possessor for the COMFORT he may enjoy in it, than for the gratification of his pride, or ambition'.[172]

Historians have defined the concept of 'home' as 'an environment which privileges comfort and convenience over grandeur and display',[173] and this eighteenth-century observation

implies that Sir Jacob had been motivated primarily by a desire to create a home he wished to live in, rather than one designed solely to show off his wealth through ostentatious display. These priorities were apparent to tourists, and helped the family gain respect among them. Although tourism at Longford might have created a dichotomy between its public and private roles, it is striking that the castle's apparently domestic nature was considered a merit when it came under public scrutiny.

Studies of eighteenth-century tourism have shown that visitors often took an interest in the items of furniture and the decorative arts within the country-house interior, as well as the paintings and sculptures.[174] At Longford, the particularly high calibre of the furnishings and decoration meant that these pieces did not escape tourists' notice. Written accounts of visits to the castle devoted space to describing wainscoting, chimneypieces, stained-glass windows, and soft furnishings including damask, chintz and tapestry.[175] In particular, a set of eighteenth-century Brussels tapestries based on the designs of the Flemish artist David Teniers the Younger (1610–1690) caught visitors' attention.

For example, Richard Pococke wrote of how one 'apartment is hung with fine Flemish tapestry of the design of Tenieres',[176] and an anonymous account published in 1762 made mention of 'an octagonal Room, hung with modern Tapestry from the droll Paintings of *Teniers*',[177] revealing the manner in which the tapestries were displayed in the eighteenth century. From the mid-seventeenth to the mid-eighteenth century, subjects from Teniers's paintings were often used as the basis for tapestry designs.[178] 'Droll' was a term used in the eighteenth century to describe a 'type of amusement which, while low in itself, appealed to the polite'.[179] The four separate panels of the Longford tapestries show a range of scenes from

Fig. 46 David Teniers the
Younger (1610–1690), *Boers
Playing Bowls at an Inn with the
Sign of a Star*, seventeenth
century, oil on panel,
40 x 52.7 cm, enlarged
below and on the left,
Longford Castle

everyday life, including the preparation of dinner at an inn (fig. 45), a vegetable and flower market, a fish market and the harvest at a farmstead. These representations of rural work chime with the subjects of some of the Dutch and Flemish paintings Sir Jacob collected for Longford, including paintings by Teniers himself.

Sir Jacob commissioned and imported these wool and silk tapestries in 1749, for a total of £148 14s.[180] Within the previous five years he had bought two paintings by Teniers at auction, and in 1750 he bought a total of seventy-nine prints after works by the artist, revealing the extent of his interest in Teniers's oeuvre.[181] Although, as we have seen, the Dutch school was less highly esteemed than the Italian by academic theorists of the time, Teniers was nonetheless well regarded, because his work was said to show a higher level of refinement.[182] A collector could demonstrate taste by an ability to overlook a painting's 'mundane or vulgar subject', and instead appreciate its technical aspects.[183]

The first painting by Teniers acquired for the Longford collection depicted *Boers playing Bowls* (fig. 46), and was bought by Sir Jacob at the 1744 auction conducted by Robert Bragge at which he also purchased Avercamp's skating scene, discussed earlier in this chapter. It was one of the more expensive items he purchased at that sale, costing £40 8s 6d.[184] The second painting, which he described as a 'return from hunting', was bought at auction in 1748, and cost £84.[185] This genre painting (fig. 47) shows two figures standing near the edge of a wood, surrounded by dogs, with some cottages to the right of the composition.

Fig. 47 David Teniers the Younger (1610–1690), *The Return from Coursing, an Old Man with a Young Sportsman carrying a Dead Hare with Hounds near Cottages at the Edge of a Wood*, seventeenth century, oil on canvas, 114.3 x 153.7 cm, Longford Castle

When John Smith catalogued the Longford art collection in 1829, he wrote that 'the figures in this excellent picture are unusually large for the master, the general effect is powerful & imposing & the execution very free & masterly'.[186] He also mentioned that the painting 'was greatly admired by our celebrated Painter Gainsborough by whom it was successfully copied', and indeed the eighteenth-century English landscape artist and portrait painter Thomas Gainsborough (*c.* 1727–1788) did make a copy after the painting when he came to stay at Longford Castle in the 1770s.[187] The works he undertook for the Bouveries at this time will be the subject of discussion later in this book (see pages 102–3). For now, however, it is interesting to note how the Longford art collection was experienced in the eighteenth century: it did not exist only for the enjoyment of the family, or tourists who visited the castle, but was also used by contemporary artists for their edification.

Sir Jacob's acquisition of a range of works of art by and after Teniers provides further evidence of his taste for the Northern schools of painting. Although today the tapestries hang in the Triangular Hall, they were originally hung in one of the castle's round tower rooms. Given that, during the Tudor period, houses were often decorated with tapestries for their warmth and portability,[188] the decision to decorate a room with contemporary examples was arguably an eighteenth-century inflection of a trend that looked back to Longford's sixteenth-century heritage. The room in which the tapestries hung came to be known as the

Tapestry Room. Similarly, during the eighteenth and nineteenth centuries, other rooms in the castle were called after the material in which they were decorated, such as the India Paper Bed Chamber, the Blue Damask Bed Chamber, and, especially importantly, the Green Velvet Drawing Room.[189]

This latter room provides one of the final case studies in this chapter. Like the Round Parlour and Gallery discussed earlier, it is one of the most important Longford interiors, and, like those rooms, was substantially refurbished in the eighteenth century under the direction of Sir Jacob. The room today appears much as it did in his day, thanks to the preservation of this remarkable interior by his successors. The Green Velvet Drawing Room is another round tower room, adjoining the Gallery at its far end. Sir Jacob contracted work to be done on this room around the same time as he refurbished the Gallery, and from the type of decoration and furnishing he commissioned it appears that he conceived of the two rooms as working together in enfilade.

This was primarily achieved through the repetition of the colour: as we have seen, the Gallery had been hung at great expense in green damask, and the Green Velvet Drawing Room continued this theme. Although the two spaces were already configured on a single axis, this choice indicates that Sir Jacob wished to enhance the vista, and to augment the sense of continuity and progression between these spaces. A suite of ten parcel-gilt mahogany chairs upholstered in green velvet had been commissioned in 1739, and four years later, the 'green flowered velvet' for the walls was purchased at a cost of £150 (fig. 48).[190]

The suite of chairs has been attributed to the renowned eighteenth-century cabinetmaker Giles Grendey (1693–1780), on the basis of the style and virtuosity of the carving, which features lion-paw feet and lion heads on the arms (fig. 49).[191] A payment in the Longford accounts to 'Greenday, chairmaker' of £68 is likely to refer to this commission.[192] Again, we can see how Sir Jacob was keen to patronise the best furniture-makers available when refurbishing Longford Castle. The carving on the chairs speaks to the fashions of the time, as similar pieces were made for other country houses including Rousham House in Oxfordshire and Holkham Hall.[193]

The continuation of the colour green across these two rooms created a sense of continuity but the change in texture from silk damask to velvet, as one traverses the threshold, subtly differentiates the spaces. John Cornforth has noted in relation to the decoration of these two rooms that drawing rooms 'were invariably more richly furnished' than picture galleries.[194] This may have been thanks to the relative sizes of the spaces: because velvet was more expensive than damask,[195] it may have been employed for the smaller room on the basis of cost. However, Sir Jacob's choice of material for each space may also have been precipitated by the rooms' respective functions.

Sumptuous velvet was arguably a highly appropriate choice for a drawing room, as it would have provided more comfort within a space that was intended to be sat in. Moreover,

Fig. 48 Green Velvet Drawing Room, Longford Castle, 2016

Above: Fig. 49 Attributed to Giles Grendey (1693–1780), Chair, eighteenth century, parcel-gilt mahogany with velvet upholstery, Longford Castle

unlike the adjacent Gallery, the principal function of the Green Velvet Drawing Room was not the accommodation of the art collection. Although eighteenth-century inventories record the presence of a few pictures in the room,[196] and indeed it is hung today with some notable works in the collection, Sir Jacob may have foreseen a sparser or more static arrangement of art in the Green Velvet Drawing Room than in the Gallery, because velvet is more easily damaged if pictures are removed, rehung or replaced[197] (although the presence of only a few paintings in the room could equally have been precipitated by the presence of the velvet). In any case, the fabric would not have been as suitable a decorative choice for the Gallery as damask, considering that room's use for the display of a constantly expanding collection of art.

Today, the Green Velvet Drawing Room contains some veritable treasures of the Longford art collection, including the portrait of Queen Elizabeth I, discussed in Chapter 1 (page 20; fig. 9). Two other paintings

Above: Fig. 50 Samuel Scott (1702–1772), *View of London Bridge*, c. 1750, oil on canvas, 48.3 x 142.2 cm, Longford Castle

Below: Fig. 51 Samuel Scott (1702–1772), *View of Westminster Bridge*, c. 1750, oil on canvas, 48.3 x 142.2 cm, Longford Castle

on display in the room, commissioned by Sir Jacob, merit particular attention at this point. In 1750 he paid the artist Samuel Scott (1702–1772), renowned for his landscapes and seascapes, for a pair of paintings depicting views of London Bridge and Westminster Bridge (figs 50 and 51). His account entry for the transaction reads: 'Mr. Scott in earnest for two Pictures bespoke of him at 25 Gs. each, but He talks of 5 Gs more each, on acct. of his being to lengthen his draughts'.[198]

Scott depicted the bridges in another pair of paintings, now in the Tate collection, which were engraved in 1758 on account of their popularity.[199] The subject matter of these two sets of paintings highlighted the differences between the newly built Westminster Bridge and the old London Bridge, which was then awaiting renovation.[200] What is 'bespoke' about the Longford pair is not only that they were painted at Sir Jacob's behest, but that they are slightly curved, enabling them to be displayed over doors in the circular tower rooms. Like the curved

Fig. 52 Luca Carlevarijs (1663–1730), *The Piazza of St Mark's, Venice, looking East, with Numerous Figures*, late seventeenth or early eighteenth century, oil on canvas, 53.3 x 119.4 cm, Longford Castle

Fig . 53 Luca Carlevarijs (1663–1730), *View on the Grand Canal, Venice, looking North, with Ca' Balbi on the Left and Numerous Figures, Gondolas and Boats*, late seventeenth or early eighteenth century, oil on canvas, 53.3 x 119.4 cm, Longford Castle

JACOB BOUVERIE, IST VISCOUNT FOLKESTONE

Fig. 54 William van de Velde the Younger
(1633–1707), *A Dutch States Yacht in a Strong Breeze
near a Jetty with Men-o'-War at Anchor*, seventeenth
or early eighteenth century, oil on panel,
34.9 x 43.8 cm, Longford Castle (acquired 1760)

marble-topped table commissioned from Goodison for the Round Parlour, discussed earlier (pages 49–50 and fig. 25), these paintings are highly significant as they fitted and complemented Longford's unique architecture. Both fine art commissions and furnishings were therefore contrived to fit the distinctive shape of the castle.

However, although they are today on display in the Green Velvet Drawing Room, in the eighteenth century they in fact hung in another round tower room: that known as the Tapestry Room, where the newly commissioned Brussels tapestries, discussed earlier (page 78 and fig. 45), were displayed. We know from descriptions in inventories of the Longford collection that they were hung over doors when in the Tapestry Room – much as they are today in the Green Velvet Drawing Room.[201] This was a display convention seen in country houses from the late seventeenth century onwards,[202] and it can be seen elsewhere at Longford.

For instance, in 1757 Sir Jacob bought a pair of landscapes depicting the Piazza of St Mark's and a view of the Grand Canal at Venice,[203] providing an Italian counterpart to Scott's depictions of the bridges on the River Thames. Once attributed to Gaspar Ochiale and today given to Luca Carlevarijs (1663–1730), they now hang in the Long Parlour (figs 52, 53); however, eighteenth-century inventories show that they once hung over doors in the Breakfast Room at Longford.[204] Therefore, although it is in the nature of country-house art collections that works of art are moved around and redisplayed as a collection evolves and a house is passed down through the generations, certain pieces are by their very materiality always hung in particular types of space.

Although Longford Castle today bears witness to many changes made by Sir Jacob's successors, much of what he did to improve the unique building he inherited, and to establish the art collection there, remains discernible today. He sympathetically respected the castle's heritage and individuality when redecorating its interiors, while following new fashions in a decorous manner. Today, those rooms continue to function as home to a world-class collection of art, and as part of a family home. This chapter has shown how Sir Jacob was concerned with improving Longford in its entirety, bringing it up to date through the modernisation of the gardens, the acquisition of important works of art from abroad and at auction, and the patronage of the best furniture-makers and contemporary artists for works of fine and decorative art of the highest quality. All of these elements worked together to articulate his wealth, taste and ascending social status.

It is testament to Sir Jacob's success as landowner and collector that his successors went on to match his achievements and even to advance the family's aristocratic status. As a patron, he looked to the past, the present and the future: he respected tradition and created a sense of continuity both at Longford Castle itself and through his political work for the surrounding community; he was at the forefront of the eighteenth-century art world through his patronage of artists and presidency of the Society of Arts; and he looked to the future and the continuation of his family dynasty at Longford, planting trees in the grounds and amassing his art collection for posterity. With these foundations laid, his son and heir, William, was able to follow in his footsteps, honouring his legacy and inserting key new acquisitions and commissions from the finest artists of his day. It is to his tenure that we now turn our attention.

Fig. 55 Probably Antonio Susini (*fl.* 1572–1624) after a model by Giambologna (1529–1608), *Nessus and Deianira*, early seventeenth century, bronze, 40.6 cm high, Longford Castle (acquired 1739)

CHAPTER 3

William Bouverie, 1st Earl of Radnor

The King has granted unto the Right Hon. William Viscount Folkstone, Baron
of Longford, and the heirs male, the dignities of a Baron and Earl of the kingdom
of Great Britain, by the title of Baron Pleydell-Bouverie, of Coleshill,
in the county of Berks, and Earl of the county of Radnor, in the principality of
Wales: and, in default of such issue, the said dignity of Earl of the county of
Radnor, to the heirs male of Jacob Viscount Folkstone, deceased.[1]

This report of grant of title appeared in *Owen's Weekly Chronicle and Westminster Journal* in
October 1765. It documents what was one of the most significant changes that occurred during
the tenure of this member of the Bouverie family at Longford Castle: the recreation of the earldom of Radnor that ennobled William Bouverie, eldest son of Jacob, 1st Viscount Folkestone.
The new 1st Earl of Radnor (1725–1776) built admirably upon the legacy he had inherited from
his father, by furthering the Bouverie family's aristocratic status and adding to the collections
of fine art and furnishings that Sir Jacob had inaugurated at the castle. As this chapter will show,
the 1st Earl stayed true to the character of the art collection, by acquiring works of art on the
secondary market by important old masters, and by continuing to patronise the best artists and
craftsmen of the day for pieces that chimed stylistically with those already at Longford.

The Radnor title had been held before by successive members of the Robartes family but
had died out during the 1750s upon the death of John Robartes, 4th Earl of Radnor (1686–1757).
The Whig grandee Charles Watson Wentworth, 2nd Marquess of Rockingham (1730–1782),
secured the earldom for William Bouverie. On 18 August 1765, he wrote in a letter that he had
'done what your Lordship wished in laying your Request before his Majesty', adding that he
was 'happy to be able to inform you that your Request is granted'.[2] He noted that 'His Majesty's
gracious manner in conferring this Favour gave me great satisfaction, as it was with the utmost
willingness that I submitted to his Majesty's consideration a Request so well supported by
Merit & Character':[3] a flattering testimonial that reveals how highly the new 1st Earl of Radnor
was esteemed.

The 1st Earl was an important patron of the arts, and continued his father's practice of
keeping meticulous accounts, recording purchases and payments for works of art. Unlike
his father, he did not always provide a lot of detail in his descriptions of items, with the result

Fig. 56 Thomas Gainsborough
(1727–1788), *William, 1st Earl of
Radnor*, 1773 (detail of fig. 66)

89

that it is sometimes not easy to trace the precise identity of the 'pictures' to which he refers. However, an examination of the art-related transactions for the years immediately following the 1st Earl's ennoblement is revealing. It shows, for instance, that many pieces of family silver were re-engraved with new coats of arms, crests and coronets after this important event.

Silver's malleable properties mean that it could be re-worked and enhanced in line with a patron's social ascend-ancy relatively easily. The Longford accounts, and 'gentlemen's ledgers' belonging to the firm owned by silversmith George Wickes (c. 1698–1761) and his successors, Edward Wakelin (fl. 1759–1777) and John Parker (dates unknown), illustrate how the Bouveries' collection of plate was reworked over the course of the eighteenth century to express the family's ever-increasing social status.

Fig. 57 Edward Wakelin (*fl.* 1759–1777), Sauceboat Engraved with the Arms of Pleydell-Bouverie impaling Clarke, 1759, silver, Longford Castle

For example, in 1766, following the ennoblement, the firm was contracted for numerous tasks, including engraving '72 Coats Supporters & Cor[onet]s and pollishg up six Dox: Plates', 'taking out and Regraving Coats of 29 Dishes' and 'taking out and regravg Cor[onet]s on the Candlesticks'.[4] The 1st Earl paid a bill of £45 to 'Edward Wakelin & Co: Silver Smiths' in July 1766, one of £22 13s to 'Parker & Wakelin Goldsmiths' in 1767 and further bills of similar sums in the years thereafter.[5] These payments show how the Bouveries' collection of silverware was a primary arena in which their identity was articulated. After all, plates, dishes, candlesticks and cutlery were items seen and used on a regular basis by the family and their guests, and would have taken their place alongside the redecorated interiors, family portraits and fine art acquisitions at Longford Castle to express their wealth and status. The payments also hint at the maintenance and upkeep that had to be undertaken to keep a collection of plate looking its best. Silversmiths' firms would regularly undertake repair work for aristocratic patrons,[6] evincing the fact that plate was indeed in regular practical use, as well as revealing owners' concerns with caring for their heirlooms for posterity.

As this chapter and the next will demonstrate, the 1st and 2nd Earls of Radnor were loyal patrons to particular artists, craftsmen and firms, to whom they entrusted multiple commissions on a repeat basis. This was very much the case for the firm of silversmiths and goldsmiths begun by Wickes, continued by Wakelin and Parker, and taken over by Robert Garrard (*fl.* 1792–1802) in 1802. This company produced a multitude of items for the Bouverie family, which can still be seen and appreciated at Longford today (fig. 57).

The Bouveries' patronage of the firm had begun in 1737, when Sir Jacob commissioned from Wickes a collection of plate and engraving services, totalling over £1,000 in value. It will not escape the reader's notice that this patronage took place at the same time as Sir Jacob's inheritance of Longford and his work on its interior decoration, and was another way in which he invested in material goods to set himself up as a member of the elite. Similarly, following his elevation to the viscountcy, Sir Jacob paid Wickes for 'altering the arms and adding the Coronet to almost all the other Plate'.[7] Like his father, the 1st Earl recognised the importance of plate as a medium through which to convey his increasing social status.

A few years after the earldom was recreated for William Bouverie, a new Bouverie family motto came into use: 'Patria Cara Carior Libertas' ('My country is dear, but my liberty is dearer').[8] The motto is revealing, as it provides a reminder that although the family were loyal to their adopted country, England – as had been confirmed by the establishment of their family seat at Longford, their political and charitable work and their ennoblement into the ranks of the aristocracy – their belief in freedom was nonetheless of greater import.

This belief is also evident in the particular interest the 1st Earl showed in constitutional history going back to the Anglo-Saxons and King Alfred the Great (849–899). It is worth considering this aspect of the Earl's background, as it influenced some of his artistic patronage. Whig historians particularly revered the Anglo-Saxon period during the eighteenth century. The French Huguenot nobleman Paul de Rapin de Thoyras (1661–1725) had written an illustrated *Histoire d'Angleterre* ('History of England') dedicated to King George I (1660–1727) in the 1720s, wherein he stated that the principle of liberty and 'the foundations of constitutionalism' could be dated back to Anglo-Saxon times.[9] King Alfred's reign was seen to embody some of the key characteristics of eighteenth-century identity as pinpointed by the historian T. C. W. Blanning – Protestantism, commercial prosperity, imperial expansion and, most importantly for our purposes, liberty.[10]

The 1st Earl and three of his sons attended University College, Oxford, supposedly founded by King Alfred, for whom graduates held a great deal of respect.[11] The Earl's interest in the Anglo-Saxon King may be attributed to the time he spent at the college but, equally, it must be remembered that the values of liberty and freedom from oppression that were associated with King Alfred held a particular resonance for the Bouverie family, whose Huguenot ancestors had fled persecution. A desire to pay tribute to King Alfred is visible in the 1st Earl's patronage. In 1767, he bought a statue of *Fame* by the sculptor John Michael Rysbrack for the garden at Longford, and commissioned the artist's pupil, Gaspar van der Hagen (*d.* 1769), to add a depiction of King Alfred to the medallion held by the figure of Fame.[12] An inscription, evoking the sentiment of liberty, accompanied this depiction:

> Whoever you may be, lover of liberty or letters, regard with reverent eyes the Portrait of this Man, who, when his Country was threatened by the Foe from abroad and struggling under Barbarian and shameful ignorance within, did raise it up by Arms, temper it by Laws, and embellish it by Learning. If you be a Briton, you may be proud, also, that the military prowess of Romulus, the politick Wisdom of

Numa, and the philosophick Nobility of Aurelius, are uniquely comprehended in the name of BRITTANIC ALFRED.[13]

A number of other patrons had commissioned images of King Alfred throughout the eighteenth century, from Queen Caroline (1683–1737) to Richard Temple, 1st Viscount Cobham (1675–1749), for various political ends.[14] However, when assessed alongside the new Bouverie family motto, the way in which the 1st Earl refashioned Rysbrack's statue of *Fame* to convey admiration of King Alfred suggests that he was not simply following fashionable regard for the King but that he wished to pay tribute to the Anglo-Saxon emphasis on liberty, as it resonated with his family's pursuit of freedom.

The 1st Earl followed in his forebears' footsteps by continuing to invest in land and property in England, and the extent of his landholdings was made clear in his will.[15] In addition, he became involved in a number of philanthropic initiatives on a national scale. He was a governor of the Foundling Hospital[16] and was closely involved in the Huguenot charity known as the French Hospital (see page 44); he was the first of many members of the Bouverie family to be elected governor of this organisation.[17] He retained links with the Levant Company, following a precedent set by both his Bouverie forebears and his maternal grandfather, becoming a governor in 1771.[18] By taking on this less active and more ceremonial role, rather than a position at the heart of the business overseas, as his predecessors had done, the 1st Earl demonstrated his family's social escalation, as those of high social status usually held governorships.[19]

To understand the full scope of the 1st Earl's work and patronage, it is important to look back at his earlier adult life, before he came to inherit Longford in his mid-thirties. One important life event that is worth our attention is his first marriage, to the heiress Harriot Pleydell, in 1748. As happened on the occasion of his father's first marriage, the union was commemorated through a portrait commission. The artist Thomas Hudson (1701–1779) painted two pairs of portraits of William and Harriot, which have been dated to 1749, and which are on display at Longford today.

The first set comprises two half-length portraits showing the sitters against dark backgrounds and facing one another, framed within feigned ovals. The second pair are three-quarter-lengths,

Fig. 58 Thomas Hudson (1701–1779), *William, 1st Earl of Radnor*, *c.* 1749, oil on canvas, 124.5 x 99.1 cm, Longford Castle

Fig. 59 Thomas Hudson
(1701–1779), *Harriot Pleydell*,
c. 1749, oil on canvas,
127 x 100.3 cm,
Longford Castle

showing the two sitters in seventeenth-century costume, again facing towards one another with a swathe of red drapery in each painting serving to unite the two compositions (figs 58, 59). Hudson regularly depicted his sitters wearing what is known as Van Dyck costume in portraits of the period,[20] and, as will be shown, the style was one repeatedly employed in representations of the Bouverie family.

The portraits cannot be matched firmly to entries in the Longford accounts, which were at this time, of course, kept by the incumbent, Sir Jacob. One of the sets may have been commissioned by William himself, or perhaps by Harriot's father, Sir Mark Stuart Pleydell (*c.* 1693–1768), for display at his country seat, Coleshill House in Berkshire. Acquiring two sets of portraits would have enabled the family at large to capitalise on the hours the pair had sat for Hudson. Sir Jacob was an important patron to this artist, and the Bouverie family entrusted multiple portrait commissions to him over the years. Hudson is said to have bridged the gap between 'the craftsmen-painters of Kneller's generation' and the 'gentlemen-artists of the Royal Academy', and was at the height of his prominence in the late 1750s.[21] The Bouveries thus followed a common course in their patronage, employing painters who were most fashionable at the time, a theme to which we will return.

William's marriage to Harriot brought further landholdings to the Bouverie family. She was heiress to Sir Mark's estate at Coleshill, and after the birth of William and Harriot's son, Jacob (later 2nd Earl of Radnor), her father (fig. 60) added a codicil to his will, leaving his land and fortune to his new grandchild.[22] Coleshill House, which no longer survives, was designed by the influential architect Inigo Jones (1573–1652) and built by Sir Roger Pratt (1620–1684) in around 1660. With Coleshill, Jones and Pratt pioneered the double-pile house type, a model that was much emulated,[23] and Coleshill's architecture has consistently been held in high regard.

Coleshill was Sir Mark's family seat but appears in general to have taken second place to Longford under Bouverie ownership. For instance, during the 1st Earl's lifetime, it was used predominantly as a staging post, providing a temporary resting point for family members travelling between Longford and Oxford, or Bath.[24] In the nineteenth century, some members of the family occupied Coleshill on a more permanent basis (see pages 121–2). Aside from this period, however, it seems that Longford has consistently been treated as the main family seat.

WILLIAM BOUVERIE, 1ST EARL OF RADNOR

Furthermore, it seems that the majority of the art collection amassed by the family has always been held at Longford.

Works of art commissioned during and after William and Harriot's marriage brought to the fore and celebrated her role as heiress, and paid tribute to the strength of the bond the couple shared. For instance, a small oil portrait of Harriot in the collection at Longford Castle shows her on a terrace, with Coleshill House in the background. She was painted gesturing to her right, with her index finger pointing at and turning the viewer's attention to the property (fig. 61). The painting therefore directly associates Harriot with her inheritance, even going so far as to adopt the classic gesture of the male landowner. It was executed by the artist Edward Haytley (*fl.* 1740–1764), who was known as a journeyman artist, as he would travel to his clients' homes and observe them in their milieu, showing off his sitters' wealth or status by representing them outdoors, alongside their property, to depict its scale and therefore their status.[25] It was unusual, however, for a portrait of the time to be so explicit in acknowledging a woman's inheritance, ownership or transmittal of property to her husband,[26] making this a particularly intriguing work of art.

Fig. 60 Circle of Thomas Gibson (*c.* 1680–1751), *Sir Mark Stuart Pleydell*, eighteenth century, oil on canvas, 73.7 x 61 cm, Longford Castle

It is uncertain who commissioned this painting, but it is notable that other depictions of Harriot can be deemed less conventional and more innovative than other contemporary representations of women, as they portray her in an independent or even superior position. For example, a small oval wax portrait in the collection at Longford Castle, showing Harriot and the 1st Earl in profile, is striking, as it inverted the traditional means of depicting husband and wife by putting Harriot's profile in the foreground, showing it overlapping that of her husband, rather than the other way round (fig. 62).

This portrait has been attributed to the sculptor John Michael Rysbrack, and may have been made as part of the design process for a piece of monumental sculpture commissioned by the 1st Earl for All Saints Church, Coleshill, in 1750. This monument, which was included in Horace Walpole's list of Rysbrack's twenty-two 'best works',[27] commemorated Harriot following her tragically early death, just two years after her marriage. The monument, like the wax model, features overlapping relief portraits of the couple, which the art historian Matthew Craske has argued 'constitute the most patent inversion of an established visual tradition aimed at communicating patriarchal power in marriage and the family' and were '[unique] in the sculpture of the period'.[28] This notable stylistic deviation from the norm may be attributed to the fact that the monument was intended for display on Harriot's ancestral estate, and a feeling that it was appropriate to commemorate her in relation to her own inheritance and identity, rather than subsumed under that of her husband.

PATRIA·CARA·CARIOR·LIBERTAS

LVII

C·PHILIPS·

Fig. 61 Edward Haytley
(*fl.* 1740–1764), *Harriot Pleydell*,
mid-eighteenth century, oil on
panel, 49.5 x 34.3 cm,
Longford Castle

WILLIAM BOUVERIE, IST EARL OF RADNOR

A pen and ink sketch for the monument, showing Harriot's profile superimposed over that of her husband, survives in the archive of the Victoria and Albert Museum, and a scribbled note on its reverse reveals that the 1st Earl sanctioned this design: 'This drawing is approv'd of by Mr Bouverie, who wou'd have the Monument executed in every particular according to it which is agreeable to the Contract sign'd by Mr Rysbrack.'[29] The Earl's desire to pay tribute to his wife by representing her in this less conventional manner probably stems from his great love and respect for her, and the design of the monument has been described as 'flagrantly emotive'.[30] In the late nineteenth century, a member of the Bouverie family transcribed some letters written by the pair, and these transcriptions survive in the Longford archive, paying testimony to the strength of their relationship. For example, in August 1749, Harriot wrote to her husband:

> I have my most hearty wishes that God almighty will bestowe on you all kind of blessing in this world & give you eternal happiness in the life to come. I also return you my thanks for all the tenderness & affection you have shewn me . . . [I] will only add, my love . . . that till death & in death I am yours H.B.

Fig. 62 Possibly John Michael Rysbrack (1694–1770), *Harriot Pleydell and William Bouverie, 1st Earl of Radnor*, mid-eighteenth century, wax, 19.7 x 16.5 cm, Longford Castle

This marriage did not only occasion the production of important and innovative works of art, and bring Coleshill House to the Bouverie family: it also brought them the Pleydell family name. Sir Mark's will had decreed that his inheritors should 'assume ye Sirname of Pleydell',[31] and so Harriot and William's son, Jacob, was the first of the family to use the surname Pleydell-Bouverie. When eighteenth-century aristocratic families were faced with what was known as a 'name and arms clause' – decreeing that the wife's surname be retained – it was customary for a new, double-barrelled surname to be created, especially when the husband was unwilling to give up his own.[32] In this case, it was essential that a double-barrelled surname be brought into use. When Sir Jacob, 1st Viscount Folkestone, wrote his will, he decreed that his descendants inheriting his estates, hereditaments and title – including Longford Castle itself – and their heirs in turn should bear the surname Bouverie: if not, the will stated that the inheritor should be considered 'as if he or they were actually dead', and the inheritance passed on.[33]

The extremity of this sanction indicates how strongly Sir Jacob felt about the future security of the Bouverie surname, which, having been anglicised, acted as a symbolic vehicle incorporating the family's Huguenot heritage with its newer English identity. This clause of the will was tested on the 1st Earl's first marriage, but the creation of a double-barrelled surname meant that future members of the family could lay claim to both their Longford and Coleshill inheritances. Significantly, the Bouverie name was made the suffix, as Sir Jacob had specifically directed that, should another name be attached to his, it should be placed 'before and proceeding' Bouverie, 'to the Intent that Bouverie may be deemed the Chief family name'.[34] Indeed, scholars have argued that the suffix within a double-barrelled surname was considered the 'critical' name.[35] Therefore, the joining together of these two families and estates did not overshadow the significance of the Bouverie name, one of the central facets of the family's identity, but instead enriched it.

The 1st Earl married his second wife, Rebecca Alleyne (1725–1764), a second cousin and close friend of Harriot, in 1751.[36] The eminent eighteenth-century society portraitist Sir Joshua Reynolds painted Rebecca in 1760, and this work is one of many treasures of the Longford collection commissioned by the 1st Earl. The latter not only demonstrated his wealth and status by patronising the best artists of the day but also ensured that there was a sense of stylistic harmony throughout the family portrait collection, by transferring his patronage between artists who had learnt from one another. Reynolds, for example, had been apprenticed to Hudson,[37] who had painted a number of Bouverie family members, including the 1st Earl and Harriot.

Reynolds's portrait of Rebecca (fig. 63) is a three-quarter-length depiction, showing her standing with a classical sculpted urn decorated with hunting nymphs.[38] Anglo-Italian motifs were frequently employed in the Bouveries' decorative arts commissions (see pages 50–51), and the inclusion of a reference to both the classical past and English country sporting pursuits within this portrait demonstrates how the motif was used within fine art commissions as well, creating a sense of iconographic cohesion across the interiors and the art collection at Longford.

It appears that Rebecca attended sittings at the artist's studio for the portrait, as Reynolds's pocket book details six appointments between March and May.[39] The timing of the commission, at what has been understood as the artist's peak, is significant. The art historian Ellis Waterhouse noted that Reynolds 'reached full artistic maturity in 1753'; moreover, his practice became fully professionalised in 1760, when he took a house in Leicester Fields, London, in order to be able to receive sitters and showcase his work for potential patrons, and he also exhibited his work at the first exhibition in the Great Room of the Society of Arts in this year.[40] The 1st Earl's patronage of Reynolds at this time reminds us how the Bouverie family were at the forefront of patronage trends.

It is interesting to consider how this portrait of Rebecca was placed alongside some of the other Bouverie family portraits by important contemporary artists at Longford Castle. In the eighteenth century, four handwritten inventories of works of art at Longford were created, indicating the family's need and desire to document and keep track of their collection of treasures and heirlooms. Although some of the inventories contain repetitions, crossings-out

and layers of rewriting, providing a reminder that works were rearranged or redisplayed as the art collection grew, the most detailed and complete of them helps us reconstruct a picture of how paintings were shown at the castle during the tenure of the 1st Earl.

This particular inventory has been dated to between 1760 and 1780, and appears to be in the handwriting of Jacob Pleydell-Bouverie, 2nd Earl of Radnor, the 1st Earl's eldest son. Given the presence within the document of works acquired during the 1st Earl's tenure but a lack of items collected by the 2nd Earl, it may have been the case that this inventory was compiled as a working document, allowing the latter to assess and take stock of the art collection, perhaps once it had passed into his ownership following the death of his father in 1776.

The inventory documents a comprehensive set of family portraits on display in the ground-floor Long Parlour, arranged harmoniously, despite the fact that they were not all part of a set and were painted at different times by different artists. That these portraits were displayed at Longford Castle, the family's country seat, rather than at the London town houses they rented, for instance, shows that they were thinking in accord with other eighteenth-century country-house owners, whose 'ancestors were always in the country'.[41] Family portraits were usually stored at rural seats both for 'reasons of space' and because, there, they evoked the 'family's roots in the land'.[42] It was, moreover, not uncommon to see such portraits grouped together within the same room,[43] as had traditionally been the case in Elizabethan and Jacobean long galleries.

Here, the family's decision to patronise artists who worked in similar styles and who had learnt from one another – such as Hudson and Reynolds – meant that their respective outputs hung happily together, and that the overall display had stylistic integrity. Paintings of husbands and wives were, unsurprisingly, hung next to one another, but it is notable that the picture hang acknowledged deceased as well as living spouses. For instance, the inventory notes that a painting of the 1st Earl by Hudson was accompanied on one side by Hudson's likeness of his first wife, Harriot, and on the other by the portrait of his second wife, Rebecca, by Reynolds.

As we saw earlier, Hudson produced two sets of paintings of the 1st Earl and Harriot: it is not clear from the inventory which set was displayed in the Long Parlour. However, it is most likely to be the pair showing the sitters dressed in Van Dyck costume, as they are of the same dimensions as Reynolds's portrait of Rebecca as well as many of the other paintings in the room, and they would thus have hung most comfortably in tandem. The three portraits are united by a similar format and dark backgrounds filled with rich red drapery. Moreover, although Rebecca is not portrayed in Van Dyck dress, the dresses of the two wives are in shades of blue and grey. The patronage of artists who worked within the same idiom therefore helped to create a 'house style', presenting a coherent image of the Bouveries as fashionable patrons.

The 1st Earl appears to have used the Long Parlour as a space to highlight his family tree for the benefit of family members and their guests, who would have used the room every day,

Fig. 63 Sir Joshua Reynolds (1723–1792), *Rebecca Alleyne*, 1757, oil on canvas, 124.5 x 99.1 cm, Longford Castle

WILLIAM BOUVERIE, 1ST EARL OF RADNOR

and to showcase his and his father's extensive patronage of the best portrait painters of the time. Another important painting on display in this room, according to the inventory, was a portrait of Jacob (later 2nd Earl of Radnor) as a child, again by Reynolds (fig. 64). This shows Jacob wearing Van Dyck costume, situated within a landscape. It is often difficult to assess the extent of a patron's involvement in the stylistic decisions pertaining to a commission, particularly when written evidence such as letters or diary entries dealing with that aspect of the commission cannot be traced. However, it is reasonable to assume that the Bouverie patrons had some level of input into the final appearance of these commissioned works of art, and to conclude that these pieces are particularly revealing of their personal tastes.

In this case, the 1st Earl's involvement in the commission is hinted at by the fact that, between sittings for the portrait, he called at Reynolds's studio, possibly to check on the progress of this and the other portraits he was commissioning from the artist.[44] Van Dyck dress may have been requested deliberately to help create a sense of stylistic continuity throughout the portrait collection at Longford. The adoption of this type of costume in this particular work was apposite, as it would not have dated the portrait, instead ensuring that it appeared timeless in posterity. This was arguably particularly important in a work of art that was presumably commissioned to foreshadow the sitter's aristocratic inheritance and future role within the family dynasty.

Fig. 64 Sir Joshua Reynolds (1723–1792), *Jacob Pleydell-Bouverie* [later 2nd Earl of Radnor] *as a child*, 1757, oil on canvas in an overmantel frame, 125.7 x 99.1 cm, Longford Castle

According to the late eighteenth-century inventory of works of art, this portrait was hung in the most prominent position within the Long Parlour: the space over the chimneypiece. In 1768 the architect Isaac Ware wrote that 'the conspicuous side of a room is that in which a chimney is placed',[45] demonstrating the importance of this location in the eyes of contemporaries. Chimneypieces were often crowned with portraits of venerated members of a family, since the hearth was understood in the eighteenth century as 'sacred to rites of patriarchal succession'.[46] Hanging a portrait of his heir in this significant position suggests the 1st Earl's anticipation of the continuation of the family dynasty into the future. Since ancient times, the hearth had evoked notions of home, ancestry and hospitality, and, in the eighteenth century, functioned as the focus of domesticity.[47] When considering that parlours especially were a location of everyday domestic interaction within the country house during Georgian times, it is significant that the picture hang within this room alluded to familial descent by focusing on the image of the heir in the foreground.

Fig. 65 Sir Joshua Reynolds
(1723–1792), *The Hon. Harriot
Bouverie, Lady Tilney-Long*,
c. 1763–4, oil on canvas,
80 x 91.4 cm, Longford Castle

Works of art by Reynolds were also hung in the prominent overmantel position in other rooms at Longford. In 1763 and 1764, Reynolds painted another member of the Bouverie family: the 1st Earl's younger sister, Harriot Bouverie (1736–1777), who later became Lady Tilney-Long upon her marriage in 1775 to Sir James Tilney-Long (1736–1794). This half-length portrait (fig. 65), today on display in the Long Parlour, shows the sitter in a white dress with a sash and scarf, resting her left elbow on a pedestal, and is displayed in a mid-eighteenth-century over-mantel frame.[48] According to the late eighteenth-century inventory, this painting used to hang above the chimneypiece in the Tapestry Room, again showing how works by the best masters were deemed appropriate for this important location within a room.

Throughout the eighteenth century, the Bouverie family continually employed the most popular and highly esteemed artists to paint their likenesses, demonstrating an awareness of shifts in taste that speaks of their knowledge of and involvement in the contemporary art scene. The 1st Earl, for example, maintained links with the Society for the Encouragement of Arts, Manufactures and Commerce, which Sir Jacob had helped to found. Although he was not President of the Society, like his father, he was elected Vice-President in March 1776.[49] In addition,

Left: Fig. 66 Thomas Gainsborough (1727–1788), *William,
1st Earl of Radnor*, 1773, oil on
canvas, 73.7 x 62.2 cm,
Longford Castle

Right: Fig. 67 Thomas Gainsborough (1727–1788), *The Hon.
William Henry Pleydell-Bouverie*,
1773, oil on canvas,
74.3 x 61.6 cm,
Longford Castle

he played an important role in helping to facilitate the production of a commemorative portrait of Sir Jacob for the Society.[50] During the early 1770s he lent an existing portrait of his father by Hudson from the Longford collection for copying, first to the artist Nathaniel Dance (1735–1811), and then to Thomas Gainsborough, when the former was no longer able to execute the commission. The resultant portrait still hangs today in the Great Room of what is now the Royal Society of Arts, at the Adelphi Buildings in the Strand, London.

The 1st Earl himself commissioned a number of family portraits by Gainsborough, demonstrating how he achieved a sense of continuity in representations of the Bouveries – both alive and deceased – by entrusting their image to the same important artist. Gainsborough produced a set of six portraits documenting members of the family, including the 1st Earl (fig. 66) and his three sons by his second wife, Rebecca (figs 67, 68 and 69): William Henry (1752–1806), Bartholomew (1753–1835) and Edward (1760–1824).

These paintings have a more intimate feel to them than many of the other family portraits at Longford, including another depiction of the 1st Earl by Gainsborough, dated to 1772, where he is shown wearing a wig and peer's robes, with an authoritative stance and gaze and with a column and drapery in the background (fig. 70). Instead, the slightly later portrayal, of smaller proportions and containing a relative lack of accoutrements, depicts the sitter in a plainer style of dress; it concentrates the viewer's attention more fully on the 1st Earl's physiognomy,

demanding that he be confronted as an individual, rather than in an official capacity. The art historian Malcolm Baker has argued that, in focusing more intensely on sitters' features, the bust and head-and-shoulders formats of many eighteenth-century portraits in both marble and oil required the viewer to engage primarily with the sitter's likeness and sense of self, and less with his or her identity as expressed through external attributes such as props or costume.[51] Gainsborough's series appears to achieve this aim.

This set of portraits was purchased for a total sum of £252 in 1774,[52] and at least some of the sittings may have taken place at Longford Castle itself, when Gainsborough made a visit in 1773. He made a copy after a painting by David Teniers the Younger in the Longford collection on this occasion (see pages 79–80). Encountering other works of art in the collection, such as paintings by Van Dyck, may have exerted an influence upon the style of the portraits he produced for the 1st Earl. He adopted a seventeenth-century format, the feigned oval, for his portraits of the Bouveries, and included some references to Van Dyck costume, most notably in his portrayal of Edward. This portrait is especially celebrated, as it has been suggested that the dress in which Edward was depicted – a buttoned blue silk jacket with slashes in the sleeves, a white lace collar and cuffs – was based on a real-life costume owned by Gainsborough and also used as a model for his famed portrait *The Blue Boy*.[53]

It is likely that Gainsborough saw the paintings by Van Dyck at Longford depicting Queen

WILLIAM BOUVERIE, 1ST EARL OF RADNOR

Henrietta Maria and Gaston, Duke of Orléans (see figs 17 and 18 and page 35). Moreover, at the time, the 1st Earl had recently acquired a further painting by the seventeenth-century master for the Longford collection (fig. 71): a portrait of Katherine Wootton, Countess of Chesterfield (1609–1667). This full-length portrait shows the sitter wearing a grey satin dress, her right elbow resting upon a rock. She is situated within a wooded glade with a landscape receding into the background, and the sky can be glimpsed to the right of the composition. The work has been described as 'decorative, elegant and somewhat manneristic', and an example of 'the typical English style of Van Dyck's later years'.[54] The painting was previously understood to be a work of Van Dyck and his studio but has now been reassessed and deemed to be substantially autograph.

This particular acquisition provides an important case study. First, the portrait's provenance was especially notable. It had previously been owned by Sir Robert Walpole, who amassed an important collection of art, hanging it at his newly built country seat, Houghton Hall in Norfolk. He had bought eight portraits by Van Dyck for Houghton in 1725, and it has been suggested that his combining of seventeenth-century portraits with works of other genres in the Common Parlour at the Hall may have been a 'deliberate attempt . . . to give his splendid but very new "palace" a greater sense of history'.[55] Acquiring historical works by artists such as Van Dyck helped collectors to fill in gaps if their art collection was less well established. The portrait of the Countess of Chesterfield had been sold from the Walpole collection in 1751, however, to an individual known only as West. It was later bought from a London auction in April 1773 by the 1st Earl for £55 13s.[56]

Fig. 70 Thomas Gainsborough (1727–1788), *William Bouverie, 1st Earl of Radnor*, c. 1770, oil on canvas, 127 x 99.1 cm, Longford Castle

The portrait now hangs in the Gallery at Longford Castle, where it is accompanied by other works by Van Dyck, including the portrait of Gaston, Duke of Orléans, and a full-length portrait of another seventeenth-century countess (fig. 72): Martha Cranfield, Countess of Monmouth (1601–1677). It is believed that it was also the 1st Earl who acquired this work of art for the Longford collection.[57] This portrait and that of the Countess of Chesterfield were painted during the same period, having been dated to between 1636 and 1640,[58] and are of a similar size. They hang neatly upon the walls of the Gallery, the proportions of which were, of course, originally designed to accommodate a single row of full-length pictures in the tradition of an Elizabethan long gallery.

The portrait of the Countess of Monmouth is an important and influential work by the

Fig. 71 Sir Anthony Van Dyck
(1599–1641), *Katherine Wootton,
Countess of Chesterfield*, c. 1636,
oil on canvas, 215.9 x 127 cm,
Longford Castle

WILLIAM BOUVERIE, IST EARL OF RADNOR

artist, having been described as a 'prime example of a Van Dyckian pattern which passed almost instantly into the repertoire of lesser painters working in England'.[59] The keen viewer will notice that, as in the Longford portrait of Queen Henrietta Maria (see page 35 and fig. 17), the sitter is depicted with one hand cradling the other, and holding a rose. Again, it is believed that this motif was included to hint at the sitter's pregnancy.[60] As in the portrait of the Countess of Chesterfield, a glimpse of sky is visible in the background of the composition. An orange tree frames the vignette of sky, and the fruits upon the tree glow with the same golden hue as the sitter's dress. The use of colour within this portrait has been described as 'unusually rich', with the juxtaposition of the orange dress and 'clear green curtain' creating a striking contrast.[61] This effect is augmented when one views the portrait against the green damask wall hangings of the Gallery.

Here, we have a significant example of the intersection between the Bouveries' acquisitions on the secondary market and their patronage of contemporary artists. We have already seen that the family favoured a seventeenth-century aesthetic in their portrait commissions, with members of the family being portrayed in Van Dyck costume by artists that included Hudson and Reynolds. However, the 1st Earl's purchase of a painting by Van Dyck concurrently with Gainsborough's adoption of a historicising aesthetic in his portrait commissions for the family shows how the two mechanisms of collecting went hand in hand for the Earl, and each informed the other.

Gainsborough may well have seen and been inspired by the works by Van Dyck at Longford on the occasion of his visit there, and had certainly shown an interest in the master's oeuvre prior to the 1770s. For instance, he had produced portraits in this historicising style since he left Suffolk in the late 1750s.[62] It is thought that when he was working in Bath throughout the 1760s, the artist may have been reading manuals of seventeenth-century painting techniques, and even going so far as to revive some of their methods.[63] During his time in Bath he visited Wilton House, close to Longford in the county of Wiltshire, where he was greatly influenced by Van Dyck's portraits of members of the Pembroke family. The importance of this style of painting to the artist is therefore clear.

It is surely no coincidence that the 1st Earl chose to patronise Gainsborough at a time when his acquisitions demonstrate a clear interest in the work of Van Dyck. He may well have consciously wished to harness Gainsborough's ability to appropriate seventeenth-century styles, as this would have ensured that the new portrait series did not date but instead blended harmoniously into the Longford art collection. A number of Gainsborough's clients shared a concern that their portrait commissions did not quickly become dated.[64] For example, the same sense of continuity had been achieved at Arundel Castle in West Sussex, home to the Norfolk family: portraits by Gainsborough of Charles Howard, 11th Duke of Norfolk (1746–1815), and Bernard Howard, 12th Duke (1765–1842), were hung in the Drawing Room alongside portraits by Van Dyck.[65]

Fig. 72 Sir Anthony Van Dyck
(1599–1641), *Martha Cranfield,*
Countess of Monmouth,
c. 1638–40, oil on canvas,
218.4 x 127 cm,
Longford Castle

WILLIAM BOUVERIE, IST EARL OF RADNOR

For a socially ascending family such as the Bouveries, the role of historicising portraits in achieving a 'conscious evocation of the past both suggest[ing] noble lineage and lend[ing] distinction to the status of the family'[66] was especially pertinent. This case study shows how the 1st Earl stayed at the forefront of patronage trends by commissioning Gainsborough, already fashionable, yet also looked to the past stylistically, thereby helping to secure the on-going relevance of the Longford portrait collection for posterity.

We know from an inventory of pictures at Longford made in 1814, which was accompanied by a small sketch plan illustrating the arrangement of works of art on the castle's walls, that Gainsborough's paintings of William Henry, Edward and Bartholomew were hung at one point close to the paintings of King Charles I and Henrietta Maria by Van Dyck, in a room known as the Green Bedchamber.[67] The Bouveries, therefore, seem to have been conscious of the stylistic influence at play in Gainsborough's work, and desirous of amplifying it through juxtaposition with Van Dyck's output. In a discussion of the Bouveries' patronage of Gainsborough, the art historians Deborah Cherry and Jennifer Harris noted that his portraits 'would have been fitting companions to works by Van Dyck' but also that 'we have as yet little information on how these collections were hung'.[68] The inventory and sketch plan therefore provide a valuable insight into the fact that these treasures of the Longford collection were indeed displayed close to one another at the castle.

Although there is little surviving evidence in the Longford archive to illuminate Gainsborough's visit to the castle and his execution of the portrait series, an anecdotal letter written by the connoisseur and art collector Sir George Beaumont provides an amusing insight into the occasion:

> At the Earl of R——'s, where it was the custom to have morning prayers, [Gainsborough] was loath to attend for fear of laughing at the chaplain. . . . Receiving a hint from his Lordship that service was performed at nine . . . a few days after that first announcement of the pious custom, the painter not having made his appearance at the chapel, his Lordship reminded him again, saying, 'Perhaps, Mr Gainsborough, you geniuses having wandering memories, you may have forgotten.'[69]

This letter goes a small way towards reconstructing a sense of what it was like for a patron to host an artist at his country house: it certainly seems that, alongside the time he spent studying the art collection at Longford and undertaking his own work, Gainsborough was expected to join in with the family's daily routines by attending chapel. The episode hints at the importance that the 1st Earl attached to family prayers, and provides a reminder of his piety. Indeed, he considered religious observance to be an integral part of everyday life, and it is worth pausing to consider how this impacted on his patronage.

During the early 1770s, the 1st Earl had been engaged in the restoration of the church in nearby Britford, and in the construction of a family vault there: a number of payments in his account books for the period relate to works undertaken in this connection.[70] Moreover, during this time a new chapel was built outside the garden front of Longford Castle, at the behest of the Earl: a task that involved much expenditure.[71] Although this chapel was later destroyed by his successor, the 2nd Earl, the construction works do attest to the 1st Earl's devoutness, and his desire to resolve the issue of the location of the family chapel at the castle.

Significantly, this was the second change in the Bouverie family's chapel arrangements since their purchase of the castle, and this catalogue of change could reflect dissatisfaction or a lack of resolution within Longford's original architecture regarding the placement of a chapel. The original situation of the chapel at the castle's moment of construction is unknown. Sir Jacob used one of the first-floor round tower rooms, located at the end of the Gallery, for this purpose but the 1st Earl's ambition to move the place of worship to the castle's exterior suggests that he was keen to make it more public and outward-facing.[72]

Aside from these examples, the 1st Earl did not undertake any significant building projects at Longford Castle during his time in charge there. Like his father, he does not seem to have felt it imperative to remodel the castle in line with the neo-Palladian architectural ideals fashionable at the time. His marriage to Harriot Pleydell, and the resultant transfer of the Coleshill estate to the Bouverie family, may have led him to believe such works to be unnecessary. Coleshill House, although a seventeenth-century creation, had been built in a style that underpinned the aesthetic of many eighteenth-century buildings, and had left an impression upon influential Georgian builders, including Richard Boyle, 3rd Earl of Burlington (1694–1753), who had drawings made of its ceilings by the architect and translator of Palladio, Isaac Ware.[73] Writing around the turn of the nineteenth century, the antiquarian John Britton (1771–1857) described Coleshill as 'a *perfect* and unaltered specimen of the architectural taste of Inigo Jones',[74] and the Bouverie family's inheritance of this important house may well have precluded any obligation on their part to subscribe to more up-to-date styles at Longford. With an Elizabethan family seat, evoking a sense of establishment and longevity, a fashionable and well-known seventeenth-century house acting as a secondary country home, and properties in town, the family covered all bases.

The 1st Earl followed the wishes of his father in maintaining Longford Castle in good repair, contracting glass painters, carvers, surveyors, masons, glaziers and a 'chimney doctor', among other tradesmen,[75] to look after his property. We can find clear evidence of the sense of pride he felt in his ownership of Longford Castle in its inclusion in the fifth volume of the architectural treatise *Vitruvius Britannicus*. This volume was published in 1771 by the architects John Woolfe (d. 1793) and James Gandon (1742/3–1823), and was an imitation of the original series published by the architect Colen Campbell (1676–1729) earlier in the eighteenth century.[76] The 1771 volume continued the earlier books' tradition of cataloguing important country houses,

Fig. 73 Tobias Miller
(*fl.* 1744–1790) after T. Milton,
*Longford in Wiltshire, the Seat of
the Earl of Radnor*, 1766,
engraving, sheet 48.3 x 63.5 cm,
plate mark 33 x 55.9 cm,
Longford Castle

giving written descriptions alongside printed elevations and plans.[77] Engravings of the south and garden fronts of Longford Castle (fig. 73) and ground plans of its first and second floors were published, showing off the castle as an architectural exemplar.

These images had been engraved by Tobias Miller (*fl.* 1744–1790) after drawings by an unknown T. Milton in 1766, and their existence and later publication demonstrate the 1st Earl's keenness to document and promote the castle among a contemporary readership. The written description that accompanied the plates in *Vitruvius Britannicus* is revealing, both of the castle's contemporary appearance and of the Earl's attitude to sharing his family seat. It describes how Longford Castle 'is a large and commodious habitation, elegantly fitted up and furnished, being decorated with many very capital pictures' and how the Earl, 'as a great promoter and encourager of this work, made us a present of these plates, with those of Coleshill, and likewise favoured us with the description of both'.[78]

The 1st Earl and his eldest son, then Viscount Folkestone, were both subscribers to the volume.[79] As the Earl had himself supplied the accompanying descriptions of both Longford Castle and Coleshill House, they were perhaps somewhat biased. However, they are none-theless revealing of how highly esteemed the houses were by their owner. The description of Coleshill adds to our understanding of the house's exemplary worth in the eyes of the 1st Earl:

> It is, perhaps, the most perfect work now remaining of that great architect, Inigo
> Jones, having undergone no alteration since the year 1650, when it was compleated:
> it is remarkable for the magnificence of the entrance, the height with the fine

proportion of the rooms, and the richness of the ceilings. . . . It is situated on a hill, above the river Cole (which parts Wiltshire from Berkshire, and from which the village derives its name) commanding an extensive prospect over the vale of White Horse, and part of the adjoining counties of Wilts and Gloucester.[80]

The 1st Earl also allowed certain works of art from his collection to be reproduced in engraved form, helping to spread their fame and perhaps acting as a draw for visitors to the castle. For example, Claude Lorraine's *Pastoral Landscape with the Arch of Titus* was engraved several times, once by William Woollet (1753–1785), whose version was published by John Boydell (1720–1804) in 1772.[81] Similarly, Reynolds's portrait of young Jacob was engraved by James McArdell (*c.* 1729–1765) soon after its completion, and copies survive both at Longford Castle and in the Prints and Drawings collection at the British Museum.

Various payments to engravers appear in the 1st Earl's account books, alongside payments for pictures, sculptures and frames.[82] For instance, he paid the balance of a total sum of £87 7s to 'Tobias Miller Engraver' in March 1767,[83] possibly for the plans and elevations of Longford Castle that were later reproduced in *Vitruvius Britannicus*. Although he did not undertake any substantial refurbishment works in any of the rooms at Longford, the account books reveal that the Earl continued to contract important and fashionable designers, furnishers and craftsmen. For example, he bought a number of pieces of 'Staffordshire Ware' from Wedgwood & Co. in 1772 and 1774.[84] He paid a bill in May 1765 to 'Messrs. Vile & Cobb Cabinet Makers' of £52 9s 6d and one of £28 to 'Cobb Cabinet Maker' in July 1767.[85] The furniture historian Margaret Jourdain has described John Cobb (*c.* 1710–1778) as one of 'the leading cabinetmakers of the middle years of the eighteenth century', along with Benjamin Goodison, William Hallett (*c.* 1707–1781) and William Vile (*c.* 1700–1767), all of whom were also patronised by the Bouverie family.[86] As with their portrait commissions, therefore, the family continually commissioned the best artists of the day.

The Longford collection contains a great many important pieces of English furniture of the Georgian period, and although the account books are not entirely clear on the matter of exactly when particular pieces were bought, some may well have been acquired by the 1st Earl as additions to the interiors that his predecessor had redecorated. For example, a serpentine commode in the Round Parlour has been associated with the cabinetmaker Cobb, so may relate to one of the payments noted above. Also in the Round Parlour is a marquetry commode dated to the same period (fig. 74), which is possibly the work of William Ince (1737–1804) and John Mayhew (1736–1811). Its intricate design features two oval panels depicting cupids, topped with laurel festoons tied with ribbons, on the front, a further cupid on the top and radial fan designs on the sides. It is likely that this piece was, like Goodison's marble-topped side table, made especially for either the Round Parlour or another of the circular tower rooms, as it is slightly curved in response to the shape of the room.

Another important piece of English furniture at Longford worth noting is a gilded commode attributed to William Vile (fig. 75), although, again, it is not certain when precisely this piece was bought. The commode features carvings in low relief, with flowers, leaves, basketwork and scrolls among other ornament. It sits harmoniously today alongside other gilt furniture in the Green Velvet Drawing Room, which includes other pieces by the English school such as the set of chairs commissioned from Giles Grendey (see page 81 and fig. 49), as well as a German gilt commode.

The portraitist and Royal Academician Francis Cotes (1726–1770) was another important and fashionable eighteenth-century artist commissioned by the 1st Earl. For instance, he painted a half-length portrait of the Earl's eldest son, Jacob, when the sitter was in his late teens. The account books list two payments, of £10 10s each, for 'Folkestone's Picture', in 1767 and 1768.[87] The 1st Earl later commissioned another portrait of Jacob, when the sitter was in his

Fig. 75 Attributed to William
Vile (*c.* 1700–1767), Gilded
Commode, gilt, mahogany and
Japanese black and gold lacquer,
81.3 x 94 x 54.6 cm,
Longford Castle

mid-twenties, this time from the Royal Academician Nathaniel Dance. This portrait cost £42 in 1774,[88] and is a three-quarter-length painting, showing the sitter holding a cane and with a fashionable tricorn hat. This example again shows the extent of the 1st Earl's patronage network.

Cotes had also painted a portrait of the 1st Earl's third wife, Anne Hales, Dowager Countess of Feversham (1736–1795). The pair had married in 1765, following the death a year earlier of Rebecca Alleyne, and the portrait (fig. 76) was paid for in two instalments: the first, of £21, in 1765, and the second, again of £21, in 1767.[89] The portrait of Anne shows her dressed in blue silk, leaning against a vase and gazing into the distance. The background is filled with rich red drapery, and an accompanying inscription identifies the sitter.

This marriage brought another property into the Bouveries' ownership: a London town house, 52 Grosvenor Street, which remained in the family until 1897.[90] Prior to this, they had lived in a number of rented houses in the capital.[91] For instance, in 1764, the 1st Earl paid £250 for 'a years Rent for the House I live in in Burlington Street'.[92] The Bouverie family made use of London residences in the conventional manner of their aristocratic peers.[93] Landowners were required to attend Parliament during the winter season – and indeed made use of this time to engage in the social and cultural opportunities London had to offer the fashionable *beau monde*[94] – but retired to the countryside during the summer months.[95]

For example, Sir Jacob had tended to chair meetings of the Society of Arts in London during the winter, and kept up with the business and proceedings of the Society remotely during the summer.[96] Similarly, the 1st Earl appears to have adhered to these standard aristocratic living arrangements. Cellar accounts for his London town houses run from January to June, indicating that he was in town during the first half of the year, perhaps hosting and entertaining guests, before returning to Longford for the summer and autumn.[97] Many at the time saw the town house as a less permanent fixture, and one less closely associated with the family's identity, than their country seat, which they treated as their

primary home: for instance, individual members of a family might occupy different town houses.[98] The degree to which the Bouveries moved between various town houses, settling in one location only in the event of an inheritance, is notable but serves to reinforce the importance that Longford held in their eyes.

Although the 1st Earl is especially notable for his patronage of contemporary artists, he did also acquire many works of art on the secondary market. More often than not, when listing his acquisitions in his account books, he referred to them only as 'pictures', making it difficult to identify precisely which works of art he acquired when. However, on certain occasions, he did provide greater detail, making it easier for the historian to trace the provenance of particular paintings in the Longford collection.

For instance, in December 1773, he noted a payment of £100 made for a 'Picture of Reubens's Son'[99] (fig. 77). This is a full-length portrait of Frans Rubens (baptised 1633), the eldest son of the Flemish Baroque painter Peter Paul Rubens (1577–1640) and his second wife, Helena (Hélène) Fourment (1614–1673). Today it hangs in the Green Velvet Drawing Room at Longford, and provides another reminder of the Bouveries' interest in seventeenth-century portraiture. It was previously given to Rubens's studio, but Nicholas Penny has reassessed it as the work of Rubens himself, although a strip down the left side of the painting is a later addition. A painting in oil on panel depicting *Diana and her Nymphs*, now on display in the Picture

Fig. 77 Sir Peter Paul Rubens
(1577–1640), *Frans Rubens*,
early seventeenth century, oil on
panel with early additions,
123.8 x 66 cm, Longford Castle

Gallery at Longford, is also by Rubens (fig. 78). It is not certain when precisely the Bouverie family bought this work. A piece described as 'A Sketch representing ye Painter's three Wives in the Characters of Diana, & her attendant nymphs . . . Sir Peter Paul Reubens' appears in a late eighteenth-century inventory of the collection,[100] so it may be one of the unnamed 'pictures' that the 1st Earl bought and recorded in his accounts.

One acquisition that we can firmly associate with the 1st Earl is a series that he described as 'four Pictures by Old Bassan', bought for £34 13s in May 1771.[101] This set of four pictures, painted in oil on panel, and now said to be by the Flemish school after the Italian painter Jacopo Bassano (1510–1592), depicts the four seasons (figs 79, 80, 81 and 82). Like his father, the 1st Earl did not apparently travel abroad on the Grand Tour to collect works of art but he did acquire

Fig. 78 Sir Peter Paul Rubens (1577–1640), *Diana and her Nymphs with Hounds and Satyrs Returning from the Chase*, c. 1615, oil on panel, 29.2 x 38.1 cm including an original addition, Longford Castle

an important work of the Italian school with the help of a London-based dealer, Gerard van der Gucht (1696/7–1776): a large-scale painting of the *Adoration of the Shepherds*, then attributed to the Bolognese painter Annibale Carracci (1560–1609) or a member of his school, and now given to Giacomo Cavedone (1577–1660), another Bolognese painter of the period.[102] The Earl listed a number of transactions with Van der Gucht in his account books, for buying and exchanging pictures and engaging his services as a picture cleaner.[103]

It is important to remember that money and effort were concentrated not only upon buying new works of art for the Longford collection during this time but also upon cleaning, restoring and conserving those already in the collection. The 1st Earl had inherited a great many pictures from his father, and part of his duty as heir was to keep them in good repair. For this he enlisted the help of picture restorers, including Van der Gucht and Isaac Collivoe,[104] who had previously cleaned Sir Jacob's painting of flowers on copper by Brueghel.

In conclusion, the 1st Earl of Radnor did much for the collection of treasures at Longford Castle, especially through his patronage of some of the best artists of the day, including Gainsborough and Reynolds, for additions to the family portrait collection. He died at the age of fifty-one in 1776, and the castle, collection and earldom were transferred to Jacob. The 2nd Earl of Radnor continued in his predecessors' footsteps by making important additions to the art collection, including some unique or unusual treasures. His approach to art collecting, and to Longford Castle itself, however, took on a more independent and individual character, as the next chapter will show.

When writing his will, the 1st Earl declared a specific wish that his hearse be 'attended only by one mourning Coach without Escutcheons and without Supporters to my Pall or any Appearance of funeral pomp'.[105] His desire for a more modest funeral reflects the trends of the time. Matthew Craske has suggested that a tendency towards unwarranted heraldic display and 'dynastic pomp' in funerals led some members of the eighteenth-century nobility to hold small, private funerary ceremonies, rather than traditional public ones involving the local community in the seventeenth-century tradition.[106] This enabled families to communicate their intrinsic nobility in a subtler manner. Although his elevation to the earldom had led to the creation of new heraldry for the family – a coat of arms featuring a double-headed eagle having been permitted in 1768[107] – it is revealing that the 1st Earl seems to have been conscious of, and subscribed to, contemporary ideals about noble behaviour in this context, eschewing ostentation and instead quietly communicating his newly heightened social position through a modest and intimate funerary ceremony.

His remains, and those of the rest of his family, were interred in the new family vault at St Peter's Church in Britford, thus linking the family with the locality in perpetuity.[108] A year after his death, his son, the 2nd Earl, wrote the following words, as part of an inscription for the vault, providing a reminder of the family's journey thus far:

Figs 79, 80, 81 and 82 Flemish school after Jacopo Bassano (1510–1592), *The Seasons* (a set of four, left to right: Spring, Summer, Autumn, Winter), *c.* 1620, oil on panel, 24.1 x 32.4 cm, Longford Castle

To God, most good, most great and most bountiful, Jacob, Earl of Radnor, caused this Testimony (such as it is) of the heartfelt gratitude of himself and Family to be erected near the Vault, destined for receiving their remains, because besides those good things which He so liberally bestows on all mankind, He has in a peculiar manner been indulgent to his [*sic*] family, which, when banished from their native land on account of their having embraced the Reformed Religion, destitute of wealth and loaded with reproaches, His providence placed in this Land (The seat as well of religious as of civil liberty) and has from that time continued to cherish and increase in wealth . . . by the fair gains of prosperous trade, by fortunate marriages, and the bounty of different Testators, and finally has raised to honors, and to an hereditary seat among the British Peers . . . Radnor 1777.[109]

CHAPTER 4

Jacob Pleydell-Bouverie, 2nd Earl of Radnor

> There are great expenses . . . which possibly it may be suggested to you that I have
> done wrong, (and if you listen to the suggestion, I certainly have done wrong) to
> render necessary; I mean the Building at Longford; But to this Point I leave my
> Answer in one Word; I have done this; & every Thing else, which I have done
> respecting my Family Possessions with the View, & the Intention of extending,
> and improving them for our permanent Benefit, Consequence, & Credit.[1]

Jacob Pleydell-Bouverie, 2nd Earl of Radnor (1750–1828), is often remembered for the independent and somewhat whimsical and eccentric attitude he took towards Longford Castle and its art collection during his tenure, which lasted from 1776 until 1828. He proposed the idea of rebuilding the castle to a hexagonal ground plan but only partially executed the scheme, leaving it to later generations to complete the building works to a different design. The quotation above hints at the dissatisfaction with these works that was felt among the family, and which was acknowledged by the Earl, but also provides an important reminder that the project was conceived with the intention of augmenting the family's most important heirloom, their hereditary seat. Indeed, much of what he achieved at Longford was driven by an independent and free-spirited attitude, which saw, for instance, the addition of more unusual works of art to the collection, but which also demonstrated a concern on the part of this collector with the preservation and improvement of the family's possessions for posterity. It is the 2nd Earl who can be credited with bringing important pieces of fine and decorative art to the collection, including an Elizabethan cabinet, a unique Renaissance iron chair, and the famous painting by Hans Holbein the Younger now known as *The Ambassadors.*

The 2nd Earl was, as we have seen, also heir to Coleshill House in Berkshire. However, it seems that he used this property only on an *ad hoc* basis: for example, installing his sons there while he travelled in France.[2] He allowed some members of the family to reside at this secondary country estate on a longer-term basis. A letter written by his nephew, Edward Bouverie (dates unknown), in the early nineteenth century reveals that the Earl had offered Edward 'the Living of Coleshill' and that he was expected 'to reside there . . . so long as I keep the living'.[3] Similarly, the Earl encouraged his eldest son and heir, William, later 3rd Earl of Radnor

Fig. 84 Richard Cosway (1742–1821), *Jacob Pleydell-Bouverie* [2nd Earl of Radnor], *c.* 1812 (detail of fig. 87)

121

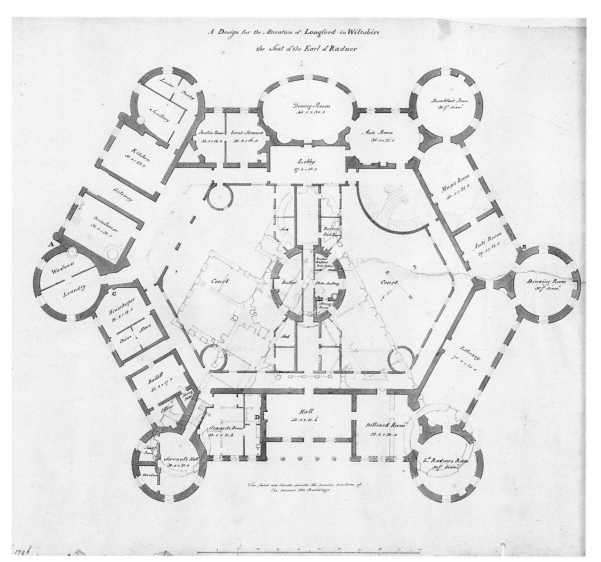

A Design for the Alteration of Longford in Wiltshire
the Seat of the Earl of Radnor

1796

Fig. 85 James Wyatt (1746–1813), *Plan for the Enlargement of Longford Castle*, 1796, pen and grey and dark red ink, grey and red wash, 49.5 x 50.8 cm, Longford Castle

(1779–1869), to inhabit the main house at Coleshill on a more permanent basis. He wrote to William in April 1814 that he 'wished you to occupy Coleshill as the most respectable situation you could have . . . it is to be occupied . . . as a gentleman's House'.[4] It seems that the Earl considered Longford Castle to be the main family seat, and Coleshill House an appropriate home for a younger member of the family.

The art historian Shearer West has argued that 'frequent architectural and decorative change in country houses was part of the owner's bid for power',[5] and the 2nd Earl seems to have been the first of the Bouveries to attempt to undertake substantial architectural works, perhaps to create his own legacy for the future. This imperative was played out at Longford, rather than at Coleshill, and the changes attest to the notion that the Earl wished to stamp his own mark upon his family seat. The new building scheme was initially presided over by the architect James Wyatt (1746–1813) during the 1790s, two decades into the Earl's ownership of Longford.

Wyatt may have been employed for the project because he had an existing connection with the Bouverie family, having been responsible for works recently undertaken at Salisbury Cathedral, to which the 2nd Earl had donated money. The latter may also have been aware of the architect's work at other country houses. For example, Wyatt had constructed some offices at Strawberry Hill in Twickenham for Horace Walpole in 1790, and had been employed by William Windham (1750–1810) at Felbrigg Hall, Norfolk, although it has been noted that, in the latter case, the architect 'did little except exasperate his client'![6] Wyatt in fact abandoned the Longford project in 1796 to undertake work at Fonthill Abbey in Wiltshire, and the architect Daniel Alexander (1768–1846) took over at Longford in his stead in 1802.[7] Alexander's plans, however, stayed more or less true to the original designs drawn up by Wyatt.

Wyatt had produced plans of the proposed new layout (fig. 85), as well as an architectural model of the hexagonal structure, which can still be seen today at the castle (fig. 86), and the bill for which can be found in the Longford archive.[8] It was not common for architects to produce models of buildings in the late eighteenth century. Sir John Soane pioneered the practice but few others engaged in it.[9] The Longford model is comparatively plain, in that it does not open up to suggest the way in which the interior would be decorated. In this way, it contrasts with a model made earlier in the eighteenth century by John Marsden (fl. 1735) of a proposed new palace at Richmond, Surrey, for Queen Caroline: the detailed interiors of this model suggest its maker's consideration of the ways in which its (female) patron would live within the space.[10]

The lack of interior detail in the Longford model implies that, from the beginning, the main impetus behind the architectural works was to make a bold exterior statement and to remodel the overall form and structure of the castle. Wyatt is said to have 'suppress[ed] purely ornamental detail and concentrat[ed] on the effect of large masses' in his designs,[11] which may account for the appearance of the model. However, its relative plainness might also reflect the fact that it was produced fairly early on in the process: had Wyatt not left the project to undertake work at Fonthill instead, he might have been commissioned to produce a more advanced model to follow up what was perhaps a preliminary prototype. In any case, the model provides a clear and striking reminder of the new design.

It might seem unexpected, particularly within the antiquarian climate of the late eighteenth and early nineteenth centuries, which looked upon Elizabethan architecture more favourably,[12] that the 2nd Earl proposed to strip the castle of one of its defining original features: its triangular shape. However, although the castle's shape had been integral to its identity, in planning a hexagonal structure the Earl arguably did not detract from its individuality but instead made changes in keeping with its unusual geometric character.

Furthermore, it is notable that, in line with his predecessors, the Earl decided neither to replace nor transform the castle in the neo-Palladian style: instead, the changes he proposed and partially executed appear to have shown a respect for, and even amplified, Longford's individuality and distinctiveness. This is also suggested by the fact that he seems to have looked abroad for inspiration for the designs, much as Longford's original builders had done. For example, plans of various continental castles, including one composed of two triangles, can be found stored among the designs for the project.[13] Moreover, the alterations appear to have been designed to retain the original aesthetic of the building's fabric. For instance, a specification for the works dating to 1797 contains a note decreeing that the 'Towers to be like the present Garden Front – 2 Stone, & Flint',[14] and an 'Elevation of the complete round of one of the Circular Towers supposing it open'd out into a flat surface' in the Longford archive shows the proposed exterior colours and materials, which remain in keeping with Longford's vernacular aesthetic of stone and flint, discussed in Chapter 1 (see page 16).[15]

The historicising tendency within these architectural plans was counterbalanced, however, by plans to bring Longford up to date in certain regards, particularly in relation to the accommodation of the art collection. A new, larger Picture Gallery was planned, and although the plans never reached fruition, they are still worth consideration, as they demonstrate the 2nd Earl's at least theoretical ambitions for Longford, and provide a reminder of the size and importance of its art collection by this time. Many eighteenth-century country-house building projects, such as at Ickworth House in Suffolk, Kedleston Hall in Derbyshire and Holkham Hall in Norfolk, had been conceived with the express aim of housing a notable art collection.[16] The Bouverie family had successfully adapted and decorated the existing rooms at Longford Castle to house their expanding collection of paintings and sculptures in line with eighteenth-century ideals, but it appears that the 2nd Earl was even more ambitious. Designs drawn up in 1802 by Alexander label each of the round towers at either end of the Picture Gallery as 'Upper part of the ends of the Gallery', showing how these spaces were intended to be incorporated into the room, increasing the space available for the display of works of art.[17] In this vein,

Fig. 87 Richard Cosway
(1742–1821), *Jacob
Pleydell-Bouverie* [2nd Earl of
Radnor], *c.* 1812, oil on
canvas, 184.6 x 128.3 cm,
Longford Castle

the antiquarian John Britton noted how the art collection, currently 'disposed in different rooms', was to be consolidated along one of the sides of the proposed hexagon.[18] Perhaps the 2nd Earl did not deem the existing Picture Gallery big enough for the collection he had inherited, to which he was adding his own acquisitions and commissions.

The Earl purchased some important works of art around the time that the architectural plans were drawn up, and had acquired a few key pieces in the years preceding the project. He continued his predecessors' habit of keeping detailed accounts of his expenditure, including that pertaining to works of art, and these accounts survive today in the Longford archive. His art-collecting activity was not as extensive as that of his grandfather, Sir Jacob, who had, of course, established the Longford collection almost from scratch, through the purchase of a large number of works of different schools. Like his predecessors, the Earl appreciated the value conferred upon a work of art by provenance, but he instead focused predominantly on acquiring key paintings and items of furniture to insert into the collection, many of which spoke to connoisseurial trends and fashions, but some of which spoke of more individual tastes and personal interests.

Some intriguing correspondence between the Earl and Lord Dacre – presumably Thomas Barrett-Lennard, 17th Baron Dacre (1717–1786) – survives from 1776, the year in which the former inherited Longford Castle. It refers to the fact that he had recently purchased some portraits depicting members of the Forster and Barrett families, from whom he was descended, at a sale at Aldermaston in Berkshire.[19] Judging by the letters, it seems that Lord Dacre, who himself was descended from the Barretts, had also been keen to buy the portraits, even going so far as to enquire about the Earl's amenability to selling them on.[20] This enquiry seems to have been met with a negative response, and the fact that 'Lord Radnor bought all the pictures in a Lot' suggests that this was an important purchase for the Earl.[21] These portraits of ancestors would have worked as part of a 'visual family tree',[22] helping to communicate important notions of lineage and dynasty within the country house. It was not uncommon for families missing a portrait of a certain forebear to look to purchase or even commission one to fill the gap in a collection:[23] indeed, this imperative seems to have been felt by both the Earl and Lord Dacre.

JACOB PLEYDELL-BOUVERIE, 2ND EARL OF RADNOR

One portrait that is likely to have formed a part of this 'Lot' is a depiction of Sir Humphrey Forster (*d.* 1602), who had married a member of the Barrett family, was a High Sheriff for Berkshire and later became a Member of Parliament during the reign of Queen Elizabeth I (fig. 88). The Earl might have bought this portrait because it was expressive of his familial connections in Berkshire: his mother's estate, Coleshill, being located in that county. In addition, it foreshadowed the family's later political work, and would also have chimed stylistically with other sixteenth-century paintings at Longford.

Acquiring an image of a forebear may also have been precipitated by the Earl's marked interest in genealogy. In the late eighteenth century, it was fashionable to take an interest in one's ancestry, and the Earl nurtured an interest in his family's origins. We have seen that Sir Jacob and his brother had sought to learn more about their Huguenot origins earlier in the century (see page 44), but the Earl's engagement with his family history was undertaken in a somewhat different manner. This is hinted at within some notes he compiled, which have been dated to around 1800, and which demonstrate that he investigated his family history through the methods of professionalised antiquarian study, such as the correct use of historical evidence:

Fig. 88 English school, *Sir Humphrey Forster* [d. 1602], early seventeenth century, oil on panel, 47 x 33 cm, Longford Castle

> I have adverted at different Periods of my Life to the Task of giving a satisfactory Pedigree of my Family, of which an erroneous, unadvised & curtailed sketch has appeared in different Publications . . . Instead of looking back to the Land whence they emigrated & searching the History of their Ancestors, appealing to Evidence of Authority . . . they contented themselves with a compilation . . . what was recollected by their then living Relations & Connexions which has been treated the origin of the Family ever since . . . In pursuance of this wish to ascertain, & establish as correct an account of the Family as I can, I have in addition to the Papers I find in my Fathers Possession collected such Information as from Time to Time lay in my Way – From Books, Writings, Registers, & Individuals.[24]

These notes imply that the Earl considered his predecessors' more amateur approach not to have done justice to their family history; however, it must be remembered that the more professionalised approach he took was likely to have been conditioned by changing cultural circumstances, and born of the antiquarian climate of the late eighteenth century.

This interest in family history was not only manifested in art acquisitions but also in a genealogical tree drawn up in 1779, tracing the ancestry to King Edward I (1239–1307) of the 2nd

Earl and his wife, Anne Duncombe (1759–1829), whom he had married in 1777.[25] The Plantagenet kings were the subjects of extended antiquarian interest in the late eighteenth century. For instance, in 1771, Edward I's tomb at Westminster Abbey had been exhumed, and the medieval period was widely esteemed for having seen the foundation of the English constitution and common law.[26] The Earl even appealed to this period of history in a 1795 debate in the House of Lords on the Treasonable Practices Bill, by 'seriously recommend[ing] to the attention of government, the statute of Edward 3d', as it formed the basis of the law of treason.[27]

Despite his evident interest in history, the Earl also kept up to date with the fashions of the time, and followed in his father's footsteps by continuing to build strong patronage relationships with some of the most important contemporary artists of the late eighteenth century. These included Thomas Gainsborough and Joshua Reynolds, both of whom had, of course, been commissioned by the 1st Earl of Radnor to paint likenesses of members of the family (see pages 97–103 and figs 63–69). This repeat patronage of the same artists appears to have arisen out of a desire for visual continuity, as well as of artistic excellence, in the family's lineal self-representation. For instance, Gainsborough painted a portrait of Anne Duncombe, Countess of Radnor, in 1778, most probably to commemorate her marriage the previous year.[28] This three-quarter-length portrait (fig. 89), which today hangs in the Billiard Room at Longford Castle, shows Anne seated, wearing an orange-yellow dress, leaning against a piece of furniture upon which a red curtain is draped. In her left hand she is holding an open book, and she is inclined forwards, catching the viewer's gaze.

Just under a decade later, Reynolds painted Anne, in a commission that cost £105 (fig. 90).[29] The resultant portrait was painted in what has been assessed as the artist's late style: it features a 'very freely executed' landscape background, softly painted in blues and greens, demonstrating stylistic progression.[30] Today this portrait hangs in the Long Parlour, near other works by Reynolds including his likeness of the 2nd Earl as a child (see page 100 and fig. 64) and

a portrait of Lady Catherine Pelham-Clinton (1776–1804), to be discussed in the next chapter (see page 157 and fig. 107). Although, as we have seen, the portrait of the Earl as a child was painted in a historicised style, featuring the sitter wearing seventeenth-century dress, it hangs appropriately alongside Reynolds's likeness of Anne, being the output of the same artist, and, in addition, being of approximately the same dimensions. The family's extensive patronage of the best artists, including Reynolds, means that the portrait collection at Longford Castle forms a harmonious whole.

Anne was the daughter of Anthony Duncombe, 1st Baron Feversham (*c.* 1695–1763), and his third wife, Anne Hales. Anne Hales was later remarried to the 1st Earl of Radnor after the death of his second wife, Rebecca Alleyne, making Anne Duncombe the 2nd Earl's stepsister. Their marriage further consolidated the links between these important families. Anne Duncombe brought with her to Longford Castle an extensive porcelain dinner service decorated with the arms of the Duncombe family, quartering Cornwallis and impaling Verney (fig. 91). This decoration recalls the provenance of the service, which had been made for Anne's father and his first wife, the Honourable Margaret Verney (dates unknown). Unlike the arms upon the collection of silver plate at Longford, discussed in Chapter 3 (see pages 90–91), the decoration upon this porcelain dinner service could not be amended to reflect changes in ownership or title. However, the permanent links between the Bouveries, Duncombes and Verneys that the service displayed were arguably just as important in conveying their new owners' social status as were the updated crests and coronets upon their silverware.

Helen Matilda Chaplin, who catalogued the Longford art collection in the early twentieth century, noted how Anne Duncombe was 'a good business woman' who 'virtually managed the property for some years before her husband's death in 1828'.[31] An insight into female patronage and the use of works of art by female members of the family can be gleaned from references to Anne. For instance, between 1813 and 1815, she was provided with gold thimbles, a gold pencil case, 'a pair of Amber Waist Clasps' and various items of jewellery including 'a pr of garnet Earrings', and received services including 'colouring a long Golde Neckchain' from the firm Garrard & Co.[32] The company's ledgers clearly differentiate between payments associated with Anne and her husband, as a note detailing a payment for 'Repairing a Teapot & furnishing a padlock (Lord R)' specifically documented the Earl's involvement in a separate transaction.[33] The historian Amanda Vickery has noted that, during the Georgian period, 'in all ledgers, named female customers are in a minority'.[34] However, this evidence provides a rare glimpse into an instance in which the Countess of Radnor can be identified as responsible for particular commissions.

In addition, some notebooks survive in the Longford archive containing drawings and copies by Anne after paintings by 'Woverman' – possibly the seventeenth-century Dutch artist Philips Wouwerman (1619–1668).[35] Paintings associated with this artist's circle are today present at Longford Castle, but Anne's drawings cannot be firmly matched with them, although

Facing: Fig. 90 Sir Joshua Reynolds (1723–1792), *The Honourable Anne Duncombe*, c. 1787, oil on canvas, 127 x 99.1 cm, Longford Castle

JACOB PLEYDELL-BOUVERIE, 2ND EARL OF RADNOR

Fig. 91 A *famille verte* Armorial Service featuring the Arms of Duncombe quartering Cornwallis impaling Verney, *c.* 1724, enamelled porcelain, Longford Castle

the subject matter – dogs, horses and people – is similar. The practice of making copies after paintings in a collection can be seen in the context of eighteenth-century feminine pursuits, or 'amusements', within the country house,[36] and the existence of these copies is revealing of the way in which the then Countess of Radnor also took an interest in fine art.

In the early nineteenth century, the Earl and his wife encouraged Margaret Sarah Carpenter (1793–1872), a young female artist from Salisbury, to visit Longford Castle and study the picture collection, much as Gainsborough had done some years earlier (see pages 80 and 103–4).[37] Carpenter was then an aspiring artist, and went on to enjoy a career as a portraitist, exhibiting with the Royal Academy,[38] an indication of how women also used the collection at Longford in a professional capacity. Her work, including a copy of Nathaniel Dance's 1774 portrait of the 2nd Earl, and a full-length posthumous portrait of Lady Barbara Pleydell-Bouverie (1783–1798), one of his daughters, who died young, can still be seen at Longford Castle.

The 2nd Earl's tenure at Longford saw a number of other important family portraits added to the collection, to which we will return later. However, at this point it is interesting to consider some of the acquisitions he made on the secondary market. What unites many of the Earl's purchases is the fact that they had previously been owned by other important art collectors or interesting individuals, providing further grounds for the argument that the Bouveries valued the prestige conferred by provenance on a work of art. For instance, two important paintings that entered the Longford art collection thanks to the 2nd Earl had previously been owned by the diplomat, antiquarian and archaeologist Sir William Hamilton (1730–1803).

Provenance, however, did not necessarily guarantee the authorship of a work of art. For example, in 1796, the Earl bought a painting of *Venus disarming Cupid* (fig. 92), then thought to be by the Italian Renaissance painter Correggio (1489–1534) but now attributed to Luca Cambiaso (1527–1585). He spent the large sum of £630 on acquiring the painting at a post-humous sale of works of art in the collection of the dealer Benjamin van der Gucht.[39] However, this amount was nowhere near the sum its previous owner had hoped to reach.[40] Hamilton had hoped to sell it through Van der Gucht for £3,000, to help clear his debts.[41]

The lower price it achieved may reflect the fact that doubts had recently arisen over the attribution of the painting.[42] The desire to see the hand of Correggio at work is demonstrative of the esteem in which collectors of the time held this artist, who was admired for his perceived supremacy in the art of chiaroscuro.[43] Ownership of a painting by Correggio was, for many connoisseurs and art collectors, a point of pride and honour, which the Earl may well have not wanted to miss out on. For example, a painting by the artist had been housed at nearby Wilton House since 1669, when Cosimo III de' Medici, Grand Duke of Tuscany (1642–1723), had presented it to Philip Herbert, 5th Earl of Pembroke (1621–1669).[44]

Although this painting did not turn out to be the work of Correggio, the Earl later bought another masterpiece once in the ownership of Hamilton: a portrait of *Juan de Pareja* by the Spanish artist Diego Velázquez (1599–1660).[45] This painting (fig. 93), now in the Metropolitan Museum of Art in New York, depicts Velázquez's 'enslaved assistant', who was later liberated, and worked as an 'independent painter'.[46] In his account book, the Earl listed a payment of £151 14s 5d for the 'Picture by Velasquez Etc' in May 1811.[47] Early nineteenth-century catalogues of pictures at Longford suggest that this painting was hung at different times in the 'India Paper Bed-chamber', the Gallery and possibly also a 'Closet room', and in 1829 the art dealer John Smith described it as 'very excellent'.[48]

The 2nd Earl therefore showed a taste for works of art from both the Italian and Spanish schools but his artistic interests were wide-ranging. For example, in 1791, he had bought a painting then attributed to the Flemish master Peter Paul Rubens, and now given to Pieter Verhulst (dates unknown), depicting *A View of the Escorial with a Hermit, his Ass and Deer and a Crucifix in the Foreground* (fig. 94).[49] As we have seen, the 1st Earl acquired works of art by Rubens (see pages 114–16), and the presence of this artist's output among the collection the 2nd Earl inherited may have contributed to the latter's interest in his oeuvre. His desire to buy this particular painting may also have been influenced by the fact that the artist-collector Richard Cosway (1742–1821), with whom the 2nd Earl had had a number of dealings, had previously owned it.

Cosway was commissioned to produce a range of portraits of members of the Bouverie family for the 2nd Earl. One particularly interesting example is a full-length portrait he

Fig. 92 Luca Cambiaso (1527–1585), *Venus disarming Cupid*, sixteenth century, oil on canvas, 149.9 x 106.7 cm, Longford Castle

Facing: Fig. 93 Diego Velázquez (1599–1660), *Juan de Pareja*, 1650, oil on canvas, 81.3 x 69.9 cm, Metropolitan Museum of Art, New York

JACOB PLEYDELL-BOUVERIE, 2ND EARL OF RADNOR

Fig. 94 Pieter Verhulst (dates unknown), *View of the Escorial with a Hermit, his Ass and Deer and a Crucifix in the Foreground*, in a mid-eighteenth-century continental (Flemish?) carved and gilded frame, 154.9 x 254 cm, Longford Castle

produced of his patron holding the architectural plans for the proposed transformation of Longford Castle into a hexagon, evincing the Earl's confidence in the designs (fig. 87). Letters from Cosway survive in the Longford archive, including one recounting the artist's visit to see the art collection at nearby Fonthill Abbey, which reveals that he had wished to pay a visit to Longford Castle.[50] This artist–patron relationship may have owed its roots to the influence of the Society for the Encouragement of Arts, Manufactures and Commerce in Cosway's early artistic development. William Shipley (1715–1803), founder of the Society, had supported the artist upon his arrival in London in 1754, and Cosway had won a premium for a chalk drawing in the under-fourteen-year-old category.[51] It is perhaps unsurprising that one of the family's most significant examples of their loyalty as patrons was towards Cosway, given that they would have been alerted to his genius from an early date through their involvement in the Society of Arts.

Moreover, the mutual self-respect of the Earl and Cosway as art collectors may have strengthened this relationship. Sir Robert Walpole was another collector who bought works of art from the collections of artists whose patron he was: in his case, the sculptor and wood-carver Grinling Gibbons (1648–1721) and the portraitist Charles Jervas (c. 1675–1739).[52] The Earl perhaps bought from Cosway's personal collection because he wished to be associated with his taste. A copy of the 1791 catalogue to the sale of Cosway's collection survives in the Longford archive, and contains some pencil annotations next to certain paintings.[53] For instance, a cross appears next to an entry labelled as 'A landscape – A view of the palace of the Escurial',[54] suggesting that this work of art had perhaps been singled out for attention prior to the sale.

The Earl's taste for artworks associated with Rubens is further evinced by the fact that he also purchased a painting of *Cupids Harvesting* by the master's circle at this sale. This acquisition is significant when assessing the Longford art collection as a whole, as it again demonstrates a confluence between the family's patronage of contemporary artists and acquisitions on the secondary market. This painting, and Rubens's portrait of his son Frans, already in the collection, would have harmonised in terms of their subject matter and style with portraits the Earl had commissioned from Cosway himself. Cosway was known to have 'excelled' in the field of child portraiture, and he produced likenesses of the Earl's children over a number of years, one of which has been linked to a 'Rubensian prototype'.[55] The fact that paintings by Rubens's circle, the master himself, and by Cosway, working in the same idiom, co-existed at Longford Castle demonstrates again how the family achieved a sense of continuity across their art collection. It also shows how the 2nd Earl was keen to follow the precedent set by Sir Jacob and the 1st Earl, keeping the family portrait collection up to date.

Cosway painted five portraits of the Earl's children during the 1780s and 1790s. Two, portraying 'my 3 eldest Children', were paid for in 1785, for the total sum of £115 10s.[56] The first depicts the family's son and heir at the time, William (later the 3rd Earl of Radnor), and the eldest child, Lady Mary Anne Pleydell-Bouverie (1778–1790), together (fig. 95); the second, the next son in age, the Honourable Duncombe Pleydell-Bouverie (1780–1850). Both paintings are idealised representations, depicting the children in relaxed, informal poses, situated within landscape settings. When the portraits were paid for, the children were aged, respectively, six, seven and four.

The next portrait commissioned cost the Earl £50 in 1789, and portrayed the next son, the Honourable Laurence Pleydell-Bouverie (1781–1811), who was then aged seven (fig. 96).[57] He appears again in a landscape setting but in a comparatively dynamic composition, depicted surrounded by dogs, evocative of Gainsborough's painting of 1783, *Two Shepherd Boys with Dogs Fighting*.[58] Two final portraits, depicting further children, were commissioned together and paid for in 1799.[59] Although they were not all painted at the same time, the repeat patronage of Cosway, and the fact that most of the paintings are of the same dimensions, suggest that the Earl wished the series to appear unified and coherent. They may have been painted at different times so that the Earl's offspring were all depicted as children of similar ages, rather than some as adolescents and others as babies. In engaging the artist to paint in the same style and size across a period of almost fifteen years, the portraits appear to posterity as a set, recording a generation of Bouveries.[60]

Fig. 95 Richard Cosway (1742–1821), *William Pleydell-Bouverie* [later 3rd Earl of Radnor] *and Lady Mary Anne Pleydell-Bouverie*, c. 1785, oil on canvas, 100.3 x 125.7 cm, Longford Castle

The portraits that the Earl commissioned from Cosway take on further significance when assessed in the light of his keen interest in genealogy and family history. The art historian Marcia Pointon has noted the prevailing belief within scholarship that a 'child-centred ideology' formed a substitute for a 'genealogical one' in the eighteenth century,[61] and child portraiture was a fashionable genre among patrons of the time. In particular, there was a tendency among artists to portray children's personalities, showing them engaged in games and connecting with animals and the natural world.[62] The Cosway works for the Earl are in line with this trend, and can be profitably seen in the context of the Swiss-born French philosopher Jean-Jacques Rousseau's (1712–1778) ideas about child-rearing, which were, by the 1780s, well established.[63]

Fig. 96 Richard Cosway (1742–1821), *The Honourable Laurence Pleydell-Bouverie*, c. 1788, oil on canvas, 124.5 x 99.1 cm, Longford Castle

Fig. 97 / Unknown artist, Rectangular Bijouterie Cabinet, late eighteenth century with some sixteenth-century metalwork, cedarwood and gilt metal on a giltwood stand, cabinet 38.1 x 45.7 cm, stand 87.6 x 58.4 cm, Longford Castle

Cosway was not only a distinguished painter of children but has also been assessed by his contemporaries and posterity as the eighteenth century's 'pre-eminent' miniaturist.[64] His portrait miniatures have been praised as 'glamorous and intimate', and described as 'the mirror in which fashionable Regency society saw itself reflected'.[65] Cosway produced a number of portrait miniatures for the Bouveries, including a depiction of the 2nd Earl in Van Dyck costume, and a small-scale copy, in watercolour on ivory, after Gainsborough's 1773 portrait of the 1st Earl, described as a 'free interpretation of the original'.[66]

These small-scale commissions complemented some important historical portrait miniatures acquired by the 2nd Earl. Works of art of this genre formed part of a patronage tradition dating back to the Tudor and Stuart eras, and he had bought several important Elizabethan portrait miniatures by the goldsmith and limner Nicholas Hilliard (c. 1547–1619) in 1799. They were housed within a cabinet understood to be Elizabethan, which the Earl acquired at the same time (fig. 97).[67] A note obtained with the set stated that 'The Cabinet was given by Queen Elizabeth to Lady Rich – and by her Ladyship it was given to the family of the present Possessor – And has never been in any other hand'.[68] Although the art historian Roy Strong has disputed parts of this provenance account, the royal heritage is undisputed,[69] and, in any case, the perception of a highly illustrious and apparently unbroken ownership history may well have constituted a large part of these items' appeal for the Earl at the time.

The cabinet also contained two letters written by Queen Elizabeth I herself; it is housed today in the Green Velvet Drawing Room at Longford Castle, which is a particularly apposite location, as, according to the poem about Longford by Henry Hare, 2nd Baron Coleraine, this was the room where the Queen once stayed.[70] The presence of the cabinet within this room therefore serves to highlight Longford Castle's Elizabethan heritage. The intricate workmanship and professed historical significance of the piece arguably imbued this item of furniture with the status of a curiosity, something that seems to have appealed strongly to the 2nd Earl as a collector. For instance, in 1797–8 he journeyed to St Petersburg via Hamburg, Hanover, Brunswick, Berlin, Dresden, Copenhagen and Stockholm, visiting palaces and cathedrals and writing down his observations in a journal.[71] His notes record his impressions of a cabinet of

Fig. 98 Thomas Rucker (*c.* 1532–1606), the Renaissance Iron Chair of The Holy Roman Emperor Rudolph II, 1574, iron with dark red silk damask dais, 143.5 cm high excluding dais, 69.9 cm wide, Longford Castle

curiosities at the ducal palace in Brunswick, 'objects of curiosity' at Dresden, and a 'cabinet given to Gustavas Adolphus by the town of Angsburgh' in Sweden.[72] His fascination with objects of technical brilliance or historical importance in continental collections may have spurred him on to acquire similarly unusual items for the Longford collection when he returned home.

Another notable piece at Longford that fits into this category is a unique iron chair, made in 1574 by Thomas Rucker (*c.* 1532–1606) and given to the Holy Roman Emperor Rudolph II (1552–1612) for the Imperial *Kunstkammer* in Prague by the city of Augsburg (fig. 98).[73] The Earl bought this distinctive item of furniture for the sum of £1,000 from the merchant, naturalist and director of the Bank of England, Gustavus Brander (1720–1787), who had brought it to

Fig. 99 Thomas Rucker
(c. 1532–1606), The Renaissance
Iron Chair of the Holy Roman
Emperor Rudolph II, 1574
(detail of chair in fig. 98)

England in the 1770s. The chair's striking appearance and fascinating provenance make it a true treasure of the Longford collection. It features exquisite reliefs depicting a number of subjects and historical events, inviting close and detailed inspection by the viewer (fig. 99).

The chair was undoubtedly acquired to function not as a piece of usable furniture but rather as an expression of the Earl's antiquarian tastes. As Nicholas Penny has noted, the chair's contemporaneity with Longford Castle itself may well be significant,[74] much like that of the Elizabethan cabinet. The chair's arresting appearance has continually stopped visitors to Longford in their tracks and invited commentary, with many considering it a piece of sculpture in its own right. This may be because of both the number of highly detailed reliefs that the chair features, and also the difficulty of working in the material.[75] For instance, the German art historian Gustav Waagen (1794–1868), who visited Longford Castle in the mid-nineteenth century, described the chair as 'a truly magnificent specimen of sculpture in iron' and 'the richest and most tasteful work of the kind that I am acquainted with'.[76]

In addition, the German librarian and travel writer Samuel Heinrich Spiker (1786–1858), who visited Longford Castle during a tour of England, Wales and Scotland in 1816, devoted three hundred words to a description of the chair and its provenance.[77] Elsewhere, it was introduced as 'another interesting object in this mansion' and 'quite a work of art',[78] signifying its parity, in the eyes of some visitors, with the works of fine art in the collection at Longford. Jocelyn Anderson has observed that the authors of eighteenth-century country-house guidebooks would elaborate on a piece of furniture only if it was a one-off production, or had particular historical significance.[79] The chair met both these criteria, and was displayed not for use but for show, and so it was described at length in *The Salisbury Guide*, a comprehensive volume of regional attractions and local points of interest including Longford Castle, Salisbury Cathedral and Stonehenge, published in its nineteenth edition in 1797.[80]

A letter written to the Earl in 1781 by the chair's previous owner, Brander, contained recommendations for keeping it in good condition but also revealed its perceived status as a curiosity.[81] Brander wrote, 'The coat of Black Lead given to it, I apprehend obscures its Beauty, and degrades the still more singular material of which it is Compos'd, and which constitutes a principal part of its Curiosity.'[82] He then added that, should 'a little discoloration <u>only</u> by Rust' occur, this should be understood 'as the Virtuosi do the Patina on a Brass Medal', as part of 'the genuine lacquer of Antiquity'.[83] Although some rust might have been valued for adding the patina of age to the chair, other evidence suggests that the Earl was keen to preserve the structure in as good a condition as possible.

When he journeyed to France in 1786, he left some written instructions to the Longford housekeeper to ensure that it was well looked after during his absence: 'particularly care must be taken against any the least damp getting on the imperial Chair – I would have the Chair stand, where I have now placed it – opposite the Gallery Chimney'.[84] Locating the chair opposite the chimneypiece represents a pragmatic decision, as the heat from the fire would have helped to prevent damp from adversely affecting its structure. However, the instruction is also interesting as it implies that the Earl was keen for the chair to be displayed in pride of place in the Gallery, alongside the fashionable bespoke eighteenth-century furniture commissions already located there (see pages 54–5 and fig. 28). The chair can still be seen in this position at the castle today. It appears that the Bouverie family have always deemed the Gallery to be a space appropriate for the display of unusual and interesting items in their ownership, as well as their most fashionable and prestigious works of fine and decorative art.

One important addition to the Gallery during the tenure of the 2nd Earl was the famed full-length double portrait by Hans Holbein the Younger now known as *The Ambassadors*, and today on display at the National Gallery in London (fig. 100). The Earl bought this painting from the well-known art dealer William Buchanan (1777–1864) at some point in 1808 or 1809: a payment to 'Buchanan (& his apignee Haldon)' for £1,000 listed in 1809 is cross-referenced in the Earl's accounts with an entry in 1808, when 'Buchanan Picture-Dealer' was given £100 'on Account'.[85]

His interest in Holbein may have been aroused by the presence at Longford of the portraits of *Erasmus* and *Aegidius* that had been acquired by his grandfather, Sir Jacob (see pages 67–70 and figs 38 and 39), and speaks of a shared taste among the Longford collectors that ran across generations. Holbein still represented a less mainstream interest in the early nineteenth century, however, although his work was more in vogue among certain collectors, such as Horace Walpole, who dedicated a room to him at Strawberry Hill House.[86] Buchanan had

Fig. 100 Hans Holbein the Younger (1497–1543), *The Ambassadors*, 1533, oil on oak, 207 x 209.5 cm, National Gallery, London

JACOB PLEYDELL-BOUVERIE, 2ND EARL OF RADNOR

acquired *The Ambassadors* from the leading art dealer and collector Jean-Baptiste-Pierre Le Brun (1748–1813), who had included an engraving of it in the first volume of his *Galerie des Peintres Flamands, Hollandais et Allemands* in 1792.[87] The art historian Francis Haskell has noted that Le Brun was interested in 'the value of rarity and unfamiliarity', and was responsible for the '"discovery" of forgotten artists' including Holbein:[88] it seems, therefore, that the 2nd Earl was at the forefront of a revival in taste for the work of this important Tudor painter. Although still in its infancy, this burgeoning interest within the art world for Holbein's work arguably sanctioned this painting as a collectable and valuable item.

The Ambassadors is widely known for its unique and captivating composition, and much art-historical attention has gone into deciphering it, with the former Director of the National Gallery, Neil MacGregor, describing it as 'one of the most puzzling' and 'filled with objects that intrigue and perplex'.[89] The use of anamorphosis enables viewers to engage in a process of discovery upon encountering the painting,[90] and the sense of mystery ingrained in its subject matter would have been heightened during its time at Longford, when the identity of the sitters – the French diplomats Jean de Dinteville (1504–1555) and Georges de Selve (1508–1541) – was not confirmed. This uncertainty arguably lent the painting the status of a curiosity, awaiting decryption. This sense of intrigue could well have constituted a key part of its appeal for the Earl, and, indeed, the painting invited much comment from people in the early nineteenth century, who wished to decode its symbolism and postulate the identity of the figures.

For example, a letter in the Longford archive signed 'Wm Coxe' – possibly the historian and archdeacon of Wiltshire, William Coxe (1748–1828)[91] – discusses the picture, opening with the line 'I flatter myself that I have discovered the two Heroes of your celebrated Picture', before suggesting the 'Earl of Surry' and 'Cornelius Agrippa' – possibly Henry Howard, Earl of Surrey (1516/17–1547) and Heinrich Cornelius Agrippa (1486–1535), a German polymath – as potential sitters.[92] Coxe wished to test his theory 'by comparing the Portrait of the Nobleman in your Picture, with a known one of the Earl of Surry'.[93] It is not certain whether the Earl facilitated this encounter; however, the identification did not stand the test of time.

It is notable that the painting of *The Ambassadors*, like others at Longford Castle by Holbein and other sixteenth-century artists, complemented the castle's symbolic architecture, and other contemporaneous curiosities bought to furnish it, such as the Renaissance iron chair and the Elizabethan cabinet. It is known from contemporary catalogues of the collection that the painting, when at Longford, was hung in the Gallery,[94] where the green curtains painted in the background would have been complemented by the green damask wall hangings that formed the backdrop to works of art in this room.

The Earl's personal taste, noted interest in history and independent attitude may well have occasioned the purchase of such an unusual painting. It is also important to bear in mind the involvement of the dealer Buchanan in the transaction. This example sheds further light on the art world networks in which the Earl was engaged, and demonstrates the importance of dealers to the Bouveries' art collecting. The Earl might have briefed or instructed Buchanan on what to acquire on his behalf but it seems that the dealer also had an instinct for what might fit into the Longford collection, possibly triggering the purchase of the painting.

Buchanan had known of the Earl as a collector a few years before the transaction took place, and had clearly identified him as a potential client, as is evidenced by a letter the dealer sent to his London agent in May 1804. He wrote: 'The great object at present is to make a Noise about these pictures, and let all the Dillettanti know of them . . . . [I] see many real purchasers returned to Town . . . and most of them are purchasing, for instance the . . . Earls Cowper, Fitzwilliam, Egremont, Radnor . . .'.[95] The letter went on to list many more collectors, from aristocrats to figures such as the Whig statesman Charles James Fox (1749–1806), the financier and philanthropist John Julius Angerstein (1732–1823) and the connoisseur and art critic Richard Payne Knight (1750–1824).[96]

The inclusion of the 2nd Earl of Radnor in the list indicates that a leading dealer of the day considered his taste concurrent with that of many other key collectors. The pictures noted by Buchanan as of potential interest to such buyers included a Van Dyck and a Poussin: two artists prominently represented in the Longford collection by this stage. Although no evidence suggests that anything came of this episode, that Buchanan later acquired the Holbein for the Earl speaks of the dealer's knowledge of his taste and of the character of the Longford art collection as a whole.

These years were a productive period for the Earl's art-collecting activity. In 1808 he had also paid for two other important works: first, a 'Picture bought of Christies of the first Lady Winchelsea by C. Janson' – a portrait of Elizabeth Finch, Countess of Winchilsea (1557?–1634), now known to be by Marcus Gheeraerts the Younger (fig. 102) – and a 'Picture by Mabuse bought at Squibb's Auction Room' – an oil painting on panel of *The Virgin and Child* (fig. 103) attributed to the Netherlandish painter Jan Gossaert, known as Mabuse (*c.* 1478–1532).[97] These acquisitions provide further evidence of the Earl's taste for sixteenth-century art. He was also responsible for acquiring a three-quarter-length portrait of Thomas Wyndham (1510–1533), which had once been in the collection at Lumley Castle in County Durham (fig. 101). This portrait is by the artist Hans Eworth (*c.* 1520–1574), an important sixteenth-century painter of Netherlandish origin who had spent time working in England, and has been described by Roy Strong as 'the most distinguished foreign painter to work in England in the Tudor period after Holbein'.[98]

The Earl took good care of the works of art in his collection, and seems to have been responsible for having a 'Catalogue of Pictures at Longford Castle' drawn up in 1814, which recorded the locations of works of art at this point.[99] One space that is particularly worthy of attention is a room described in the catalogue as 'Anti-Room to the Gallery', on the first floor of the castle, since this document, and other inventories of the Longford art collection made in the late eighteenth and early nineteenth centuries, suggest that it housed an array of important

Fig. 101 Hans Eworth (c. 1520–1574), *Thomas Wyndham, c.* 1550, oil on panel, 85.1 x 66.7 cm, Longford Castle

works of art during this period. It has also been described as a 'Lobby', and connects the Gallery with the round tower room known today as the 'Chapel Room'. Although it is not a principal room, the number of works of art once on display within it is striking.

For instance, the late eighteenth-century inventory discussed in Chapter 3 listed a total of thirty-three works of art present in this room, and by the time the 1814 catalogue was compiled it contained forty-nine pictures.[100] These included works from a number of schools of art, depicting a range of subjects: from religious scenes to landscape paintings, still lifes and portraits. They were, in the main, small-scale oil paintings but the room also featured drawings and oil sketches at certain moments in time.[101] One painting that was a constant fixture in the space at these moments of record was Jan Brueghel the Elder's *Flowers in a Glass Vase* painted on copper,[102] bought by Sir Jacob in 1744 (see page 65 and fig. 37), and, indeed, this painting is

Facing: Fig. 102 Marcus Gheeraerts the Younger (c. 1561/2–1636), *Elizabeth Finch, Countess of Winchilsea*, 1600, oil on panel, 110.5 x 87.6 cm, Longford Castle

JACOB PLEYDELL-BOUVERIE, 2ND EARL OF RADNOR

still on display in the room today. The space at one stage also housed the family's portrait of their Huguenot ancestor Laurens des Bouverie (see fig. 13).[103] Given the potential for regular, proximate viewing that this area offered, it is important to remember that displays of art would have been configured to facilitate the family's personal enjoyment of their art collection.

Some of the late eighteenth-century inventories carefully recorded the location of each work of art within the space, suggesting that the picture hang had been thoughtfully considered. Precise details were given as to the arrangement, such as: 'over the Staircase Door . . . On the Rt. Side of the Door The Upper Picture . . . The Lower . . . The Large Picture . . . The Upper Pictures'.[104] This gives the sense of a crowded yet systematised arrangement of pictures. The mixed display and volume of artworks in the space might have caused visitors to slow down their pace on the circuit of the rooms at Longford, encouraging them to experience different kinds of art at a different tempo. The scale of the room would surely have prompted viewers to pause and engage in some close looking, contemplating some or all of the paintings and drawings individually, many of which – like the Brueghel *Flowers in a Glass Vase* – had a high level of finish and detail.

Many country houses of the time, including Corsham Court and Woburn Abbey, contained a small cabinet next to the principal picture gallery, sometimes expressly intended for the display of works of art by the Dutch school.[105] The scholar Harry Mount has suggested, however, that one might frequently find 'small, highly-finished pictures of all schools . . . hung together' at the time, and in fact division into schools was actually fairly uncommon in English private houses.[106] At Houghton Hall in Norfolk, for instance, a 'Cabinet Room' contained fifty-one small-scale paintings by artists of the Italian and Northern schools, portraying a range of both classical and religious subjects.[107] Houghton's Cabinet Room, however, had been built for purpose in the eighteenth century, while the Bouveries had appropriated an existing space within the sixteenth-century castle for the display of art in line with this trend.

This state of affairs might have been a factor prompting the Earl to plan changes to the castle's architectural structure. However, one of the sets of unrealised architectural plans drawn up for him, around 1801, depicts a proposed smaller hexagonal room adjacent to the Gallery, labelled a new 'Anti-Room to the Gallery'.[108] Although we have seen that one of the Earl's ambitions in undertaking the architectural works was to bring the art collection together in one place, this new 'Anti-Room' might well have been intended to function as a purpose-designed space for the display of smaller works of art, still in line with the fashion for having a small cabinet adjoining a picture gallery.

The 1814 catalogue of pictures reveals that, while the contents and approach to the display of art in certain rooms at Longford stayed the same over time – as was the case in the Gallery and its ante-room, for example – the 2nd Earl reconfigured some of the other rooms and changed certain picture hangs in line with his own ideas. For instance, we saw in the previous chapter that the 1st Earl had displayed a number of family portraits in the ground-floor Long

Fig. 103 Attributed to Jan Gossaert, called Mabuse (*c.* 1478–1532), *The Virgin and Child*, oil on panel, 43.8 x 31.8 cm, Longford Castle

JACOB PLEYDELL-BOUVERIE, 2ND EARL OF RADNOR

Parlour, showcasing the Bouveries' family tree and drawing attention to Reynolds's likeness of his son and heir by hanging it prominently over the chimneypiece (see pages 100–101 and fig. 64). However, according to the 1814 catalogue, the Long Parlour did not contain any family portraits in the early nineteenth century but instead an array of old master landscapes and portraits attributed to artists including Anthony van Dyck, David Teniers, Gaspard Dughet, Aelbert Cuyp (1620–1691) and Jacob van Ruisdael (1628/9–1682).[109] The 2nd Earl instead moved the family portrait collection to the Breakfast Room, updating it with additions such as Gainsborough's portrait of Anne Duncombe, described in the catalogue as 'Wife of Jacob'.[110] The overhaul of the contents and character of the Long Parlour in the early nineteenth century reminds us that the display of art at Longford has been fluid and evolving, in line with the varying predilections of different owners.

The 2nd Earl's treatment of the castle and his art-collecting activity can therefore be understood as driven by something of an independent attitude. This extended to other areas of his life, including his work in the realm of politics. In correspondence with George Washington (1732–1799), the first President of the United States of America, he described himself as one 'who enlisted in no political party here as a public man',[111] and his outlook appears to have been multivalent. Although he has been labelled a Whig with radical inclinations, 'sticking up for the rights of the people',[112] he was also involved in the establishment of the dining club at University College, Oxford, which during this period was known to be Tory.[113] Moreover, his political views have also been described as 'too idiosyncratic to bring him preferment'.[114]

He consistently upheld a belief in liberty, however, which is visible in his contribution to parliamentary debates on subjects such as America and the India Bill.[115] His libertarianism is evident in how, in 1772, as 3rd Viscount Folkestone, he spoke against the Royal Marriage Bill on the grounds of freedom and equality.[116] He also carried forward his father's interest in King Alfred (see pages 91–2), presenting a bust of the King by the sculptor Joseph Wilton (1722–1803) to University College, Oxford, instead of silver, the usual gift that well-born undergraduates would make.[117] This recurrence of Alfred as a leitmotif within the Bouverie family's patronage suggests both a subscription to a fashionable trend and their ongoing desire to associate themselves with the Anglo-Saxon period and its liberal values, in line with their family motto.

The Earl, like his predecessors, involved himself in local politics and charity near his family seat in Wiltshire. In 1810, he was contacted regarding the potential establishment of a 'Salisbury Philanthropic Bank': a surviving letter to him regarding this matter suggested that the bank's surpluses 'should go in aid of the various charitable institutions' in the surrounding area, and mentioned that ministers were 'generally too much engaged, to give Plans of this sort consideration' but that it was hoped 'your Lordship will give this Publicity'.[118] Although it is unclear what happened to this particular proposal, the letter suggests that the Earl was perceived locally as being particularly amenable to such philanthropic initiatives.

Some of his charitable work was art-related: in 1781, he had paid the large sum of £680 10s for a stained-glass window in Salisbury Cathedral, depicting *The Elevation of the Brazen Serpent in the Wilderness*.[119] His generosity is reminiscent of the Huguenot-derived practice of giving gifts to churches, and suggests that his faith had a part to play in his charitable activities. His ongoing affiliation with the Huguenot community is evident in the fact that he followed his father as a governor of the French Hospital.[120]

In 1785 the Earl donated land for a new Guildhall in Salisbury.[121] This benefaction was commemorated in a portrait, commissioned from the artist John Hoppner (1758–1810), which still hangs today at the Guildhall.[122] This year was an important one for the Bouverie family, as it also saw the then Prince of Wales – later to become King George IV (1762–1830) – pay a visit to Longford Castle. The *Salisbury Journal* reported the event on 11 July, noting how the Prince of Wales had visited the races on the Wednesday afternoon, before returning 'to an elegant entertainment at Longford'.[123] That evening, he went to the 'Assembly-Room . . . attended by the Earl and Countess of Radnor', where 'his Highness joined with great spirit and good humour' in the dancing.[124] According to the report, the following night:

> His Highness dined at Longford-Castle, and was received in the evening by a
> select party of the Nobility and Gentry of the neighbourhood, assembled there, by
> invitation, to a ball and supper. The ball was opened about eleven o'clock . . . at two
> o'clock the supper was announced, and the company sat down to a most elegant
> and splendid entertainment, consisting of a profusion of every delicacy possible to
> be procured, with the choicest wines, and a band of music from London playing
> during the repast. . . .[125]

Although relatively little archival evidence survives to shed light on the visit, menu plans drawn up for the occasion are still held in the Longford archive. They show, for instance, that the supper planned by the Earl for the Thursday evening was held in the Round Parlour, and included an array of dishes such as 'Cold Chicken w Ham', 'Prawns', 'French Beans à la Cream', 'Canapies of Tongue', 'Jelly' and 'Blanch Mange', among others.[126] Given the favourable write-up that the meal received in the newspaper, this menu was clearly deemed suitable to the occasion. The event was an expensive undertaking for the Earl. On 13 August, he noted in his account book 'Extraordinary Expenses occasioned by the Prince of Wales's Visit to Longford July last' of £339 15s 1d.[127]

It is likely that Longford Castle would have received a number of aristocratic visitors during the eighteenth century, as travel to other country houses constituted an important activity for the elites during this period.[128] It is known that the Earl himself visited a number of other country houses, as expenses for trips to Wilton House, Wardour Castle, Fonthill Abbey, Longleat House and Corsham Court, all in Wiltshire, appear in the account books he kept during his tenure at Longford, along with expenses for visiting Audley End House in Essex, Highclere Castle in Berkshire, and Hatfield House in Hertfordshire, as well as others.[129] During his time at Oxford University, as 3rd Viscount Folkestone, he also took the opportunity to travel to other country houses, perhaps taking inspiration from their architecture, gardens or art collections. For instance, a few months after his matriculation, he undertook 'an Excursion to Bleinheim' (presumably Blenheim Palace, in Oxfordshire); in 1767, he went on an 'Excursion to Buckingham & Stow'; and in 1769, he recorded his expenses for 'going to & seeing Stourhead'.[130]

The Earl and his wife appear to have paid a visit to Woburn Abbey in Bedfordshire at some stage, as a note in the Longford archive among the Earl's correspondence shows that the Duchess of Bedford presented 'her Compts to Lord & Lady Radnor & is most happy to have it in her power to oblige them, by allowing them (contrary to the usual custom) to see the Abbey today at any hour Most agreeable to Lord & Lady Radnor'.[131] This note suggests that they were granted special access but is undated, so it is uncertain which Duchess of Bedford it was at the time.

Like his predecessors, the Earl engaged a number of picture cleaners and restorers to keep the works of art in his possession in good condition. His account books show payments made, for example, to 'Parsons picture Cleaner', 'Devis Picture-Cleaner', 'De Bruijn Picture Cleaner' and 'Simpson Picture-cleaner'.[132] A letter in the Longford archive also provides recommendations for removing a 'seeming injury on the <u>Poussin</u>', involving 'a little spirits of turpentine, <u>say a drop</u>', given from an unknown 'H. Parker' who added that he 'would not presume to meddle with pictures of such consequence' had he not made the subject 'my particular study'.[133] The value that the Earl attached to the pictures in his ownership is also evident in the aforementioned instructions that he wrote to his housekeeper upon his departure for France in 1786. They note, for example, that 'especially no Picture is to be removed by any Body, on any Account', without his express permission, and that 'In Case of Fire (against which I trust every Precaution will be used)', first a closet and some cupboards were to be emptied, before 'the principal Pictures' were to be attended to.[134] He added, 'till all the Pictures are removed, No Attention is to be paid to the Furniture',[135] suggesting that he deemed the collection of paintings to be of greatest importance and worth saving first in an emergency.

The legacy the 2nd Earl left at Longford Castle differs in character from those of his predecessors. Like Sir Jacob and the 1st Earl of Radnor, he took great care of the art collection he had inherited, and continued to commission the best contemporary artists of the day, for instance for additions to the family portrait collection. He also followed in the footsteps of his father and grandfather by continuing the tradition of planting trees on the Longford estate: in the 1780s, for instance, he recorded how his two eldest children had planted horse chestnuts, acorns and beeches in the grounds.[136] Involving his children, and particularly his heir, in this endeavour underscores the way in which tree planting was symbolically bound up with the continuation of the family dynasty.

The 2nd Earl's tenure at Longford is also notable for his markedly individual approach to art collecting and to the castle itself: for instance, he is often remembered for his unfinished

attempt to reconfigure the building to a hexagonal ground plan. It was down to later generations to resolve the building works, turning Longford into the structure seen today, as the
following chapter will discuss. However, as we have seen, the Earl was fundamentally motivated by a desire to improve his family's property, and the strength of his commitment to
enhancing Longford Castle cannot be doubted, even if some of his ambitions have ultimately
been deemed misguided. He made substantial contributions to the art collection: thanks to the
2nd Earl, the collection included unique treasures such as the Elizabethan cabinet, the iron
chair, and, for a time, Holbein's famous *The Ambassadors*. These treasures, contemporaneous
with Longford Castle itself, spoke to its history, and truly enriched the collection.

Fig. 104 Studio (?) of Jan
Gossaert, called Mabuse
(*c.* 1478–1532), *The Children of
King Christian II of Denmark*, oil on
canvas, transferred from panel,
34.9 x 47.6 cm, acquired 1820,
Longford Castle

JACOB PLEYDELL-BOUVERIE, 2ND EARL OF RADNOR

CHAPTER 5

The Nineteenth and Early Twentieth Centuries

Dear Lord Radnor

Will you think me very impertinent if, as a Director of the British Gallery,

I express to you in the name of myself & my Brethren, how much gratified we

should be, if you would allow us to exhibit two or three pictures from your fine

collection in our exhibition of this year. . . . <u>We are</u> of course at the whole expense

of removing & replacing the pictures, which is done also with the greatest

possible care – under the direction of Mr Seguier, with whom I believe

you are acquainted & who will be most happy to wait upon you & give

you any information you may wish for upon the subject. . . .[1]

In 1829 William Pleydell-Bouverie, 3rd Earl of Radnor (1779–1869), received this letter from George Agar-Ellis, 1st Baron Dover (1797–1833). Lord Dover was a British politician, a patron of the arts and a trustee of both the British Museum and the National Gallery, and he was writing to the Earl to invite him to send some paintings from the collection at Longford Castle to be displayed at an exhibition in the capital.[2] The letter does not mention which particular paintings Lord Dover had in mind for the annual exhibition of old masters organised by the British Institution but it is revealing, as it shows that those active within the wider art world at this point in the nineteenth century knew of the art collection at Longford Castle and were aware of its high quality.

The previous chapters of this book have told the story of how this exemplary collection came into being, thanks to three key collectors active in the eighteenth and early nineteenth centuries: Sir Jacob Bouverie and the 1st and 2nd Earls of Radnor. After the death of the 2nd Earl in 1828, art was not again collected at Longford on such a large scale as during their lifetimes but, as demonstrated by the letter from Lord Dover, as well as other evidence to be explored throughout this chapter, the collection was deemed one of great national import. Its later owners made a few additions of their own but predominantly concentrated their efforts on cleaning, cataloguing, celebrating and sharing the treasures of Longford Castle, as this chapter will show. What follows will sketch out the lives and main interests of the 3rd, 4th and 5th Earls of Radnor, as well as their contributions and the attitudes they took towards the treasures

Fig. 105 Elisabeth-Louise Vigée-Lebrun (1755–1842), *William Pleydell-Bouverie* [3rd Earl of Radnor when Viscount Folkestone], 1799 (detail of fig. 106)

153

they inherited at the castle, throughout the rest of the nineteenth century and at the turn of the twentieth.

The 3rd Earl of Radnor inherited Longford Castle upon the death of his father in 1828. He is remembered particularly for his politics, which were the subject of a study undertaken by Ronald K. Huch in 1977, wherein it was noted that 'by the time he abandoned politics in 1848, [he] had done as much to preserve the constitution and the aristocracy's role in that constitution as any one individual could ever hope to do'.[3] Huch noted how 'the spirit of noblesse oblige was everywhere in evidence' at Coleshill House and Longford Castle during the tenure of this Earl of Radnor, with 'the equanimity of [his] country life [standing] in sharp contrast to his stormy political career'.[4] This sense of *noblesse oblige* may have precipitated the Earl's generosity towards the arts. For instance, in 1830, shortly after he came to the title, he donated to the British Museum a large number of coins, dating from Anglo-Saxon times to the Tudor and Stuart reigns and encompassing a broad geography across much of Europe.[5] This gift can be seen in the context of the Bouverie family's antiquarianism, and their role as artistic benefactors, keen to make a contribution to the arts for the benefit of wider society.

However, it appears that the Earl did not agree to Lord Dover's request, as a note appended to the bottom of his letter reads 'Declined on the ground that the pictures are technically the property of the Trustees & that there would be much trouble in making arrangements . . .'.[6] However, the request is still significant, as it shows the widespread interest in the Longford collection at this date. Moreover, as we will see, later in the nineteenth century some pictures were loaned to the Royal Academy, for some of their Winter Exhibitions.

Lord Dover, in his correspondence with the 3rd Earl, alluded to the latter's familiarity with 'Mr Seguier'.[7] This may well be a reference to John Seguier (1785–1856), who was a picture restorer and superintendent of the British Institution,[8] and who, between 1830 and 1840, was contracted to clean works of art in the Longford collection. Invoices and correspondence survive detailing the cost of cleaning individual paintings and regarding the safe transportation of the paintings between the Earl and Seguier.[9] For instance, it is recorded that the sixteenth-century portraits of *Erasmus* and *Aegidius* (figs 38 and 39) were cleaned at a cost of £1 11s 6d each; that Jan Brueghel the Elder's *Flowers in a Glass Vase* (fig. 37) cost 10s 6d to clean and that Claude's *Pastoral Landscape with the Arch of Titus* (fig. 30) cost £5 5s to clean.[10] We have seen that Longford's previous owners undertook to ensure that the art collection was kept in good condition, through the employment of various picture cleaners and restorers on an *ad hoc* basis to attend to certain paintings (see pages 65, 117 and 150). However, the 3rd Earl's approach differed from that of his predecessors. Shortly after his inheritance, he employed one individual to treat works in the collection in a complete and methodical manner.

The Earl had also had the picture collection at Longford Castle comprehensively inventoried for a private catalogue drawn up in 1829. He employed the art dealer John Smith for this purpose, and the resultant catalogue differs from earlier inventories, as it contains extended descriptions of works of art and judgements upon their quality, as well as records of their locations within the castle at the time.[11] For example, a painting by the seventeenth-century Netherlandish artist Meindert Hobbema (1638–1709), then housed in the Billiard Room, was described as 'A small Landscape exhibiting a woody scene traversed by a road which leads to a cottage in the middle ground concealed in part by clusters of trees' (fig. 114), and Smith praised the work, adding that 'This is a sparkling clever Picture'.[12]

A letter housed with the catalogue in the archive states that 'Mr Smith's charge for the Examination of his Lordships Pictures & making a Catalogue & valuation thereof will be Twenty Guineas besides his travelling Expenses'.[13] It may have been the case that the 3rd Earl wished to document the collection in full at the time of his inheritance, perhaps for insurance reasons, and to embark on a process of cleaning and restoration, to safeguard the – by now extensive – collection of fine art at the castle for the future, as he took ownership of it.

The impetus for these projects seems also to have come from the trustees of the 2nd Earl's will, Cropley Ashley-Cooper, 6th Earl of Shaftesbury (1768–1851), and Charles Marsham, 2nd Earl of Romney (1777–1845). Surviving correspondence dated to 1828 and 1829 between these two men and the 3rd Earl contains mention of the need to catalogue the collection.[14] On 2 May 1828, Lord Shaftesbury wrote to the Earl, 'I think that a Catalogue should certainly be made of the Pictures at Longford Castle and Coleshill', to which he added, 'Will you have the kindness to employ a Person to do it or shall I?'[15]

Another subject covered within this correspondence was the possibility of certain un-specified pictures being sold from Longford Castle and Coleshill House. The correspondence indicates that this would have required an 'Application to Parliament for an Act to permit the Sale of the late Lord Radnor's Pictures' but also the fact that 'it would be contrary to the Prac-tice of the House of Lords to pass such a Bill'.[16] The attempt did not come to pass: another letter to the Earl from Lord Shaftesbury, dated 5 March 1829, mentioned that the former had 'given up all thoughts of attempting the Sale of the Pictures at Longford Castle and Coleshill and [were] willing that they should remain in those Houses'.[17] The Earl's possible motivations for wishing to sell works of art remain unclear, however. Although his predecessors had made some edits to the collection, selling and exchanging particular pieces on occasion, it may have been that his attempts to dispose of works of art were deemed too extensive by the trustees, or, indeed, he himself may have had a change of heart.

One important addition to the family's art collection during the 3rd Earl's lifetime was a portrait of him painted in 1799, when Viscount Folkestone, by the French artist Elisabeth-Louise Vigée-Lebrun (1755–1842). Today it is on display in the Billiard Room at Longford Castle. This three-quarter-length depiction shows the sitter dressed in a white waistcoat, a cravat and a blue coat, leaning with his right arm against a rock (fig. 106). Vigée-Lebrun has been assessed by posterity as an artist who was 'ambitious for professional recognition, social status, and financial success, all of which she attained to a remarkable degree', and she painted

many aristocratic and royal sitters during her long career, including, most famously, Queen Marie Antoinette of France (1755–1793).[18] It has been suggested that this treasure of the Longford collection was painted in Germany, where Vigée-Lebrun then resided, to commemorate the future Earl's travels around Europe and his 'coming of age'.[19]

The 3rd Earl does not appear to have made many other artistic additions to the Longford collection, however, although one important work of art came into the family as a result of his marriage, in 1801, to Lady Catherine Pelham-Clinton (1776–1804), heiress to Henry Pelham-Clinton, Earl of Lincoln (1750–1778). Sir Joshua Reynolds had painted a full-length portrait of Lady Catherine in 1781, when she was a young child, and the portrait (fig. 107), which shows the sitter feeding chickens, now hangs in the Long Parlour at Longford Castle, alongside other paintings by Reynolds of members of the Bouverie family (figs 64, 65). The portrait had been exhibited at the British Institution in 1823, and throughout the nineteenth and twentieth centuries was exhibited on four occasions at the Royal Academy.[20]

The Earl and his first wife had one surviving child, Lady Catherine Pleydell-Bouverie (1801–1875). His heir, Jacob Pleydell-Bouverie, later 4th Earl of Radnor, was born to his second wife, Judith Anne St John-Mildmay (1790–1851), whom he married in 1814. This Countess of Radnor appears to have taken a particular interest in the gardens at Longford. A description of them written in 1831 by William Sanders (dates unknown) suggests that some elements laid out in the eighteenth century still remained in place at this time: the description recounts 'pleasure-grounds . . . intersected with romantic walks along the banks of the river' and a 'small flower-garden, laid out sixty or seventy years ago . . . occup[ying] the point between the Avon and a rivulet where they meet'.[21] However, the description also suggests that the castle's new occupants were keen to update the garden, mentioning that 'Lady Radnor, who is a warm encourager of horticulture, sent her gardener to Paris, in the summer of 1829, to see the principal gardens, &c. there, and to collect what he possibly could that was new and rare.'[22] In 1896 one of her daughters, Lady Jane Ellice (1819–1903), recalled how her mother 'remembered the learned names of flowers in a way I envied her; & how she loved them!'[23] Helen Matilda Chaplin, wife of the 5th Earl of Radnor, similarly later recounted how 'to her belongs the credit of restoring the formal garden in front of the Castle at Longford'.[24]

It seems that while the Countess occupied herself with works to the castle's gardens and grounds, the Earl was undecided how to proceed in order to resolve the architectural changes left unfinished by his father. Various people were consulted over this, including John Peniston (1778–1848), an architect and surveyor local to Salisbury, in the early 1830s, and William Burn (1789–1870), a Scottish architect, in the early 1840s.[25] In 1843, Burn produced an elevation of the castle depicting a proposed addition, which was never executed but which shows how Longford might have been (fig. 108). John Cornforth has noted how, in the end, none of these schemes was taken up, and that 'depressed with the extent and cost of the task that faced him Lord Radnor went to live at Coleshill in Berkshire'.[26]

Fig. 106 Elisabeth-Louise Vigée-Lebrun (1755–1842), *William Pleydell-Bouverie* [3rd Earl of Radnor when Viscount Folkestone], 1799, oil on canvas, 124.5 x 99.1 cm, Longford Castle

The Earl had resided at the family's second country estate upon his return to England from his travels in 1799, Coleshill then having been deemed 'an excellent setting for an elder son and heir'.[27] In the end, even once he had inherited Longford Castle, the 3rd Earl seems to have preferred to reside in Berkshire, and it was there that he demonstrated his proficiency in estate management.[28]

This state of affairs may account for how, at certain times during the 3rd Earl's tenure, it was not always easy for visitors to access and see the collection at Longford Castle, despite this period having been described as 'the first great age of country-house visiting'.[29] Gustav Waagen, Director of the Royal Gallery at Berlin, who has been praised as one of 'the pioneers of modern art history',[30] toured England during the 1830s, writing up an account of the country's major art collections entitled *Works of Art and Artists in England*, published in 1838.[31] He wished to visit Longford as part of this endeavour, and noted in his account how he had 'in vain requested Lord Radnor . . . for an order to his people to allow me to study his pictures at my leisure' and that 'when I requested the steward to admit me, I was flatly refused'.[32] Eventually he gained access, but was 'hastily driven through the collection', and consequently was unable to take comprehensive notes about the paintings on display.[33] However, the Earl had, on another occasion, given permission to the antiquarian Dawson Turner (1775–1858) to see his 'noble collection of paintings', after the latter had sent him a 'Catalogue of Rubens' effects'.[34] This suggests that visitors were accommodated on something of an *ad hoc* basis at Longford during this time, and that it was not always convenient for the castle's current owner to allow them entry.

On the other hand, the 3rd Earl's eldest son, Jacob, then Viscount Folkestone and later 4th Earl of Radnor, sometimes facilitated visits on his father's behalf, having apparently been 'installed' by his father at Longford in 1840.[35] For instance, Waagen returned to Longford in the 1850s, accompanied by his 'kind friend Mr Danby Seymour' (1820–1877), a Liberal politician and art collector.[36] He noted that it was to Seymour that he 'owed a most polite reception of the part of Lord Folkestone, eldest son of the Earl of Radnor, who allowed me to inspect the pictures in undisturbed freedom and comfort'.[37] This episode suggests that the introduction provided by a trusted intermediary enabled uninterrupted admission to the castle, and that Lord Folkestone was perhaps keener, more amenable or more able than his father to encourage such access. This visit enabled Waagen to conclude that the collection at Longford 'is not only the first in England as regards Holbein, but, considering the master-works of other schools, and also the large number of valuable pictures it contains, generally speaking, it may justly be considered one of the most important in the country'.[38]

A few years later, in 1853, the first published catalogue of the collection was created. It gave a comprehensive account of the works of art in the collection, and was accompanied by 'notes, Biographical, Critical, and Descriptive, by J.S.'.[39] This may be a reference to the dealer John Smith, who, as we saw earlier, compiled a private catalogue of the collection in 1829. However, the entries in the published catalogue cannot be matched with Smith's descriptions, so the

Fig. 107 Sir Joshua Reynolds (1723–1792), *Lady Catherine Pelham-Clinton*, 1781, oil on canvas, 139.7 x 114.3 cm, Longford Castle

Fig. 108 William Burn, *Elevation of Longford Castle with a Proposed Addition*, 1843, pencil and brown wash, 22.2 x 40.6 cm, Longford Castle

identity of the commentator cannot be concluded with any certainty.[40] The 1853 catalogue was dedicated to Lord Folkestone, providing further evidence of his interest in, and desire to promote and publicise, the art collection at Longford during this period.[41] By the 1860s, the accommodation of visitors had become more systematised at the castle, with visitors able to come and see the art collection on Tuesdays or Fridays.[42]

The 3rd Earl of Radnor died in 1869, at the age of ninety. His life was characterised by extensive political work, and he was closely involved with charities, such as the French Hospital, where he followed his predecessors by taking on the governorship.[43] He was offered the Order of the Garter by the Prime Minister, Henry John Temple, 3rd Viscount Palmerston (1784–1865), but refused it because of his age; it is said, however, that he took great pride in having received the offer, even wearing 'the Garter ribbon in his bed-cap!'[44] Following his death his son, Jacob (1815–1889), became the 4th Earl of Radnor, and it is to his tenure at Longford that we now turn our attention. The 4th Earl was particularly keen on country pursuits[45] but, like his father, did not collect art on the same scale as their eighteenth-century Bouverie forebears. As we have seen, however, he took a great interest in his inheritance at Longford. Indeed, he is said to have 'preferred Longford to Coleshill', and eventually left the latter estate to his second son, the Honourable Duncombe Pleydell-Bouverie (1842–1909), permanently dividing it from that at Longford.[46]

It is the 4th Earl who was responsible for having Longford Castle finally rebuilt, following the unsuccessful attempts by his predecessors to complete its structure. He contracted the architect Anthony Salvin (1799–1881) to undertake works in the 1870s, and elevations, specifications and correspondence relating to the works survive in the Longford archive.[47] Salvin was a member of the Society of Antiquaries, and had a 'reputation as an expert on medieval buildings': it has been argued that 'this expertise and its demonstration in his early works probably led to many of his commissions relating to the restoration and improvement of castles'.[48] Although Longford is not a medieval building, Salvin worked on a number of country houses, and the proficiency and knowledge in his field that he seems to have demonstrated from an early age[49] may have been a contributory factor in the Earl's decision to employ him at Longford.

Salvin created a new square tower and a second courtyard at Longford, and undertook to have the original central courtyard covered over with a glass ceiling.[50] The results of these changes can still be appreciated today, as the courtyard now takes the form of a Triangular Hall, framed by a gallery running round it at first-floor level (fig. 109). These rooms today play host to various works of art, including the Brussels tapestries commissioned by Sir Jacob in the 1740s (fig. 45), a number of family portraits dating from the eighteenth to the twenty-first centuries, and even Wyatt's original architectural model of the proposed hexagonal castle (fig. 86). Salvin can also be credited with reworking the entrance and garden fronts of the castle, adding, for instance, 'projecting bays' to the garden front (fig. 110), and these works have been looked upon favourably by subsequent generations, with Cornforth noting in the 1960s that, in these respects, the architect 'did an excellent job'.[51] Jacob Pleydell-Bouverie, 8th Earl of Radnor (1927–2008), in his family memoir of 2001, said of Salvin's works that 'all in all a good job was done'.[52]

The new bays on the garden front of the castle slightly affected the layout of the ground-floor Long Parlour and the first-floor Gallery, but these rooms seem to have been used consistently for the display of works of art from the late nineteenth century to the present day. A 'List of Pictures in the Long Parlour' dated to 1877 in the Longford archive contains sketch plans showing the layout of works of art here at this time.[53] It shows that the room contained a variety of landscapes, subject paintings and portraits, each evoking a different collector and period in the history of the Longford art collection. For instance, the room included Van Dyck's portrait of Queen Henrietta Maria, supposedly acquired with the castle in 1717 by Sir Edward des Bouverie (see page 35 and fig. 17); Teniers's painting of *Boers Playing Bowls*, bought by Sir Jacob in the 1740s (see page 79 and fig. 46); Rubens's portrait of his son, bought by the 1st Earl of Radnor in 1773 (see page 114 and fig. 77), and the painting of '1 Son 2 Daughters of Christian King of Denmark by Mabuse', bought by the 2nd Earl in 1820 (fig. 104).[54] The layouts also show that the two overdoors landscape paintings depicting views of Venice (figs 52 and 53) still hung in these positions in 1877.[55]

The 4th Earl was married in October 1840 to Lady Mary Augusta Frederica Grimston

Fig. 109 Triangular Hall,
Longford Castle, 2016

(1820–1879), daughter of the peer and MP James Grimston, 1st Earl of Verulam (1775–1845). Lady Mary had been, along with the Earl's sister, Lady Jane Ellice, a bridesmaid to Queen Victoria (1819–1901) at her wedding to Prince Albert of Saxe-Coburg and Gotha (1819–1861) earlier that year.[56] Some letters written by the Queen from Windsor Castle survive in the Longford archive, and attest to the strength of the new Lady Folkestone's royal connections. In one, the Queen described how 'It is with very sincere pleasure, that I have learnt . . . the marriage of Lady Mary with Lord Folkestone. Having known Lady Mary ever since we were play fellows in <u>former</u> years, & she having been my Train-bearer upon two very interesting occasions, I naturally take a lively interest in all that concerns her.'[57] A letter written by the Queen directly to the future Countess of Radnor further underlines the pair's friendship:

> As the day of your marriage is fast approaching I will no longer delay . . . offering
> you my most sincere wishes for your happiness, which I trust is assured for life in
> your marriage, knowing as I do from experience that that is the only real and

Fig. 110 Garden Front,
Longford Castle, 2016

perfect happiness in this world. That you may feel this as I̲ do is my sincere wish
. . . . The Prince joins me in my good wishes.[58]

The 4th Earl and his wife went on to have twelve children, the eldest of whom later became the 5th Earl of Radnor (1841–1900). In accordance with the tradition, begun in the first half of the eighteenth century and which continues today, of alternately naming the first-born sons of the family Jacob and William, the heir was named William, since his father had been called Jacob. He inherited Longford and the earldom in 1889, and the following year the decision was made to sell three paintings from the collection to the National Gallery in London. This action was taken in order to resolve the financial problems presented by 'newly imposed "death duties"', a decline in agricultural rents and 'Salvin's costly work' at Longford Castle.[59] The paintings sold were Hans Holbein the Younger's *The Ambassadors* (fig. 100); a portrait of Don Adrián Pulido Pareja (dates unknown), a Knight of the Order of Santiago (fig. 111), then attributed to the Spanish master Diego Velázquez (1599–1660) and now understood to be possibly the

ADRIAN
PVLIDOPAREJA

Fig. 111 Possibly by Juan Bautista Martínez del Mazo (1612/16–1667), *Don Adrián Pulido Pareja*, after 1647, oil on canvas, 203.8 x 114.3 cm, National Gallery, London, probably acquired for Longford Castle by the 2nd Earl of Radnor in 1811

work of his son-in-law Juan Bautista Martínez del Mazo (1612/16–1667); and a portrait of an unidentified gentleman (fig. 112) by the northern Italian portraitist Giovanni Battista Moroni (1520/4–1579) but once said to be by Titian (*fl.* 1506–1576).

Correspondence and documents pertaining to the sale survive in the archives of the National Gallery, and indicate that staff at the art museum had been aware of the collection at Longford Castle, and of its quality, several years prior to the sale of these three works. In July 1861 the Gallery's first director, Sir Charles Lock Eastlake (1793–1865), had travelled to '[inspect] the pictures' at Kingston Lacy, a country house in Dorset, and Longford Castle.[60] In an account of the pictures at these two houses, Eastlake noted how 'the collection at Longford Castle contains some admirable masterworks'.[61] He made a list of certain pictures from the collection, which he wrote 'would, in my judgment, be all eligible for the National Gallery'.[62]

This lengthy list included, among many other paintings, Holbein's portrait 'Called Two Ambassadors – on the whole perhaps the most remarkable work in the collection'; paintings by Claude, Poussin and Rubens; the painting of 'Pareja the Spanish Admiral' then given to Velázquez, and a work described as 'Moroni – Whole length portrait of a man called Titian'.[63] It is notable that this list makes mention of all the paintings eventually sold to the National Gallery. It also shows that Sir Charles was aware at this early date that the latter portrait was in fact by Moroni.

When the paintings were sold in 1890, the 5th Earl was keen that they were bought by the National Gallery for the benefit of the nation, and that the three works of art stayed together as a set. It had been 'one of the conditions of purchase . . . that the three pictures should be taken together in one lot'.[64] Writing from Longford Castle on 13 May 1890, the Earl stated that 'The Nat. Gallery were offered the pictures some months ago; and I should prefer that the country should acquire them, rather than some private individual; but I cant afford to spoil the sale of the three, by parting with one without the other.'[65]

The London art world was just as keen that the paintings be acquired for the nation. In a letter to the editor of *The Times* published on 10 May 1890, Sidney Colvin (1845–1927), Keeper of Prints and Drawings at the British Museum, argued at length that the pictures should be kept in the country:

> Sir, – Most of your readers have doubtless already realised more or less fully, and with more or less regret, with what rapidity England is being emptied of its treasures of art. . . . Unless something can be done quickly to arrest the process of export, there will soon be next to nothing left of that which was one of the characteristic glories of our country, and future public acquisitions in this kind, either for the nation or for our municipal galleries, will have been made impossible. I write now in no official character, but as a private lover of art, to call attention to

one of the most grievous losses of this class with which the country is immediately threatened. Among the private collections of pictures in England that of Lord Radnor at Longford Castle has long been one of the most famous.[66]

Colvin went on to describe the three paintings being offered for sale, expounding upon their importance, before noting that 'Negotiations for the sale of these three pictures abroad have been on foot for some time, and will be concluded within a few days, unless something can in the meantime be done to keep them in this country', adding, 'Is it really impossible that anything should be done? No such opportunity of enriching the nation with classical masterpieces of painting has occurred since the dispersal of the Blenheim collection, and these pictures are of a kind to command more popular appreciation than those acquired from Blenheim.'[67]

The urgency with which Colvin conveyed the significance of these potential acquisitions for the nation suggests both the perceived importance of the individual paintings themselves, and also the wider need felt at the time to prevent the country's best pictures from being moved abroad. Between 1882 and 1914 a great many works of art were sold from a number of British country houses, and public auctions often raised debates over the issue of export, as many pieces went overseas – either to America, or to Europe, from which they had often originated before being transferred to Britain in the eighteenth century by Grand Tourists.[68] The ability of the British government to justify the acquisition of works of art for the nation was sometimes complicated by the fact that these paintings often had continental origins, and were not so easily understood as 'objects of national heritage deserving of State purchase'.[69] It was thanks to Treasury grants, which topped up the National Gallery's 'annual purchase-grant' of 'a pitiful £5,000', that the purchase of the Longford pictures, and also works of art from Hamilton Palace in Lanarkshire, and Blenheim Palace, was made possible – but such grants were not common.[70] Therefore, one can understand why connoisseurs felt the need to articulate so emotively and publicly arguments for the retention of important paintings in Britain.

Correspondence alluding to negotiations on price suggests that the 5th Earl's desire to sell to the National Gallery had to be balanced with the need to achieve the best possible sum for the pictures: it was understood, for example, that 'if no restrictions are imposed as to their [the pictures'] ultimate destination they will probably fetch not less than £60,000' but that 'Lord Radnor and his eldest son Lord Folkestone are however quite prepared to sacrifice £5,000 of the purchase money in order that the country may have the pictures'.[71]

The correspondence suggests that Sir Frederic William Burton (1816–1900), who had been the director of the National Gallery since 1874, had previously proposed a sum of £51,000 on behalf of the institution for the three paintings but was then offered the pictures for the Gallery 'at the price of £55,000 subject only to the approval of the Court of Chancery being obtained'.[72] In the end, the paintings were in fact purchased for this price, with the government paying £25,000, and 'three private subscribers' – the businessman Nathaniel Rothschild, 1st

Baron Rothschild (1840–1915), the Irish philanthropist Sir Edward Cecil Guinness, later 1st Earl of Iveagh (1847–1927), and the landowner and Liberal politician Charles Cotes (1846–1898) – paying a further £10,000 each to help secure the works for the nation.[73]

The purchase was discussed in many newspapers, and invited much commentary and debate, for instance regarding the identification of the sitters in Holbein's painting *The Ambassadors*.[74] An article on 'The Longford Pictures at the National Gallery' published in *The Times* on 11 September 1890 reported that 'To-day, we understand, the three pictures . . . will be exhibited in the National Gallery . . . temporarily placed on screens in the Umbrian Room, until their final place shall have been decided – no easy matter, in the crowded state of the gallery.'[75] The fact that the pictures were initially displayed in the same room together at the Gallery would have highlighted their shared provenance and their simultaneous entry into the national collection, suggesting that their previous life as part of a private collection at Longford Castle was a lens through which they could be understood at the time of their acquisition by the Gallery. Today, however, the paintings are hung in separate rooms, alongside similar works of art by the same artists, and from the same schools and periods.

The nineteenth century saw the museological 'practice of collecting and displaying works of art in chronological sequence and/or in geographical groups' within public art museums, an approach that differed from the mode of display often adopted within the private art collections to which many of the works had once belonged.[76] In the private home, as the historian and professor of museology Christopher Whitehead has noted, paintings were instead often displayed for overall effect, working as part of a whole and functioning not 'as objects intended for close scrutiny (the modern museological model) but as units, both emblematic and decorative, within the wider composition of the room and the collection themselves'.[77] At Longford Castle, the pictures had been displayed as part of a mixed hang of works of art of different schools, styles and subject matters, within interiors richly adorned with items of furniture and decorative art, which worked as a whole to convey their owners' taste and wealth. However, as accounts left by visitors such as Waagen in the nineteenth century suggest, individual works of art were still appreciated on their own terms within the wider context of the interiors of a country house such as Longford.

The article in *The Times* also reminded readers that the pictures had been displayed in public once before, in 1873, at Burlington House, home to the Royal Academy.[78] On display at the National Gallery, however, which had been founded sixty-six years previously to establish 'a new national collection, for the enjoyment and education of all',[79] audiences could appreciate the paintings on a permanent basis. The 5th Earl continued in his father's footsteps as a benefactor of the Royal Academy as well, however, by loaning other works of art for their Winter Exhibitions. A newspaper cutting dated to 2 January 1896 kept in the Longford archive described him as 'a liberal contributor to the winter exhibition on a former occasion', and noted how he had 'sent a number of works from Longford Castle to add to the attractions of the present collection' at the Royal Academy, including the large landscape painting depicting a *View of the Escorial with a Hermit, his Ass and Deer and a Crucifix in the Foreground* by Pieter Verhulst, acquired by the 2nd Earl of Radnor (fig. 94), and David Teniers the Younger's *Return from Coursing* (fig. 47).[80]

Longford also became better known towards the end of the nineteenth and at the beginning of the twentieth century through some important publications. The gardens were profiled in an article on 'Country Homes and Gardens Old & New' for *Country Life* magazine in August 1898, which included a description of the castle, its history and its surroundings, and photographs showing, for instance, the formal garden adjacent to the building.[81] The article described Longford as 'a splendid mansion of very remarkable character . . . famous for its pictures among all the mansions of the West' and noted: 'It has the advantage of lying in a very fine country, and of overlooking a noble English park, in which beech, oak and many other trees are seen, relieved by the sombre greens of conifers and pines.'[82] The tree planting undertaken in the eighteenth century under the direction of Sir Jacob had clearly functioned in its intended manner, improving the grounds for the benefit of posterity. *Country Life* magazine, which was known for its 'long-running series of country-house profiles',[83] was later to run another series of features on Longford, this time by the architectural historian Christopher Hussey.[84] This series, published in December 1931, focused more on the contents – and particularly the furnishings – of the castle.[85]

The 5th Earl did make at least one addition to the art collection at Longford Castle, buying a painting in oil on panel of *The Magdalen* by a member of the Flemish school. One of the greatest contributions to the art collection associated with him, however, was the work undertaken by his wife, Helen Matilda, Countess of Radnor, to catalogue the art collection fully and comprehensively. A large two-volume catalogue was produced in the early twentieth century, after the death of the Earl, following extensive research on the Countess's part,[86] and the discovery, for the first time, of the eighteenth- and early nineteenth-century account books kept by the family's great collectors, Sir Jacob and the 1st and 2nd Earls of Radnor, in the Muniment Room at Longford.[87]

As Helen Matilda recounted in her memoir, 'I was fond of "poking about" among old records', and 'found a number of beautiful old books, bound in green leather . . . I saw that one of them was in the handwriting of the first Viscount Folkestone . . . I realised that I was on the right track, and also that, if I had enough patience to search these account books, I should probably find out where a great many of the pictures came from'.[88] Prior to this discovery, it was believed that 'the paintings had been bought en masse from William Seguier'[89] – the elder brother of John Seguier, who, as was shown earlier, had cleaned the Longford paintings in the early nineteenth century.

Helen Matilda was the first to piece together the provenance of the Longford paintings, through the compilation of the catalogue, and was assisted in her endeavour by the music librarian and scholar William Barclay Squire (1855–1927), Sir George Scharf (1820–1895), the first Director of the National Portrait Gallery, and Sir Frederic Burton.[90] She recounted how 'Mr Scharf gave me the most valuable help while I was compiling the Catalogue of the pictures', and that, with Barclay Squire, 'we went through every line of the Catalogue together'.[91]

Surviving letters from Scharf to Helen Matilda discuss not only the compilation of the catalogue but also the recent entry of the three Longford paintings into the National Gallery collection. For instance, in a letter of 17 September 1890, Scharf wrote that he had recently been into the Gallery to see the pictures, noting, 'They look extremely well; each in an isolated position worthy of its dignity', and adding that 'The Velasquez astonished me for its tremendous merit which never was seen before; not even when it was in Burlington House'.[92] Two months later, he wrote to commend Helen Matilda – or 'Most gracious Souveraine', as he frequently addressed her – on her work, writing that:

> It appears to your vassal that you have done excellent work in thus collecting and arranging all the pictures in your magnificent Castle. But you have much more to do, your handsomely printed pages have fixed and for ever settled the existence & <u>succession</u> of all your pictures . . . The catalogue of 1890 will thus become the perpetually <u>standard</u> catalogue of appeal . . .[93]

Helen Matilda was to recount with a sense of achievement how *The Times* 'was kind enough to say that [the catalogue] was "a pattern of what such catalogues ought to be"'.[94] It was published in 1909, and shorter editions were subsequently produced, possibly for the benefit of visitors to the castle. For instance, a paperback copy produced in 1916 could 'be obtained from the housekeeper at Longford Castle' for the price of one shilling.[95] This smaller, pocket-sized version included ground plans of the castle in its current state, following Salvin's architectural works, and in its original triangular formation, as well as a short preface on the origins of the castle and its ownership by the Gorges, Coleraine and Bouverie families.[96] It may have been used by visitors as an accompaniment on a tour of the castle in the early twentieth century, furnishing them with information on pictures as they made their way around the building, as it was divided into a list of works of art at Longford Castle arranged room by room; a short list of 'Pictures at 12 Upper Brook Street', a London residence used by the family at this time; and a comprehensive list of family portraits, which gave details of artists, as well as the identities of sitters and their parentage.[97]

In 1927 Helen Matilda wrote a family memoir, entitled *From a Great Grandmother's Armchair*; she is also notable for having bred small white pigs, imported a gondola and gondolier from Venice to row her along the River Avon, and conducted a female string orchestra.[98] *Lady Radnor's Suite for String Orchestra in F* was written for her by the composer Sir Charles Hubert Hastings Parry (1848–1918) in 1894, and a portrait of her seated at a piano was painted

Fig. 113 Sir James Jebusa Shannon (1862–1923), *Helen Matilda Chaplin, Countess of Radnor*, 1895, oil on canvas, 139.7 x 106.7 cm, Longford Castle

THE NINETEENTH AND EARLY TWENTIETH CENTURIES

by the Anglo-American society painter James Jebusa Shannon (1862–1923): it can be seen today on display in the Billiard Room at Longford Castle (fig. 113), alongside a portrait painted by the same artist a year earlier, depicting her husband, the 5th Earl, wearing peer's parliamentary robes.

Over a century later, Longford Castle continues to play host to a wealth of artistic treasures, including some additions made in recent years, as will be discussed shortly in the present owner's concluding remarks. As the preceding chapters have shown, since the Bouverie family acquired this unusual Elizabethan country house in 1717, it has continually and increasingly been filled with an array of important works of art of national and international significance, including paintings, sculpture and fine furnishings. The family's three key collectors predominantly built up this collection during the eighteenth and early nineteenth centuries, and it is thanks to Jacob, 1st Viscount Folkestone, William, 1st Earl of Radnor, and Jacob, 2nd Earl of Radnor, that many treasures – including prestigious landscape paintings by Claude, fashionable family portraits by Reynolds and Gainsborough, and unique pieces such as the Renaissance iron chair – have made their way to Longford, where they can still be appreciated today within interiors that bear traces of the styles of the Elizabethan, Georgian and Victorian eras.

From 1717, the family seem always to have looked simultaneously to the past, present and future, rooting themselves within the aristocratic traditions of their adopted country and living in a country house that looked back to the Elizabethan 'golden age', while commissioning the most fashionable artists of the day to produce works of fine and decorative art, and taking good care of their estate, home and art collection for posterity. As the Conclusion will show, the legacy of care, collecting and custodianship inaugurated early on at Longford by its first Bouverie owners is alive and well today, and the collection remains a living entity, constantly developing for future generations, in line with the Bouverie family's traditional toast:

Health and Prosperity
Peace and Posterity
Long Life and Felicity
And the joys of Eternity.

Fig. 114   Meindert Hobbema
(1638–1709), *A Wooded Landscape
with Figures on a Sandy Road with
Cottages*, seventeenth or early
eighteenth century, oil on panel,
33 x 45.7 cm, Longford Castle

THE NINETEENTH AND EARLY TWENTIETH CENTURIES

Conclusion: The Twentieth Century until Now

Unsurprisingly, the first half of the twentieth century saw no great expansion of the Longford collection. Two World Wars, and subsequent austerity, put a dampener on collecting although family members still kept up the tradition of having their portraits painted. The 6th Earl, Jacob Pleydell-Bouverie, and his wife Julian were drawn by George Frederic Watts. My grandfather William, the 7th Earl, was painted by Sir William Nicholson, and his first wife, my grandmother, by Henry Lamb, a neighbour and a friend, which also led to the acquisition of a number of his paintings.

There were also disposals: in 1945 my grandfather the 7th Earl sold two great Poussins, *The Adoration of the Golden Calf* (now in the National Gallery) and *The Crossing of the Red Sea*, now in the National Gallery of Victoria, Melbourne, Australia. Kenneth Clark, who had close connections to both institutions, being a Director of the former (1933–45) and adviser to the latter, was closely involved in these transactions.

In 1949 Longford was fortunate not to have been totally destroyed by fire, and was saved by limitless water from the River Avon being pumped into the building. However, the back of the house was burnt out, with a consequent contraction of available wall hanging space. The resulting sale of a number of lesser pictures arguably enhanced the quality of the collection.

On the death of his father, my father Jacob, 8th Earl of Radnor, was forced to sell Velázquez's magnificent portrait of Juan de Pareja to satisfy death duties; he acquired a fine Augustus John of Miss Pettigrew, and was painted several times by Emma Sergeant, as was his wife Jill. Otherwise he was not driven to collect, as he felt the house was already full of beautiful works of art, but put his energies into management of the estate.

I for my part have felt that the collection should evolve, and, stimulated by a number of years working at Christie's, and in more recent years being involved with an important contemporary art show, 'The Folkestone Triennial', part of a wider regeneration programme in Kent, have done some collecting of my own. Taken as a whole my taste has been fairly eclectic, but contains some common threads. An early passion for William Nicholson resulted in landscapes of Paris, Venice, and Spain. So-called 'Modern British Artists' are represented by the likes of Hepworth, Hilton, Hitchens, Sutherland, Piper and Scott. Visits to Australia resulted in Whiteley and Aboriginal art being added to the mix. Contemporary pieces in various media include works ranging from sculptures by Richard Long and Cornelia Parker to others by Laura

Fig 115 Sebastiano del Piombo (*c.* 1485–1547), *Portrait of a Lady*, mid-1520s, oil on wood, 117 x 96 cm, on loan from Longford Castle to the National Gallery, London

Ford and Peter Randall-Page and ceramics by Edmund de Waal. All of these seem to live happily side by side and indeed integrate comfortably with all that has gone before. I hope that the collection continues to evolve, and that future generations will leave their mark on the house in which they live, while at the same time enjoying and caring for the extraordinary works of art that were amassed by their ancestors partly for pleasure, but also to embellish Longford, their home.

WILLIAM PLEYDELL-BOUVERIE, 9TH EARL OF RADNOR

Fig 116 Sir William Nicholson (1872–1949), *Lido 5 O'Clock*, 1937, oil on panel, 38.1 x 45.7 cm, Longford Castle

Facing: Fig 117 Laura Ford (b. 1961), *Weeping Girl III*, 2009, artist's proof, painted bronze, height 114.3 cm, Longford Castle, 2016

Overleaf: Fig. 118 View of Longford Castle gardens, 2016

Fig. 119 Jan de Beer
(*c.* 1491–1527/8),
*Triptych: The Virgin
and Child with Saints*,
c. 1515–20, oil on
wood, central panel
142.8 x 111 cm, on
loan from Longford
Castle to the
National Gallery,
London

NOTES

Chapter 1

1   For this and all other extracts from Reverend Pelate's manuscript history quoted within this chapter, see Wiltshire and Swindon History Centre (hereafter WSHC) 1946/3/2C/1.
2   Radnor, 1916 , p. 6.
3   See Strong, 1998, p. 45, and Gotch, 1906, p. 17.
4   See Jackson-Stops, 1990, p. 47, and Gotch, *ibid*. On devices, symbolism and geometry in Elizabethan architecture, see Summerson, 1993, p. 72, and Girouard, 2009, p. xii.
5   WSHC 1946/3/2C/14.
6   *Ibid*.
7   Sir John Soane's Museum Library, SM_vol101, Thorpe Album. See in particular SM_vol101/155–157 plans and partial exterior elevation, SM_vol101/158 partial elevation of the exterior of the Hall block, and SM_vol101/159 unfinished partial plan of the Hall block. Scholars have been divided over the extent to which Thorpe was actually responsible for the execution of these drawings (see Hussey, 1931c, pp. 652–3, 700; Blomfield, 1910, p. 37, and Summerson, 1966, p. 31).
8   On Rushton, see English Heritage, 2016. On Lyveden New Bield, see Jackson-Stops, 1990, p. 47.
9   On potential influences upon Longford's architecture, see Blomfield, 1910, pp. 27–8, Gotch, 1906, p. 18, and Girouard, 2009, pp. 242, 300–02, 480.
10   Pevsner, 1963, p. 36.
11   WSHC 1946/3/2C/14.
12   Gotch, 1906, p. 18, and Hussey, 1931c, p. 652.
13   Blomfield, 1910, p. 36, and Pevsner, 1963, p. 307.
14   Penny with the assistance of Avery-Quash, 2012, p. 6.
15   For this and all other extracts from this poem quoted within this chapter, see WSHC 1946/3/2C/1 and transcription in WSHC 1946/3/2C/11.
16   Britton, 1809, Vol. II, p. 104.
17   Ousby, 1990, p. 66.
18   Radnor, 1916, cat. 163, p. 33.
19   See Whitelock, 2013, ch. 52.
20   Howey, 2009, p. 204.
21   WSHC 1946/3/2A/1.
22   WSHC 1946/3/2C/11.
23   On long galleries, their decoration and uses, see Jackson-Stops and Pipkin, 1985, ch. 5; Coope, 1986, pp. 43–72, 74–84; Jackson-Stops with the assistance of Russell, 1985c, p. 124, and Laing, 1995, p. 17.
24   Radnor, 1916, p. 8.
25   Penny with the assistance of Avery-Quash, 2012, p. 34.
26   WSHC 1946/3/2C/9.
27   WSHC 1946/3/1B/3.
28   Radnor, 1916, p. 9.
29   Currie, 1990, pp. 27, 42.
30   Harris has suggested that this was a technique employed by both Thacker and Winstanley (Harris, 1979, p. 105).
31   Laurence, 2003, p. 85.
32   Harris, 1979, p. 89.
33   British Library, Cartographic Items Maps K.Top.43.44.a–l.
34   Defoe, 1968, Vol. I, p. 199.
35   *Ibid*., p. 192.
36   Morris, 1949, pp. xx, xlii.
37   Fiennes, 1949, p. 57.
38   *Ibid*., p. 68.
39   Defoe, 1968, Vol. I, p. 199.
40   Radnor, 1916, p. 9.
41   On Laurens, see Radnor, 2001, pp. 11–17.
42   For a comprehensive family history, see Radnor, 2001; and on the Levant Company, see Wood, 1964, chs 6, 8 and 9.
43   WSHC 1946/4/2A/6 and Radnor, 2001, p. 29.
44   WSHC 1946/4/1A/10MS.
45   WSHC 1946/4/1H/2.
46   Stone and Stone, 1984, p. 12.
47   WSHC 1946/4/2A/6.
48   *Ibid*.
49   Hunt, 1996, p. 213.
50   *Ibid*., pp. 44, 55, 58–9, 61, 65, 72, 198, 213.
51   McKellar, 2013, pp. 4–5, 146, 152, and Summerson, 1993, p. 348.
52   Hussey, 1988, p. 10, and Christie, 2000, p. 4.
53   On Walpole at Houghton, see Morel, 2013b, p. 36.
54   Summerson, 1993, pp. 297–302.
55   Girouard, 2009, p. 457, and Girouard, 1968, pp. 15–16.
56   Mandler, 1997, p. 7.
57   *Ibid*.
58   WSHC 1946/4/2A/6.
59   WSHC 1946/3/2C/5PC.
60   WSHC 1946/3/2A/8 and WSHC 1946/4/2A/6.
61   Girouard, 2009, pp. 423, 438–9.
62   Radnor, 1916, p. 10. More recent scholarship has suggested that the change may instead be attributed to Sir Jacob Bouverie, in around 1740, as at this time he commissioned an item of furniture that was most probably intended for the entrance hall (see Murdoch, 1996, p. 92).
63   Cornforth, 2004, pp. 29, 35.
64   *Ibid*., p. 23.
65   Radnor and Barclay Squire, 1909, Part I, cat. 33, p. 18.
66   *Ibid*.
67   Douglas Stewart, 1983, p. 35.
68   *Ibid*.
69   See *Art UK*, 2016.
70   Radnor and Barclay Squire, 1909, Part I, cats 24 and 39, pp. 15, 22. See also Larsen, 1988, Vol. II, cat. 860, p. 337, and Barnes *et al*., 2004, cat. IV.115, p. 341.
71   Larsen, 1988, Vol. II, cat. 860, p. 337, and Radnor and Barclay Squire, 1909, Part I, cats 24 and 39, pp. 15, 22. On the portrait of Charles I, see Larsen, 1988, Vol. II, cat. 785, p. 311.
72   Larsen, 1988, Vol. II, cat. 860, p. 337.
73   Barnes *et al*., 2004, cat. IV.113, p. 519.
74   Larsen, 1988, Vol. II, cat. 860, p. 337, and Larsen, 1988, Vol. I, p. 296.
75   Beard and Gilbert, 1986, pp. 440–41.
76   WSHC 1946/3/2A/14.
77   See Vickery, 2009, pp. 38–42.
78   WSHC 1946/3/1B/1.
79   See WSHC 1946/4/2A/6, WSHC 1946/3/2A/8 and WSHC 1946/4/2B/1.
80   WSHC 1946/4/2B/1.

Chapter 2

1   Wiltshire and Swindon History Centre (hereafter WSHC) 1946/4/2B/1.
2   *Ibid*.
3   WSHC 1946/3/1B/1.
4   Current whereabouts unknown. *Ibid*.
5   *Ibid*.
6   Lippincott, 1983, p. 64.
7   Roethlisberger, 1961, Vol. I, p. 383.
8   Now at Mertoun House, Scotland.
9   Nisser, 1927, pp. 9, 25, and Douglas Stewart, 2008.
10   See Nisser, 1927, p. 125.
11   See Meyer, 1995, pp. 45–63.
12   Lippincott, 1983, p. 66.
13   Radnor, 2001, p. 11.
14   WSHC 1946/4/2B/1.
15   Murdoch and Vigne, 2009, p. 8.
16   WSHC 1946/3/2A/1.
17   WSHC 1946/4/1A/13.
18   Reaney, 1995, p. xv.
19   WSHC 1946/4/1A/13.
20   WSHC 1946/3/1B/1.
21   See Radnor, 2001, p. 44.
22   Everett, 1994, p. 4.
23   *Ibid*., p. 1.
24   WSHC, 1946/4/2A/6.
25   WSHC 1946/4/2B/1.
26   WSHC 1946/3/1B/1.
27   Cornforth and Fowler, 1974, p. 185.
28   WSHC 1946/3/1B/1.
29   See WSHC 1946/3/1B/2 and Hussey, 1931, p. 679.
30   Cornforth, 2004, p. 124.

31 Laing, 1989, pp. 245, 248.
32 Hussey, 1931d, p. 701.
33 WSHC 1946/3/2C/11.
34 Ware, 1768, pp. 469–70.
35 Vickery, 2010, p. 180.
36 Thornton, 1984, p. 98.
37 See Cornforth, 2004, pp. 55, 127–8. On the latter, see Victoria and Albert Museum, 'Norfolk House Music Room', 2016.
38 Thornton, 1984, p. 98.
39 Harris, 2000, p. 39.
40 See Climenson (ed.), 1899, p. 164, and Harris, 2000, p. 39.
41 Forsyth and White, 2012, p. 52.
42 Edwards and Jourdain, 1955, pp. 8, 25–6.
43 See Victoria and Albert Museum, 'Longford Table', 2016.
44 See Hussey, 1931b, p. 679, and Murdoch, 1996, p. 92.
45 WSHC 1946/3/1B/1.
46 Cornforth, 2004, p. 37, and Murdoch, 1996, p. 92.
47 See Beard, 1986, pp. 1281–1282, Murdoch, 1996, p. 92, and Cornforth, 2004, p. 37.
48 Macquoid and Edwards, 1954, Vol. III, p. 282.
49 Daniels, 1988, p. 48.
50 Cornforth, 1996, p. 33, and Moore (ed.), 1996, p. 114.
51 WSHC 1946/3/1B/1.
52 WSHC 1946/3/1B/2 and Smith, 2016b, p. 20.
53 Williamson, 1995, pp. 127–8. See also Daniels, 1988, pp. 43–53.
54 Everett, 1994, p. 106.
55 Williamson, 1995, p. 134.
56 Hanway, 1756, p. 46.
57 See Smith, 2016b, p. 20.
58 On clubs, societies, their aims and leadership, see Langford, 1991, pp. 510, 556–7, 561, and Clark, 2000, pp. 60, 85.
59 See Smith, 2016b, pp. 18–19.
60 Lippincott, 1983, pp. 62–3. For a list of old master copies made by Pond and the clients who purchased them, see Küster, 2012, p. 181.
61 WSHC 1946/3/1B/1.
62 WSHC 1946/3/2A/1.
63 See Jackson-Stops with the assistance of Russell, 1985a, p. 322, Gibson-Wood, 2000, p. 196, and Richardson, 1773, pp. 225–6.
64 See Hussey, 1931b, p. 680.
65 WSHC 1946/3/1B/1.
66 Jackson-Stops and Pipkin, 1985, p. 145, and Morel (ed.), 2013, p. 162.
67 Hill, 1981, p. 70.
68 See Hussey, 1931b, p. 680, and Macquoid, 1972, Vol. III, p. 77.
69 Macquoid, 1972, Vol. III, p. 75.
70 Cartwright (ed.), 1889, Vol. II, p. 57.
71 Anon., 1762, p. 41.
72 Cornforth, 1989, p. 165, Cornforth, 2004, p. 239, and Waterfield, 1991b, pp. 58–60.

73 Roethlisberger, 1961, Vol. I, p. 233.
74 WSHC 1946/3/1B/1.
75 Penny with the assistance of Avery-Quash, 2012, p. 22.
76 Powys Marks, 2002, pp. 28–30.
77 Climenson (ed.), 1899, p. 164.
78 Ibid., p. 165.
79 Garlick and Macintyre (eds), 1978, Vol. I, p. 223.
80 Vertue, 1938, p. 128.
81 Ibid., pp. 127–8.
82 Hanway, 1756, p. 48, Anon., 1762, p. 41, Climenson (ed.), 1899, p. 164, Gilpin, 1798, p. 73, and Passavant, 1836, Vol. I, p. 296.
83 See Wine, 2001, pp. xi–xiv.
84 Haskell, 1985, p. 53, and Wine, 2001, pp. xiii–xiv.
85 WSHC 1946/3/1B/1.
86 Ibid.
87 Jackson-Stops with the assistance of Russell, 1985e, p. 288.
88 WSHC 1946/3/1B/1. Current whereabouts unknown.
89 Ibid. and WSHC 1946/4/2A/6. Current whereabouts unknown. John Bouverie's collection of works of art by Guercino is now in the British Museum.
90 Turner, 1994, p. 93.
91 WSHC 1946/3/1B/1 and WSHC 1946/3/2A/1. Current whereabouts unknown.
92 See Sicca and Yarrington, 2000, pp. 3–4, Martin, 2000, pp. 50–51, and Christie, 2000, p. 181.
93 WSHC 1946/3/1B/1.
94 Baker, 2000, pp. 149–51.
95 WSHC 1946/3/1B/1. Current whereabouts unknown. On Bragge, see Pears, 1988, pp. 92–3.
96 Lyna, 2012, p. 103.
97 WSHC 1946/3/1B/1.
98 Avery, 1974, p. 551. On Soldani, see Jackson-Stops (ed.), 1985, cat. 215, p. 293.
99 Moore, 2004.
100 Current whereabouts unknown. WSHC 1946/3/1B/1. On Consul Smith, see Links, 1994, chs 3–11, and Ford, 1985, p. 49.
101 See Gibson-Wood, 2000, p. 13.
102 See Smith, 2016, p. 11.
103 Haskell, 1980, pp. 5, 73, 77, and Mount, 1991, pp. 113–14.
104 Mount, 1991, p. 64.
105 WSHC 1946/3/1B/1.
106 Roelofs, 2009, pp. 32–5.
107 See ibid., pp. 33, 54–9.
108 See National Gallery, 2016, and Rijksmuseum, 2016.
109 WSHC 1946/3/2A/3.
110 WSHC 1946/3/4A/1.
111 WSHC 1946/3/1B/1.
112 See Schama, 1993, p. 480.

113 MacGregor, 2007, p. 52.
114 Baker, 2000, p. 145. See also Pincus, 2001, p. 12, Paoletti, 1998, p. 97, and Blake McHam, 1998, p. 13.
115 See Lippincott, 1983, p. 5, Brewer, 1997, p. 256, Pears, 1988, pp. 158–60, and MacGregor, 1985, p. 158.
116 See Mount, 2006, p. 169, and Hanson, 2009, p. 195.
117 See definition of 'curiosity, n.' in OED Online, 2014.
118 Hanson, 2009, pp. 161, 195.
119 WSHC 1946/3/1B/2.
120 On these paintings, see Silver, 1984, pp. 105-14, 163–4 and cat. 58, pp. 235–7, and Rowlands, 1985, cat. 13, pp. 56–8, 128.
121 Penny with the assistance of Avery-Quash, 2012, p. 13.
122 Rowlands, 1985, p. 57.
123 Ibid., p. 57.
124 See Foister, 2004, p. 269, and Bätschmann and Griener, 1997, pp. 291–5.
125 Marschner, 2014b.
126 WSHC 1946/3/1B/2.
127 See Foister, Roy and Wyld, 1997, p. 12, and Foister, 2006, p. 24.
128 Hanson, 2009, pp. 178, 182.
129 See Guerrini, 2008.
130 WSHC 1946/3/1B/1.
131 Craske, 2007, p. 353.
132 Baker, 2014, pp. 79, 92.
133 Craske, 2007, pp. 359–60.
134 Harris, 1979, p. 158, and Einberg, 1970, p. 7.
135 Craske and Baker, 2008.
136 Friedman and Clifford (compilers), 1974, p. 9.
137 WSHC 1946/3/1B/1.
138 WSHC 1946/3/1B/2.
139 WSHC 1946/4/2B/1.
140 Turner, 1985, pp. 38–9.
141 Langley, 1728, p. 195.
142 Currie, 1990, p. 28, and Turner, 1985, p. 42.
143 See Anonymous, 1898, pp. 176–9, and Historic England, 2004.
144 WSHC 1946/3/1B/1.
145 Williamson, 1995, pp. 37–9.
146 Hussey, 1964, p. 610.
147 Ibid., p. 610.
148 WSHC 1946/3/2G/2.
149 Cartwright (ed.), 1889, Vol. II, p. 57.
150 Anonymous, 1970, pp. 7–8.
151 Retford, Perry and Vibert, 2013, p. 15. On Brown's work at Burghley, see Turner, 1985, pp. 110–12.
152 Climenson (ed.), 1899, p. 165.
153 Ibid., pp. 166–7.
154 Jackson-Stops with the assistance of Russell, 1985d, p. 376.
155 Penny with the assistance of Avery-Quash, 2012, p. 24.
156 WSHC 1946/3/2A/1.

157 WSHC 1946/3/1B/2.
158 Summerson, 1993, p. 341.
159 WSHC 1946/3/1B/2.
160 Hussey, 1931c, pp. 654–5.
161 Climenson (ed.), 1899, p. 165.
162 The National Archives Prob 11/863.
163 Tinniswood, 1989, p. 66, and Mandler, 1997, p. 9.
164 Moir, 1964, p. xiii, Girouard, 1978, pp. 190, 218, Ousby, 1990, p. 10, and Albert, 1972, pp. 6–13.
165 Waterfield, 1995a, p. 51. See also Stourton and Sebag-Montefiore, 2012, pp. 323–5.
166 Harris, 1968, p. 62, and Moir, 1959, p. 586.
167 Hanway, 1756, p. 48.
168 WSHC 1946/3/2C/12.
169 WSHC 1946/3/1B/2.
170 Jackson-Stops with the assistance of Russell, 1985f, p. 15.
171 WSHC 1946/3/1B/2. On the *Aedes Walpolianae*, see Walpole, 1767, and Stourton and Sebag-Montefiore, 2012, p. 325.
172 Hanway, 1756, p. 47.
173 Lewis, 2009, p. 341.
174 Anderson, 2013, pp. 210, 212, 228.
175 For example, see Hanway, 1756, p. 48, Sullivan, 1785, p. 193, and Cartwright (ed.), 1889, Vol. II, p. 57.
176 Cartwright (ed.), 1889, Vol. II, p. 57.
177 Anon, 1762, p. 41.
178 Thomson, 1973, p. 374, Göbel, 1974, p. 49, and Florisoone, 1978, pp. 89, 101.
179 Mount, 1991, p. 34.
180 WSHC 1946/3/1B/2.
181 *Ibid.*
182 Mount, 1991, p. 56.
183 Mount, 2006, pp. 178–9.
184 WSHC 1946/3/1B/1.
185 WSHC 1946/3/1B/2.
186 WSHC 1946/3/2A/3.
187 WSHC 1946/3/2A/3, and see Art Net, 2016.
188 Jackson-Stops and Pipkin, 1985, p. 139.
189 See WSHC 1946/3/2A/1.
190 WSHC 1946/3/1B/1.
191 Hussey, 1931b, p. 681.
192 See Hussey, 1931b, pp. 681–2 and WSHC 1946/3/1B/1.
193 Cornforth, 2004, p. 104.
194 Cornforth, 2004, pp. 52–4.
195 Cornforth and Fowler, 1974, pp. 131, 133.
196 WSHC 1946/3/2A/1.
197 Cornforth and Fowler, 1974, p. 202.
198 WSHC 1946/3/1B/2.
199 Tate Gallery, London (see Tate, 2004a and 2004b).
200 *Ibid.*
201 WSHC 1946/3/2A/1.
202 Harris, 1979, p. 40.
203 WSHC 1946/3/1B/2.
204 WSHC 1946/3/2A/1.

Chapter 3

1 Wiltshire and Swindon History Centre (hereafter WSHC) 1946/4/2F/2/1.
2 WSHC 1946/4/2B/3.
3 *Ibid.*
4 National Art Library (hereafter NAL) AAD/1995/7/7 (VAM 7).
5 WSHC 1946/3/1B/2.
6 Barr, 1980, pp. 95, 130.
7 NAL AAD/1995/7/3 (VAM 3) and WSHC 1946/3/1B/2.
8 Radnor, 2001, p. 52.
9 Jones and Shawe-Taylor, 2014, p. 271. On the historiography and appropriation of Alfred in the eighteenth century, see Cox, 2013.
10 See Blanning, 2002, p. 356, and Cox, 2013, p. 3.
11 Keynes, 1999, p. 321, and Cox, 2013, p. 88.
12 WSHC 1946/3/1B/2. See Keynes, 1999, pp. 320–21; Webb, 1954, p. 137; Eustace, 1982, pp. 182–4, and Cox, 2013, p. 90.
13 Translation from the Latin sourced from Keynes, 1999, p. 321, n. 456.
14 Cox, 2013, pp. 104–5.
15 The National Archives (hereafter TNA) Prob 11/1016.
16 Murdoch and Vigne, 2009, pp. 90–91.
17 For more on the 1st Earl's involvement in the French Hospital, see TNA Huguenot Library H/C6/9; TNA Huguenot Library H/A1/1 and TNA Huguenot Library H/F3/9.
18 Radnor, 2001, p. 47.
19 Wood, 1964, p. 206.
20 Miles, 1977, pp. 79–80.
21 See Weyer, 1979, unpaginated, and Miles, 1979, unpaginated.
22 Radnor, 2001, p. 47.
23 Jackson-Stops, 1990, p. 56.
24 WSHC 1946/4/2A/6.
25 See Griffiths, 2012, pp. 1, 10, and Strong, 2000, p. 75.
26 See Retford, forthcoming, Ch. 6.
27 Walpole, 1888, Vol. III, p. 37.
28 Craske, 2007, p. 327.
29 Victoria and Albert Museum (hereafter V&A) E.448–1946.
30 Craske, 2007, p. 327.
31 TNA Prob 11/943.
32 Spring, 1994, pp. 95–6.
33 TNA Prob 11/863.
34 *Ibid.*
35 Stone and Stone, 1984, p. 136.
36 WSHC 1946/4/2A/6.
37 Waterhouse, 1941, p. 4.
38 Penny (ed.), 1986, cat. 40, p. 204.
39 Mannings, 2000, cat. 225, p. 100.
40 Waterhouse, 1941, p. 9, and Penny, 1986, p. 24.
41 Perry, Retford and Vibert, 2013, p. 3.
42 Waterfield, 1995b, p. 51.
43 Cornforth and Fowler, 1974, p. 243.
44 Mannings, 2000, cat. 223 and cat. 226, p. 100.
45 Ware, 1768, p. 475.
46 Craske, 2016, unpaginated.
47 *Ibid.*
48 See Mannings, 2000, cat. 222, p. 100.
49 Royal Society of Arts (hereafter RSA) AD/MA/100/12/01/21. See also Smith, 2016b, p. 33.
50 On this see Smith, 2016b, pp. 22–31.
51 Baker, 2014, pp. 65–7.
52 WSHC 1946/3/1B/3.
53 Huntington Library, California. Cherry and Harris, 1982, pp. 299–300, 305.
54 Larsen, 1988, Vol. II, cat. 812, p. 320.
55 Cornforth, 1996, p. 32 and Edwards, Moore and Archer, 1996, p. 94.
56 On the provenance of the painting, see Getty Provenance Index, 2015, and WSHC 1946/3/1B/3 and Barnes *et al.*, 2004, cat. IV.75, p. 489.
57 Barnes *et al.*, cat. IV.166, p. 558.
58 *Ibid.*, and cat. IV.75, p. 489.
59 Barnes *et al.*, cat. IV.166, p. 558.
60 *Ibid.*
61 *Ibid.*
62 Cherry and Harris, 1982, p. 300.
63 Jones and Postle, 2002, p. 35.
64 Cherry and Harris, 1982, pp. 292–3.
65 Pointon, 1993, p. 23, and Rosenthal, 1999, p. 158.
66 Cherry and Harris, 1982, p. 305.
67 WSHC 1946/3/2A/1.
68 Cherry and Harris, 1982, p. 306.
69 Sir George Beaumont quoted in Boulton, 1905, pp. 286–7.
70 See WSHC 1946/3/1B/2 and WSHC 1946/3/1B/3.
71 See payments for 1770 in WSHC 1946/3/1B/3.
72 See Giometti, 2000, pp. 79–80.
73 Avray Tipping, 1919, p. 108.
74 Britton and Brayley, 1801, Vol. I, p. 132.
75 See WSHC 1946/3/1B/3.
76 Woolfe and Gandon, 1771, Vol. V. On the difference between Campbell's publications and his imitators', see Connor, 1997, p. 14.
77 Arnold, 1998, pp. 36–9.
78 Woolfe and Gandon, 1771, Vol. V, p. 10.
79 *Ibid.*, pp. 1, 2.
80 *Ibid.*, p. 9.
81 On Boydell and the publication of prints after works by Claude, see Clayton, 1997, pp. 170, 177–180, 209, and Brewer, 1997, p. 453.
82 See WSHC 1946/3/1B/2 and WSHC 1946/3/1B/3.
83 WSHC 1946/3/1B/2.
84 WSHC 1946/3/1B/3.
85 WSHC 1946/3/1B/2.
86 Jourdain and Rose, 1953, p. 37.
87 WSHC 1946/3/1B/2 and WSHC 1946/3/1B/3.
88 WSHC 1946/3/1B/3.
89 WSHC 1946/3/1B/2.

90   WSHC 1946/4/2A/6.
91   See Sheppard (ed.), 1963, Vols XXXI and XXXII, pp. 566–72, and Allan, 2007.
92   WSHC 1946/3/1B/2.
93   On this see Stewart, 2009, pp. 29–30, 32–4, 38, 56.
94   See Greig, 2013, pp. 1–4, 6–7.
95   On the relationship between city and countryside in the eighteenth century, see Christie, 2000, p. 2, and McKellar, 2013, p. xv.
96   See RSA PR/GE/110/1/22, RSA AD/MA/100/12/01/01 and discussion in Smith, 2016b, pp. 16–17.
97   WSHC 1946/3/4A/9.
98   Stewart, 2009, p. 56.
99   WSHC 1946/3/1B/3.
100 WSHC 1946/3/2A/1.
101 WSHC 1946/3/1B/3.
102 See Smith, 2016a, pp. 67–73.
103 See WSHC 1946/3/1B/3.
104 See WSHC 1946/3/1B/2 and 1946/3/1B/3.
105 TNA Prob 11/1016.
106 Craske, 2007, pp. 43–5, 63–71. See discussion of the rural middling classes' awareness and expectation of such events from local aristocratic families in Tadmor, 2001, p. 84.
107 Radnor, 2001, p. 52.
108 See WSHC 1946/4/2A/10.
109 Ibid.

Chapter 4

1   Wiltshire and Swindon History Centre (hereafter WSHC) 1946/4/2B/1.
2   WSHC 1946/4/2A/6.
3   WSHC 1946/4/2B/26.
4   WSHC 1946/3/3/2.
5   West, 1996, p. 77.
6   Colvin, 1954, pp. 727–31. On Wyatt, see also Jackson-Stops, 1990, p. 108.
7   WSHC 1946/4/2A/6 and WSHC 1946/3/2C/12.
8   WSHC 1946/3/2E/4.
9   Conway and Roenisch, 2005, p. 104.
10   See Marschner, 2014a, pp. 64–5, and Marschner, 2014a.
11   Jackson-Stops, 1990, p. 108.
12   See Girouard, 2009, p. 457 and Girouard, 1968, p. 18.
13   WSHC 1946/3/2E/2.
14   WSHC 1946/3/2E/6.
15   WSHC 1946/3/2E/14.
16   See Jackson-Stops, 1990, pp. 95–105, 124, and Retford, 2006, p. 168.
17   WSHC 1946/3/2E/11.
18   Britton, 1814, Vol. XV, pp. 389–90.
19   WSHC 1946/4/3F/2.
20   Ibid.
21   Ibid.
22   Retford, 2006, pp. 149–51.

23   Ibid., pp. 165–6.
24   WSHC 1946/4/3P/3.
25   WSHC 1946/4/2A/2.
26   Sweet, 2004, pp. 231, 278.
27   Cobbett and Hansard, 1795, Vol. XXXII, p. 247.
28   WSHC 1946/3/1B/3 and Penny with the assistance of Avery-Quash, 2012, p. 10.
29   WSHC 1946/3/1B/3.
30   Mannings, 2000, cat. 218, p. 99.
31   WSHC 1946/3/2A/8.
32   National Art Library AAD/1995/7/40 (VAM 37).
33   Ibid.
34   Vickery, 2010, p. 282.
35   WSHC 1946/4/2K/21.
36   On this, see Cornforth and Fowler, 1974, pp. 248–53.
37   See Smith, 2001, pp. 223–5.
38   Smith, 2004.
39   WSHC 1946/3/1B/4.
40   Jenkins and Sloan, 1996, cat. 176, p. 279.
41   Ibid.
42   Ibid. and Sloan, 1996, p. 85.
43   Gould, 1976, p. 158.
44   Lord Pembroke, 1968, p. 4.
45   Sloan, 1996, pp. 75–7. See also Metropolitan Museum of Art, 2017.
46   Metropolitan Museum of Art, 2017.
47   WSHC 1946/3/1B/4.
48   See WSHC 1946/3/2A/1 and WSHC 1946/3/2A/3.
49   WSHC 1946/3/1B/3.
50   WSHC 1946/4/2B/4.
51   Lloyd, 1995, pp. 13, 20.
52   Moore, 1996, p. 48.
53   WSHC 1946/3/4A/3.
54   Ibid.
55   Steward, 1995, pp. 20–25 and Lloyd, 1995, cat. 32, p. 116.
56   WSHC 1946/3/1B/3.
57   Ibid.
58   Kenwood House, London.
59   WSHC 1946/3/1B/4.
60   On agency and meaning within eighteenth-century child portraiture, see Pointon, 1993, p. 178.
61   Ibid., p. 177.
62   Steward, 1995, pp. 19, 90, 133.
63   See Newman and Brown, 1997, p. 119.
64   Reynolds, 1992, p. 118.
65   Lloyd, 1995, p. 13.
66   WSHC 1946/3/1B/3 and Lloyd, 1995, cat. 22, p. 115.
67   WSHC 1946/3/1B/4.
68   WSHC 1946/4/2K/1.
69   Strong, 1974, p. 257.
70   See WSHC 1946/3/2C/1 and WSHC 1946/3/2C/11.
71   Berkshire Record Office D/EPb/F28.
72   Ibid.

73   Ward, 2008, p. 294.
74   Penny with the assistance of Avery-Quash, 2012, p. 27.
75   Ibid., p. 27.
76   Waagen, 1838, Vol. III, pp. 58–9.
77   Spiker, 1820, Vol. II, pp. 173–4.
78   Passavant, 1836, Vol. I, p. 296.
79   Anderson, 2013, pp. 225–6.
80   Anonymous, 1797, pp. 83–4.
81   WSHC 1946/3/2A/27.
82   Ibid.
83   Ibid.
84   WSHC 1946/4/2C/2.
85   WSHC 1946/3/1B/4. See also Hervey, 1900, pp. vi, 6.
86   Langford, 2011.
87   Hervey, 1900, p. 5.
88   Haskell, 1980, pp. 28–32.
89   See Foister, Roy and Wyld, 1997, and MacGregor, 1997, p. 9.
90   Foister, 1997, pp. 44–55.
91   See Knight, 2009.
92   WSHC 1946/3/2A/15.
93   Ibid.
94   WSHC 1946/3/2A/1 and WSHC 1946/3/2A/3.
95   Brigstocke (ed.), 1982, pp. 294–5.
96   Ibid., p. 295.
97   WSHC 1946/3/1B/4.
98   Strong, 2004.
99   WSHC 1946/3/2A/1.
100 Ibid.
101 Ibid.
102 Ibid.
103 Ibid.
104 Ibid.
105 Jackson-Stops with the assistance of Russell, 1985b, p. 354.
106 Mount, 1991, p. 66, fn. 196, and Laing, 1995, p. 119.
107 See Mount, 1991, p. 66, fn. 196, Walpole, 1767, pp. 65–71, and Morel, 2013a, p. 138.
108 WSHC 1946/3/2E/9.
109 WSHC 1946/3/2A/1.
110 Ibid.
111 WSHC 1946/4/2B/14.
112 Radnor, 2001, p. 54.
113 On the politics and membership of the dining club, see Mitchell, 1970, pp. 352–8, and WSHC 1946/4/2G/2/16.
114 Langford, 1991, p. 573.
115 Cobbett and Hansard, 1775–76, Vol. XVIII, pp. 1019–20, 1370, and Cobbett and Hansard, 1783, Vol. XXIV, p. 194.
116 Cobbett and Hansard, 1772, Vol. XVII, pp. 418–19.
117 Pers. comm., R. Darwall-Smith to the author, 30 June 2014. The bust has been located in the Library since 1938 (Keynes, 1999, p. 324, n. 468).
118 WSHC 1946/4/2B/20.
119 WSHC 1946/3/1B/3. See also WSHC

1946/4/2G/2/7.

120   On his work for the French Hospital, see The National Archives (hereafter TNA), Huguenot Library H/A1/2, TNA Huguenot Library H/E9/1 and Murdoch and Vigne, 2009, p. 44.
121   Radnor, 2001, pp. 59–60.
122   See WSHC 1946/4/2B/4.
123   WSHC 1946/3/2D/1.
124   *Ibid.*
125   *Ibid.*
126   *Ibid.*
127   WSHC 1946/3/1B/3.
128   Beckett, 2002, p. 237.
129   WSHC 1946/3/1B/3 and WSHC 1946/3/1B/4.
130   WSHC 1946/4/2D/2.
131   WSHC 1946/4/2B/20.
132   WSHC 1946/3/1B/3.
133   WSHC 1946/3/2A/13.
134   WSHC 1946/4/2C/2.
135   *Ibid.*
136   WSHC 1946/3/2G/2.

Chapter 5

1   Wiltshire and Swindon History Centre (hereafter WSHC) 1946/3/2A/13.
2   On Lord Dover, see Barker, 2004.
3   Huch, 1977, p. 169.
4   *Ibid.*, p. 3.
5   WSHC 1946/4/2B/6.
6   WSHC 1946/3/2A/13.
7   *Ibid.*
8   Laing, 2004.
9   WSHC 1946/3/2A/4.
10   *Ibid.*
11   WSHC 1946/3/2A/3. On Smith, see Sebag-Montefiore with Armstrong-Totten, 2013.
12   WSHC 1946/3/2A/3.
13   *Ibid.*
14   WSHC 1946/4/2B/37.
15   *Ibid.*
16   *Ibid.*
17   *Ibid.*
18   Baillio, 1982, p. 6.
19   Penny with the assistance of Avery-Quash, 2012, p. 10.
20   Mannings, 2000, cat. 380, p. 136.
21   WSHC 1946/3/2G/5.
22   *Ibid.*
23   See WSHC 1946/3/2A/8 and WSHC 1946/4/2A/13.
24   WSHC 1946/3/2A/8.
25   See WSHC 1946/3/2C/12 and WSHC 1946/3/2E/31.
26   WSHC 1946/3/2C/12.
27   Huch, 1977, p. 10.
28   Huch, 1977, pp. 10–11.
29   Mandler, 1997, p. 4.
30   Bailey, 1978, p. vi. On Waagen, see Haskell, 2000, pp. 83–4.
31   Waagen, 1838, Vols I–III.
32   Waagen, 1838, Vol. III, p. 52.
33   *Ibid.*, Vol. III, pp. 52, 54.
34   WSHC 1946/3/2A/11.
35   Radnor, 2001, p. 70.
36   Waagen, 1857, Vol. III, p. 353.
37   *Ibid.*, Vol. III, p. 353.
38   *Ibid.*, Vol. III, p. 362.
39   WSHC 1946/3/2A/5.
40   See WSHC 1946/3/2A/3 and WSHC 1946/3/2A/5.
41   WSHC 1946/3/2A/5.
42   Mandler, 1997, p. 86.
43   Penny with the assistance of Avery-Quash, 2012, p. 40.
44   *Ibid.*, p. 40.
45   *Ibid.*, pp. 73–4.
46   *Ibid.*, p. 74.
47   See WSHC 1946/3/2E/38, WSHC 1946/3/2E/40MS, WSHC 1946/3/2E/41H, WSHC 1946/3/2E/41PC and WSHC 1946/3/2E/42PC.
48   Holder, 2004.
49   *Ibid.*
50   Radnor, 2001, p. 76.
51   WSHC 1946/3/2C/12.
52   Radnor, 2001, p. 76.
53   WSHC 1946/3/2A/6.
54   *Ibid.*
55   *Ibid.*
56   Penny with the assistance of Avery-Quash, 2012, p. 41.
57   WSHC 1946/4/2B/31.
58   *Ibid.*
59   Penny with the assistance of Avery-Quash, 2012, p. 41.
60   National Gallery Archive (hereafter NGA) NG5/339/1.
61   *Ibid.*
62   *Ibid.*
63   *Ibid.*
64   NGA NG17/5.
65   NGA NG7/127/6.
66   NGA NG24/1890/4.
67   *Ibid.*
68   Mandler, 1997, pp. 124–6.
69   *Ibid.*, p. 126.
70   *Ibid.*, pp. 126–7.
71   NGA NG7/127/9.
72   *Ibid.*
73   NGA NG17/5.
74   See WSHC 1946/4/2E/16.
75   *Ibid.*
76   Whitehead, 2005, p. 4.
77   *Ibid.*, p. 4.
78   WSHC 1946/4/2E/16.
79   National Gallery, 2017.
80   WSHC 1946/3/2A/16.
81   Anonymous, 1898, pp. 176–9.
82   *Ibid.*, p. 176.
83   Mandler, 1997, p. 287.
84   See Hussey, 1931a, 1931b, 1931c, 1931d, 1931e.
85   *Ibid.*
86   See Radnor and Barclay Squire, 1909.
87   Penny with the assistance of Avery-Quash, 2012, p. 42.
88   Radnor, 1927, p. 177.
89   Penny with the assistance of Avery-Quash, 2012, p. 42.
90   On Barclay Squire, see Cobbe, 2006 and on Scharf, see Jackson, 2004.
91   Radnor, 1927, p. 179.
92   WSHC 1946/3/2A/20.
93   *Ibid.*
94   Radnor, 1927, p. 184.
95   Radnor, 1916.
96   *Ibid.*, pp. 5–13.
97   *Ibid.*
98   Penny with the assistance of Avery-Quash, 2012, p. 42. See Radnor, 1927.

BIBLIOGRAPHY

Manuscripts
Berkshire Record Office
D/EPb/F28 Diary of a journey from Yarmouth to Gothenburg …
1797–8

Sir John Soane's Museum Library
SM_vol101, Thorpe Album: SM_vol101/155-157 plans and partial
exterior elevation, SM_vol101/158 partial elevation of the exterior
of the Hall block, and SM_vol101/159 unfinished partial plan of the
Hall block

The National Archives
Prob 11/863 Will of … Jacob Lord Viscount Folkestone, Baron of
Longford
Prob 11/943 Will of Sir Mark Stuart Pleydell
Prob 11/1016 Will of … William [1st] Earl of Radnor
Huguenot Library H/A1/1–3 Minutes of the Court's quarterly and
extra-ordinary meeting (Livres de Délibérations des Assemblées
Générales de la Corporation Françoise), 3 Vols., 1770–1835
Huguenot Library H/C6/9 Note of Lord Radnor's election as Director
1770
Huguenot Library H/E9/1 Act of Parliament for enabling the Hospital
Corporation to grant part of their site and lands upon building
leases 1808
Huguenot Library H/F3/9 Appeal for funds for rebuilding the
bakehouse wing, addressed to the Earl of Radnor c. 1763

National Art Library
AAD/1995/7/3 (VAM 3) Gentleman's Ledger 1746–1751
AAD/1995/7/7 (VAM 7) Gentleman's Ledger 1765–1776
AAD/1995/7/40 (VAM 37) Gentleman's Ledger 1811–1818

National Gallery Archive
NG5/339/1 List of pictures at Longford Castle and Kingston Lacy,
July 1861
NG7/127/6 Letter from Lord Radnor to the Earl of Carlisle stating that
Philip Coxe of Bompas, Bischoff, Dodgson & Coxe would act on
his behalf in the sale of the Radnor pictures (1314–1316), 13 May
1890
NG7/127/9 Letter from Philip Coxe to Sir Frederic Burton re the sale
of the Radnor pictures (1314–1316), 28 May 1890
NG17/5 National Gallery Reports 1887–1897
NG24/1890/4 Press cuttings 11 April–29 July 1890
NG17/5 National Gallery Reports 1887–1897
NG24/1890/4 Press cuttings 11 April–29 July 1890

Royal Society of Arts
AD/MA/100/12/01/01 Minutes of the Society, 1754–1757
AD/MA/100/12/01/21 Minutes of the Society, 1775–1776
PR/GE/110/1/22 Letter from Lord Folkestone … 2nd June 1755

Wiltshire and Swindon History Centre
1946/3/1B/1 House book [of household and personal expenses of
Sir Jacob Bouverie] 1723–1745
1946/3/1B/2 House book [of household and personal expenses of
Sir Jacob Bouverie and William, 1st Earl of Radnor] 1745–1768
1946/3/1B/3 Account book [of personal expenditure of the 1st and 2nd
Earls of Radnor] 1768–1795
1946/3/1B/4 Account book [of personal expenditure of Jacob, 2nd Earl
of Radnor] 1797–1828
1946/3/2A/1 Early catalogues of paintings at Longford 1748–1828
1946/3/2A/3 Catalogue of paintings at Longford Castle 1829
1946/3/2A/4 Survey and cleaning of paintings at Longford Castle
1830–1840
1946/3/2A/5 Catalogues of paintings at Longford Castle 1849–1853
1946/3/2A/6 Picture galleries, mid–late nineteenth century
1946/3/2A/8 Research volumes for the Countess of Radnor's catalogue
of paintings [c. 1890–c. 1930]
1946/3/2A/11 Correspondence and research notes for the Countess of
Radnor's catalogue 1839–1907
1946/3/2A/13 Correspondence about paintings 1804–1877
1946/3/2A/14 Letter [from Robert Hodson to Sir Edward des
Bouverie] 1724
1946/3/2A/15 Correspondence 1807–1876
1946/3/2A/16 Royal Academy exhibitions 1872–1876
1946/3/2A/20 Correspondence 1889–1893
1946/3/2A/27 [Letters, descriptions and photographs of] The Steel
Chair 1781– c. 1820
1946/3/2C/1 History of buildings 1678, 1694
1946/3/2C/5PC History of buildings [Longford Castle] 1766
1946/3/2C/9 History of buildings [Longford Castle] 1644–1962
1946/3/2C/11 History of buildings [Longford Castle] 1889
1946/3/2C/12 Article on history of Longford Castle [including letter by
John Cornforth] 1967–1968
1946/3/2C/14 History of buildings [Longford Castle] 18th century,
1989
1946/3/2D/1 Royal visit [of the Prince of Wales to Longford Castle]
1785
1946/3/2E/2 Designs for building work at Longford Castle
1790s–1800s
1946/3/2E/4 Vouchers 1792, 1797
1946/3/2E/6 Specification 1797
1946/3/2E/9 Plans 1801
1946/3/2E/11 Plans 1802
1946/3/2E/14 Plans [c. 1802], 1812
1946/3/2E/31 Correspondence 1831–1832
1946/3/2E/38 Specifications, correspondence and accounts for
alterations to Longford castle 1871–1878
1946/3/2E/40MS Plans [c. 1872]
1946/3/2E/41H Plan 1856 [c. 1872]
1946/3/2E/41PC Plans [c. 1872]
1946/3/2E/42PC Plans 1872
1946/3/2G/2 Alterations to the garden and grounds [c. 1760]–1814
1946/3/2G/5 Alterations to the garden and grounds 1831–1832

1946/3/3/2 Correspondence 1814

1946/3/4A/1 Auction catalogue 1743–1744

1946/3/4A/3 Catalogue of pictures & letter 1791

1946/3/4A/9 Cellar accounts for London houses 1768–1777

1946/4/1A/10 MS Patent of baronetcy 1714

1946/4/1A/13 Act of Parliament for change of name [1737]

1946/4/1H/2 Passport & portfeuille 1700–1713

1946/4/2A/2 Descent from Edward I [c. 1270]–1779

1946/4/2A/6 Family History by Nancy Steele [16th century–c. 2000]

1946/4/2A/10 Family vault in St Peter's, Britford 1765–1923

1946/4/2A/13 Correspondence 1889–1896

1946/4/2B/1 Volume of family history documents 1623–1834

1946/4/2B/3 Letter 1765

1946/4/2B/4 Correspondence … 1771–1821

1946/4/2B/6 Correspondence 1774–1830

1946/4/2B/14 Correspondence of Jacob, 2nd Earl of Radnor: George Washington's letter 1797

1946/4/2B/20 Correspondence of Jacob, 2nd Earl of Radnor 1804–1812

1946/4/2B/26 Correspondence … 1806–1811

1946/4/2B/31 Correspondence 1808–1923

1946/4/2B/37 Correspondence 1828–1829

1946/4/2C/2 Notebook of Jacob, 2nd Earl of Radnor 1786

1946/4/2D/2 Account books … 1767–1776

1946/4/2E/16 Sale of 3 paintings to National Gallery 1890–1997

1946/4/2F/2/1 Report of grant of title 1765

1946/4/2G/2/7 Correspondence about stained-glass windows in Salisbury Cathedral 1776–1880

1946/4/2G/2/16 Printed memorial 1804

1946/4/2K/1 Lady Rich's cabinet contents and documents 1589–1996

1946/4/2K/21 Anne, Countess of Radnor 1793–1794

1946/4/3F/2 Letters about Foster & Barrett portraits 1776

1946/4/3P/3 Genealogical notes 3 [819–c. 1800]

Victoria and Albert Museum

E.448–1946 Design for a memorial (front and side elevations) to the Hon. Harriet Bouverie, Viscountess of Folkestone (d. 1750)

Unpublished secondary manuscripts

Anderson, J., 'Remaking the Country House: Country House Guidebooks in the Late Eighteenth and Early Nineteenth Centuries', unpublished PhD thesis, The Courtauld Institute of Art, University of London, 2013

Cox, O., '"Rule, Britannia!" King Alfred the Great and the Creation of a National Hero in England and America, 1640–1800', unpublished PhD thesis, University College, Oxford, 2013

Miles, E.G., 'Thomas Hudson, 1701–1779: Portraitist to the British Establishment', unpublished PhD thesis, Yale University, 1977

Mount, H., 'The Reception of Dutch Genre Painting in England 1695–1829', unpublished PhD thesis, Corpus Christi College, Cambridge, 1991

Publications

Albert, W., *The Turnpike Road System in England 1663–1840*, Cambridge: Cambridge University Press, 1972

Allan, D.G.C., 'Bouverie, Jacob, first Viscount Folkestone (*bap.* 1694, *d.* 1761)' in *Oxford Dictionary of National Biography*, Oxford University Press, October 2007, online edn, January 2008, http://www.oxforddnb.com/view/article/38924 (accessed 21 October 2015)

Anonymous, *The Beauties of England Displayed, in a Tour through the Following Counties … Exhibiting A View of whatever is curious, remarkable, or entertaining*, London, 1762

Anonymous, 'Country Homes and Gardens Old & New: Longford Castle, Wiltshire, the Seat of the Earl of Radnor' in *Country Life*, Vol. 4, No. 84, 13 August 1898, pp. 176–9

Anonymous, *The Rise and Progress of the Present Taste in Planting Parks, Pleasure Grounds, Gardens, Etc*, a facsimile with an introduction by J. Harris, Newcastle upon Tyne: Oriel Press, 1970

Anonymous, *The Salisbury Guide, giving an Account of the Antiquities of Old Sarum, and of the Subterranean Passage lately discovered there: the Ancient and Present State of New Sarum, or Salisbury, with a Copious Description of the Council-House, and a Correct List of the Corporation: the Cathedral, Stonehenge, and Seats of the Nobility and Gentry: the coming in and going out of the Post, Coaches, Waggons, and Carriers: with the Distances of the principal Towns and Villages on the High Roads from Salisbury*, nineteenth edn, Salisbury: printed and sold by J. Easton, London, 1797

Arnold, D., 'The Country House and its Publics' in D. Arnold (ed.), *The Georgian Country House: Architecture, Landscape and Society*, Stroud: Sutton, 1998, pp. 20–42

Art Net, 'Past Auction', 2016, http://www.artnet.com/artists/thomas-gainsborough/the-return-from-shooting-after-teniers-skYxqueol507h93HJzTZbg2 (accessed 3 August 2016)
Art UK, 'Hugh Hare (1668–1707), Translator', 2016

http://artuk.org/discover/artworks/hugh-hare-16681707-translator-212801 (accessed 13 October 2016)

Avery, C., 'John Cheere at Marble Hill' in *The Burlington Magazine*, Vol. 116, No. 858, September 1974, pp. 551–3

Avray-Tipping, H., 'Coleshill House. Berkshire. I' in *Country Life*, Vol. XLVI, 26 July 1919, pp. 108–16

Bailey, C.J., 'Introduction' in M. Passavant, *Tour of a German Artist in England, with Notices of Private Galleries, and Remarks on the State of Art*, originally published in 2 vols., Wakefield: EP Publishing, 1978, Vol. I, pp. v–xx

Baillio, J., *Elisabeth Louise Vigée-Lebrun, 1755–1842*, Fort Worth: Kimbell Art Museum, 1982

Baker, M., *Figured in Marble: The Making and Viewing of Eighteenth-Century Sculpture*, London: V&A Publications, 2000

Baker, M., *The Marble Index: Roubiliac and Sculptural Portraiture in Eighteenth-Century Britain*, New Haven and London: Yale University Press for the Paul Mellon Centre for Studies in British Art, 2014

Barker, G.F.R., 'Ellis, George James Welbore Agar-, first Baron Dover (1797–1833)', rev. H.C.G. Matthew in *Oxford Dictionary of National Biography*, Oxford University Press, 2004, online edn, May 2006, http://www.oxforddnb.com/view/article/8693 (accessed 29 February 2016)

Barnes, S.J., De Poorter, N., Millar, O. and Vey, H., *Van Dyck: A Complete Catalogue of the Paintings*, New Haven and London: Yale University Press for the Paul Mellon Centre for Studies in British Art, 2004

Barr, E., *George Wickes 1698–1761: Royal Goldsmith*, London: Studio Vista/Christie's, 1980

Bätschmann, O. and Griener, P., *Hans Holbein*, trans. C. Hurley and P. Griener, London, 1997

Beard, G., and Gilbert, C. (eds), *Dictionary of English Furniture Makers 1660–1840*, London: Furniture History Society, 1986

Beard, G., 'William Kent's Furniture Designs and the Furniture Makers' in *The Magazine Antiques*, Vol. CXXIX, New York: Straight Enterprises, June 1986, pp. 1278–291

Beckett, J.V., 'Country House Life' in *The Historical Journal*, Vol. 45, No. 1, March 2002, pp. 325–44

Blake McHam, S., 'Introduction' in S. Blake McHam (ed.), *Looking at Italian Renaissance Sculpture*, Cambridge: Cambridge University Press, 1998, pp. 1–17

Blanning, T.C.W., *The Culture of Power and the Power of Culture: Old Regime Europe 1660–1789*, Oxford: Oxford University Press, 2002

Blomfield, R., *A Short History of Renaissance Architecture in England 1500–1800*, London: Bell, 1910

Boulton, W.B., *Thomas Gainsborough: His Life, Work, Friends and Sitters*, London: Methuen, 1905

Boyer, J.-C., 'Some Identifications of Paintings in the Collection of "le grand Colbert"' in *The Burlington Magazine*, Vol. 156, No. 1333, April 2014, pp. 212–18

Brewer, J., *The Pleasures of the Imagination: English Culture in the Eighteenth Century*, Chicago: University of Chicago Press, 1997

Brigstocke, H. (ed.), *William Buchanan and the 19th Century Art Trade: 100 Letters to His Agents in London and Italy*, London: published privately for the Paul Mellon Centre for Studies in British Art, 1982

Britton, J., *The Architectural Antiquities of Great Britain, represented and illustrated in a series of Views, Elevations, Plans, Sections, and Details of Various Ancient English Edifices with Historical and Descriptive Accounts of Each*, 9 vols., London: Longman, Hurst, Rees & Orme, 1809

Britton, J., *The Beauties of England and Wales; or Original Delineations, Topographical, Historical, and Descriptive, of Each County, Embellished with Engravings*, 18 vols., London, 1814

Britton, J., and Brayley, E.W., *The Beauties of England and Wales; or Delineations, Topographical, Historical, and Descriptive, of Each County, Embellished with Engravings*, 18 vols., London, 1801

Cartwright, J.J. (ed.), *The Travels through England of Dr Richard Pococke*, 2 vols., London: Camden Society, 1889

Cherry, D., and Harris, J., 'Eighteenth-Century Portraiture and the Seventeenth-Century Past: Gainsborough and Van Dyck' in *Art History*, Vol. 5, No. 3, September 1982, pp. 287–309

Christie, C., *The British Country House in the Eighteenth Century*, Manchester and New York: Manchester University Press, 2000

Clark, P., *British Clubs and Societies 1580–1800: The Origins of an Associational World*, Oxford: Clarendon Press, 2000

Clayton, T., *The English Print 1688–1802*, New Haven and London: Yale University Press, 1997

Climenson, E.J. (ed.), *Passages from the Diaries of Mrs Philip Lybbe Powys of Hardwick House, Oxon. A.D. 1756 to 1808*, London: Longmans, Green, and Co., 1899

Cobbe, H., 'Squire, William Barclay (1855–1927)' in *Oxford Dictionary of National Biography*, Oxford University Press, 2004, online edn, May 2006, http://www.oxforddnb.com/view/article/36228 (accessed 2 March 2016)

Cobbett, W., and Hansard, T.C. (eds), *Cobbett's Parliamentary History of England from the Norman Conquest, in 1066 to the year 1803*, 36 vols., London: R. Bagshaw, 1806–1820

Colvin, H.M., *A Biographical Dictionary of English Architects, 1660–1840*, London: J. Murray, 1954

Connor, T.P., 'The Making of "Vitruvius Britannicus"' in *Architectural History*, Vol. 20, 1997, pp. 14–30, 81

Conway, H., and Roenisch, R., *Understanding Architecture: An Introduction to Architecture and Architectural History*, second edn, London: Routledge, 2005

Coope, R., 'The 'Long Gallery': Its Origins, Development, Use and Decoration' in *Architectural History*, Vol. 29, 1986, pp. 43–72, 74–84

Cornforth, J., and Fowler, J., *English Decoration in the 18th Century*, London: Barrie and Jenkins, 1974

Cornforth, J., 'A Georgian Patchwork' in G. Jackson-Stops, *The Fashioning and Functioning of the British Country House*, Washington: National Gallery of Art, 1989, pp. 155–74

Cornforth, J., *Early Georgian Interiors*, New Haven and London: Yale University Press, 2004

Cornforth, J., 'The Genesis and Creation of a Great Interior' in A. Moore (ed.), *Houghton Hall: The Prime Minister, the Empress, and the Heritage*, London: Philip Wilson Publishers, 1996, pp. 29–40

Craske, M., and Baker, M., 'Cheere, Sir Henry, first baronet (1702–1781)' in *Oxford Dictionary of National Biography*, Oxford University Press, 2004, online edn, January 2008, http://www.oxforddnb.com/view/article/5207 (accessed 9 January 2015)

Craske, M., 'Conversations and Chimneypieces: the Imagery of the Hearth in Eighteenth-Century English Family Portraiture' in *British Art Studies*, Issue 2, 2016, http://dx.doi.org/10.17658/issn.2058-5462/issue-02/mcraske (accessed 20 September 2016)

Craske, M., *The Silent Rhetoric of the Body: A History of Monumental Sculpture and Commemorative Art in England, 1720–1770*, New Haven and London: Yale University Press, 2007

Currie, C., 'Fishponds as Garden Features, *c.* 1550–1750' in *Garden History*, Vol. 18, No. 1, Spring 1990, pp. 22–46

Daniels, S., The Political Iconography of Woodland in Later Georgian England' in D. Cosgrove and S. Daniels (eds), *The Iconography of Landscape: Essays on the Symbolic Representation, Design and Use of*

Past Environments, Cambridge: Cambridge University Press, 1988, pp. 43–82

Defoe, D., *A Tour Thro' The Whole Island of Great Britain Divided into Circuits or Journies Giving A Particular and Diverting Account of whatever is Curious and worth Observation. Particularly fitted for the Reading of such as desire to Travel over the Island*, 2 vols., originally published 1724–6, new impression of new edn, Frank Cass & Co. Ltd, 1968

Douglas Stewart, J., *Sir Godfrey Kneller and the English Baroque Portrait*, Oxford: Clarendon Press, 1983

Douglas Stewart, J., 'Dahl, Michael (1659–1743)' in *Oxford Dictionary of National Biography*, Oxford University Press, online edn, January 2008, http://www.oxforddnb.com/view/article/7005 (accessed 14 July 2016)

Edwards, R., and Jourdain, M., *Georgian Cabinet-Makers c. 1700–1800*, London: Country Life Ltd, 1955

Edwards, S., Moore, A., and Archer, C., 'The Common Parlour' in A. Moore (ed.), *Houghton Hall: The Prime Minister, the Empress, and the Heritage*, London: Philip Wilson Publishers, 1996, pp. 94–6

Einberg, E., 'George Lambert (1700–1765)' in Iveagh Bequest, Kenwood, *George Lambert (1700–1765) First Exhibition devoted to one of England's Earliest Landscape Painters*, Greater London Council, 1970, pp. 5–12

English Heritage, 'Rushton Triangular Lodge', 2016, http://www.english-heritage.org.uk/visit/places/rushton-triangular-lodge/ (accessed 6 October 2016)

Eustace, K., *Michael Rysbrack, Sculptor, 1694–1770*, Bristol: City of Bristol Museum and Art Gallery, 1982

Everett, N., *The Tory View of Landscape*, New Haven and London: Yale University Press, 1994

Fiennes, C., *The Journeys of Celia Fiennes*, ed. and with an introduction by C. Morris, with a foreword by G.M. Trevelyan, O.M., London: The Cresset Press, 1949

Florisoone, M., 'Classical Tapestry from the 16th to the Early 20th Century' in P. Verlet, M. Florisoone, A. Hoffmeister and F. Tabard, *The Book of Tapestry: History and Technique*, trans. from the French, London: Octopus Books, 1978, pp. 62–114

Foister, S., 'Death and Distortion: The Skull and the Crucifix' in S. Foister, R. Ashok and M. Wyld, *Making and Meaning: Holbein's Ambassadors*, London: National Gallery Publications and Yale University Press, 1997, pp. 44–57

Foister, S., *Holbein and England*, New Haven and London: Yale University Press, 2004

Foister, S., *Holbein in England*, London: Tate Publishing, 2006

Foister, S., Ashok, R., and Wyld, M., *Making and Meaning: Holbein's Ambassadors*, London: National Gallery Publications and Yale University Press, 1997

Foister, S., Ashok, R., and Wyld, M., 'Introduction' in S. Foister, R. Ashok and M. Wyld, *Making and Meaning: Holbein's Ambassadors*, London: National Gallery Publications and Yale University Press, 1997, pp. 11–13

Ford, B., 'The Englishman in Italy' in G. Jackson-Stops (ed.), *The Treasure Houses of Britain: Five Hundred Years of Private Patronage*

and Art Collecting, Washington, DC: National Gallery of Art; New Haven and London: Yale University Press, 1985, pp. 40–49

Forsyth, M., and White, L., *Interior Finishes and Fittings for Historic Building Conservation*, Hoboken: Wiley-Blackwell, 2012

Friedman, T., and Clifford, T. (compilers), *The Man at Hyde Park Corner: Sculpture by John Cheere 1709–1787*, Leeds and Twickenham: Temple Newsam and Marble Hill House, 1974

Garlick, K., and Macintyre, A. (eds), *The Diary of Joseph Farington*, 17 vols., New Haven and London: Yale University Press, 1978

Getty Provenance Index, Lot 0051 from Sale Catalogue Br-A1108, http://piprod.getty.edu/starweb/pi/servlet.starweb (accessed 24 February 2015)

Gibson-Wood, C., *Jonathan Richardson: Art Theorist of the English Enlightenment*, New Haven and London: Yale University Press for the Paul Mellon Centre for Studies in British Art, 2000

Gilpin, W., *Observations on the Western Parts of England, Relative Chiefly to Picturesque Beauty*, London: T. Cadwell and W. Davies, 1798

Giometti, C., 'Gentlemen of Virtue: Morality and Representation in English Eighteenth-Century Tomb Sculpture' in C. Sicca and A. Yarrington (eds), *The Lustrous Trade: Material Culture and the History of Sculpture in England and Italy, c. 1700–c. 1860*, London and New York: Leicester University Press, 2000, pp. 77–93

Girouard, M., 'Attitudes to Elizabethan Architecture, 1600–1900' in J. Summerson (ed.), *Concerning Architecture: Essays on Architectural Writers and Writing presented to Nikolaus Pevsner*, London: Allen Lane, 1968, pp. 13–27

Girouard, M., *Elizabethan Architecture: Its Rise and Fall, 1540–1640*, New Haven and London: Yale University Press, 2009

Girouard, J., *Life in the English Country House*, New Haven and London: Yale University Press, 1978

Göbel, H., *Tapestries of the Lowlands*, trans. R. West, New York: Hacker Art Books, 1974

Gotch, J.A., 'Three Notable Houses' in A. Dryden (ed.), *Memorials of Old Wiltshire*, London: Bemrose & Sons Limited, 4 Snow Hill, E.C. and Derby, 1906

Gould, C., *The Paintings of Correggio*, London: Faber and Faber, 1976

Greig, H., *The Beau Monde: Fashionable Society in Georgian London*, Oxford: Oxford University Press, 2013

Griffiths, R., 'The Life and Work of Edward Haytley' in *The Walpole Society*, Vol. LXXIV, 2012, pp. 1–60

Guerrini, A., 'Mead, Richard (1673–1754)' in *Oxford Dictionary of National Biography*, Oxford: Oxford University Press, 2004, online edn, January 2008, http://www.oxforddnb.com/view/article/18467 (accessed 29 September 2014)

Hanson, C.A., *The English Virtuoso: Art, Medicine, and Antiquarianism in the Age of Empiricism*, Chicago: University of Chicago Press, 2009

Hanway, J., *A Journal of Eight Days Journey from Portsmouth to Kingston upon Thames … in a series of sixty-four letters: addressed to two ladies of the partie. To which is added, An essay on tea …*, London: H. Woodfall, 1756

Harris, J., *The Artist and the Country House: A History of Country House and Garden View Painting in Britain 1540–1870*, London: Sotheby Parke Bernet Publications, 1979

Harris, J., 'The Duchess of Beaufort's *Observations on Places*' in *The Georgian Group Journal*, Vol. X, 2000, pp. 36–42

Harris, J., 'English Country House Guides, 1740–1840' in J. Summerson (ed.), *Concerning Architecture: Essays on Architectural Writers and Writing presented to Nikolaus Pevsner*, London: Allen Lane, 1968, pp. 58–74

Haskell, F., and Penny, N., *Taste and the Antique: The Lure of Classical Sculpture 1500–1900*, New Haven and London: Yale University Press, 1981

Haskell, F., 'The British as Collectors' in G. Jackson-Stops (ed.), *The Treasure Houses of Britain: Five Hundred Years of Private Patronage and Art Collecting*, Washington, DC: National Gallery of Art; New Haven and London: Yale University Press, 1985, pp. 50–59

Haskell, F., *The Ephemeral Museum: Old Master Paintings and the Rise of the Art Exhibition*, New Haven and London: Yale University Press, 2000

Haskell, F., *Rediscoveries in Art: Some Aspects of Taste, Fashion and Collecting in England and France*, Oxford: Phaidon Press, second edn, 1980

Hervey, M.F.S., *Holbein's 'Ambassadors': The Picture and the Men: An Historical Study*, London: George Bell and Sons, 1900

Hill, D., 'James Pascall and the Long Gallery Suite at Temple Newsam' in *Furniture History*, Vol. 17, 1981, pp. 70–74

Historic England, 'Longford Castle', 2004, https://historicengland.org.uk/listing/the-list/list-entry/1000424 (accessed 21 November 2016)

Holder, R., 'Salvin, Anthony (1799–1881)' in *Oxford Dictionary of National Biography*, Oxford University Press, 2004, http://www.oxforddnb.com/view/article/24585 (accessed 21 February 2017)

Howey, C.L., 'Dressing a Virgin Queen: Court Women, Dress and Fashioning the Image of England's Queen Elizabeth I' in *Early Modern Women*, Vol. 4, Fall 2009, pp. 201–8

Huch, R., *The Radical Lord Radnor: The Public Life of Viscount Folkestone, Third Earl of Radnor, 1779–1869*, Minneapolis: University of Minnesota Press, 1977

Hunt, M., *The Middling Sort: Commerce, Gender, and the Family in England, 1680–1780*, Berkeley and London: University of California Press, 1996

Hussey, C., *English Country Houses: Mid Georgian 1760–1800*, London: Antique Collectors' Club, first published by Country Life Ltd, 1955, 1988

Hussey, C., 'Drawing-Room Furniture in Longford Castle' in *Country Life*, 26 December 1931a, Vol. 70, pp. 715–18

Hussey, C., 'For the Connoisseur: Furniture at Longford Castle – I' in *Country Life*, 12 December 1931b, Vol. 70, pp. 678–82

Hussey, C., 'An Historic English Garden: Parterres at Longford Castle, Wiltshire' in *Country Life*, 10 September 1964, Vol. 136, pp. 608–11

Hussey, C., 'Longford Castle – I. Wilts. The Seat of the Earl of Radnor' in *Country Life*, 12 December 1931c, Vol. 70, pp. 648–55

Hussey, C., 'Longford Castle – II. Wilts. The Seat of the Earl of Radnor' in *Country Life*, 19 December 1931d, Vol. 70, pp. 696–702

Hussey, C., 'Longford Castle – III. Wilts. The Seat of the Earl of Radnor' in *Country Life*, 26 December 1931e, Vol. 70, pp. 724–30

Jackson, P., 'Scharf, Sir George (1820–1895)' in *Oxford Dictionary of National Biography*, Oxford University Press, 2004, online edn, September 2010, http://www.oxforddnb.com/view/article/24796 (accessed 5 April 2016)

Jackson-Stops, G., *The Country House in Perspective*, London: Pavilion, 1990

Jackson-Stops, G., and Pipkin, J., *The English Country House: A Grand Tour*, Boston: Little, Brown and Company; Washington: National Gallery of Art, 1985

Jackson-Stops, G., with the assistance of F. Russell, 'Augustan Taste' in G. Jackson-Stops (ed.), *The Treasure Houses of Britain: Five Hundred Years of Private Patronage and Art Collecting*, Washington, DC: National Gallery of Art; New Haven and London: Yale University Press, 1985a, pp. 322–53

Jackson-Stops, G., with the assistance of F. Russell, 'The Dutch Cabinet' in G. Jackson-Stops (ed.), *The Treasure Houses of Britain: Five Hundred Years of Private Patronage and Art Collecting*, Washington, DC: National Gallery of Art; New Haven and London: Yale University Press, 1985b, pp. 354–75

Jackson-Stops, G., with the assistance of F. Russell, 'The Jacobean Long Gallery' in G. Jackson-Stops (ed.), *The Treasure Houses of Britain: Five Hundred Years of Private Patronage and Art Collecting*, Washington, DC: National Gallery of Art; New Haven and London: Yale University Press, 1985c, p. 124

Jackson-Stops, G., with the assistance of F. Russell, 'Landscape and the Picturesque' in G. Jackson-Stops (ed.), *The Treasure Houses of Britain: Five Hundred Years of Private Patronage and Art Collecting*, Washington, DC: National Gallery of Art; New Haven and London: Yale University Press, 1985d, pp. 376–95

Jackson-Stops, G., with the assistance of F. Russell, 'The Sculpture Rotunda' in G. Jackson-Stops (ed.), *The Treasure Houses of Britain: Five Hundred Years of Private Patronage and Art Collecting*, Washington, DC: National Gallery of Art; New Haven and London: Yale University Press, 1985e, pp. 288–321

Jackson-Stops, G., with the assistance of F. Russell, 'Temples of the Arts' in G. Jackson-Stops (ed.), *The Treasure Houses of Britain: Five Hundred Years of Private Patronage and Art Collecting*, Washington, DC: National Gallery of Art; New Haven and London: Yale University Press, 1985f, pp. 14–21

Jackson-Stops, G. (ed.), *The Treasure Houses of Britain: Five Hundred Years of Private Patronage and Art Collecting*, Washington, DC: National Gallery of Art; New Haven and London: Yale University Press, 1985

Jenkins, I., and Sloan, K., *Vases and Volcanoes: Sir William Hamilton and his Collection*, London: British Museum Press, 1996

Jones, K., and Shawe-Taylor, D., '"An Amiable Philosopher": Queen Caroline and the Encouragement of Learning' in D. Shawe-Taylor (ed.), *The First Georgians: Art and Monarchy, 1714–1760*, London: Royal Collection Trust, 2014, pp. 269–317

Jones, R., and Postle, M., 'Gainsborough in his Painting Room' in M. Rosenthal and M. Myrone (eds), *Gainsborough*, London: Tate Publishing, 2002, pp. 26–39

Jourdain, M., and Rose, F., with a foreword by R. Edwards, *English Furniture: The Georgian Period (1750–1830)*, London: B. T. Batsford Ltd, 1953

Keynes, S., 'The Cult of King Alfred the Great' in *Anglo-Saxon England*, Vol. 28, Cambridge: Cambridge University Press, December 1999, published online 26 September 2008, http://journals.cambridge.org/abstract_S0263675100002337 (accessed 27 March 2015)

Knight, J., 'Coxe, William (1748–1828)' in *Oxford Dictionary of National Biography*, Oxford University Press, 2004, online edn, May 2009, http://www.oxforddnb.com/view/article/6540 (accessed 10 February 2017)

Küster, B., 'Copies on the Market in Eighteenth-Century Britain' in C. Gould and S. Mesplède (eds), *Marketing Art in the British Isles, 1700 to the Present*, Farnham: Ashgate, 2012, pp. 179–93

Laing, A., *In Trust for the Nation: Paintings from National Trust Houses*, London: The National Trust in association with National Gallery Publications, 1995

Laing, A., 'Seguier, William (1772–1843)' in *Oxford Dictionary of National Biography*, Oxford University Press, 2004, http://www.oxforddnb.com/view/article/25045 (accessed 20 February 2017)

Laing, A., 'The Eighteenth-Century English Chimneypiece' in *Studies in the History of Art*, Vol. 25, Symposium Papers X: 'The Fashioning and Functioning of the British Country House', 1989, pp. 241–54

Langford, P., *Public Life and the Propertied Englishman 1689–1798*, Oxford: Clarendon Press, 1991

Langford, P., 'Walpole, Horatio, fourth earl of Orford (1717–1797)' in *Oxford Dictionary of National Biography*, Oxford University Press, 2004, online edn, May 2011, http://www.oxforddnb.com/view/article/28596 (accessed 11 March 2015)

Langley, B., *New Principles of Gardening, or the laying out and planting Parterres … with … directions for raising fruit-trees, etc.*, London: A. Bettesworth and J. Battey, 1728

Larsen, E., *The Paintings of Anthony Van Dyck*, 2 Vols., Luca Verlag Freren, 1988

Laurence, A., 'Space, Status and Gender in English Topographical Paintings, *c.* 1660–*c.* 1740' in *Architectural History*, Vol. 46, 2003, pp. 81–94

Lewis, J.S., 'When a House is not a Home: Elite English Women and the Eighteenth-Century Country House' in *Journal of British Studies*, Vol. 48, No. 2, April 2009, pp. 336–63

Links, J.G., *Canaletto*, second edn, London: Phaidon, 1994

Lippincott, L., *Selling Art in Georgian London: The Rise of Arthur Pond*, New Haven and London: Yale University Press for the Paul Mellon Centre for Studies in British Art, 1983

Lloyd, S., *Richard and Maria Cosway: Regency Artists of Taste and Fashion*, Edinburgh: Scottish National Portrait Gallery, 1995

Lyna, D., 'In Search of a British Connection: Flemish Dealers on the London Art Market and the Taste for Continental Painting (1750–1800)' in C. Gould and S. Mesplède (eds), *Marketing Art in the British Isles, 1700 to the Present*, Farnham: Ashgate, 2012, pp. 101–17

MacGregor, A., 'The Cabinet of Curiosities in Seventeenth-Century Britain' in O. Impey and K. Arnold (eds), *The Origin of Museums: The Cabinet of Curiosities in Sixteenth and Seventeenth Century Europe*, 1985, pp. 147–58

MacGregor, A., *Curiosity and Enlightenment: Collectors and Collections from the Sixteenth to the Nineteenth Century*, New Haven and London: Yale University Press, 2007

MacGregor, N., 'Foreword' in S. Foister, R. Ashok and M. Wyld, *Making and Meaning: Holbein's Ambassadors*, London: National Gallery Publications and Yale University Press, 1997, p. 9

Macquoid, P., and Edwards, H.C.R., *The Dictionary of English Furniture*, 3 vols., revised and enlarged by R. Edwards, London: Country Life Ltd, 1954

Macquoid, P., *A History of English Furniture*, 4 Vols., New York: Dover Publications, 1972

Mandler, P., *The Fall and Rise of the Stately Home*, New Haven and London: Yale University Press, 1997

Mannings, D., *Sir Joshua Reynolds: A Complete Catalogue of His Paintings*, New Haven and London: Yale University Press, 2000

Marschner, J., *Queen Caroline: Cultural Politics at the Early Eighteenth-Century Court*, New Haven and London: Yale University Press, 2014a

Martin, F., 'Camillo Rusconi in English Collections' in C. Sicca and A. Yarrington (eds), *The Lustrous Trade: Material Culture and the History of Sculpture in England and Italy, c. 1700–c. 1860*, London and New York: Leicester University Press, 2000, pp. 49–66

McKellar, E., *Landscapes of London: The City, the Country and the Suburbs 1660–1840*, New Haven and London: Yale University Press for the Paul Mellon Centre for Studies in British Art, 2013

Metropolitan Museum of Art, 'Juan de Pareja (1606–1670)', http://www.metmuseum.org/art/collection/search/437869 (accessed 20 January 2017).

Meyer, A., 'Re-dressing Classical Statuary: The Eighteenth-Century "Hand-in-Waistcoat" Portrait' in *The Art Bulletin*, Vol. 77, No. 1, March 1995, pp. 45–63

Miles, E.G., 'Introduction' in Iveagh Bequest, Kenwood, *Thomas Hudson 1701–1779: Portrait Painter and Collector: A Bicentenary Exhibition*, London: Greater London Council, 1979

Mitchell, L., 'The First Univ. Dining Club' in *University College Record*, August 1970, Vol. 5, 1966–1970, pp. 351–58

Moir, E., *The Discovery of Britain: The English Tourists 1540–1840*, London: Routledge and Kegan Paul, 1964

Moir, E., 'Touring Country Houses in the 18th Century' in *Country Life*, Vol. 126, 22 October 1959, pp. 586–88

Moore, A., 'Fountaine, Sir Andrew (1676–1753)' in *Oxford Dictionary of National Biography*, Oxford University Press, 2004, www.oxforddnb.com/view/article/9994 (accessed 1 December 2014)

Moore, A. (ed.), *Houghton Hall: The Prime Minister, the Empress, and the Heritage*, London: Philip Wilson, 1996

Moore, A., 'Sir Robert Walpole: The Prime Minister as Collector' in

A. Moore (ed.), *Houghton Hall: The Prime Minister, the Empress, and the Heritage*, London: Philip Wilson, 1996, pp. 48–55

Morel, T., 'The Cabinet Room' in T. Morel (ed.), *Houghton Revisited*, first published for the exhibition 'Houghton Revisited: The Walpole Masterpieces from Catherine the Great's Hermitage', 2013, London: Royal Academy of Arts, 2013a, p. 138

Morel, T., 'Houghton Revisited: An Introduction' in T. Morel (ed.), *Houghton Revisited*, first published for the exhibition 'Houghton Revisited: The Walpole Masterpieces from Catherine the Great's Hermitage', London: Royal Academy of Arts, 2013b, pp. 31–43

Morel, T. (ed.), *Houghton Revisited*, first published for the exhibition 'Houghton Revisited: The Walpole Masterpieces from Catherine the Great's Hermitage', London: Royal Academy of Arts, 2013

Morris, C., 'Introduction' in C. Fiennes, *The Journeys of Celia Fiennes*, ed. and with an introduction by C. Morris, with a foreword by G.M. Trevelyan, O.M., London: The Cresset Press, 1949, pp. xiii–xliii

Mount, H., 'The Monkey with the Magnifying Glass: Constructions of the Connoisseur in Eighteenth-Century Britain' in *Oxford Art Journal*, Vol. 29, No. 2, 2006, pp. 167+169–84

Murdoch, T., and Vigne, R., *The French Hospital in England: Its Huguenot History and Collections*, Cambridge: John Adamson, 2009

Murdoch, T. ,'Side Table, British, circa 1740' in C. Wilk (ed.), *Western Furniture: 1350 to the Present Day in the Victoria and Albert Museum, London*, London: Philip Wilson, 1996, p. 92

National Gallery, 'About the Building', 2017, https://www.nationalgallery.org.uk/paintings/history/about-the-building/about-the-building (accessed 21 March 2017)

National Gallery, 'A Winter Scene with Skaters near a Castle', 2016, https://www.nationalgallery.org.uk/paintings/hendrick-avercamp-a-winter-scene-with-skaters-near-a-castle (accessed 16 November 2016)

Newman, G., and Brown, L.E., *Britain in the Hanoverian Age, 1714–1837: An Encyclopedia*, Taylor & Francis, 1997

Nisser, W., *Michael Dahl and the Contemporary Swedish School of Painting in England*, Uppsala: Almqvist & Wiksells Boktryckeri-Aktiebolag, 1927

OED Online, Oxford University Press, December 2014, http://www.oed.com/view/Entry/46038?redirectedFrom=curiosity (accessed 20 February 2015)

Ousby, I., *The Englishman's England: Taste, Travel and the Rise of Tourism*, Cambridge and New York: Cambridge University Press, 1990

Paoletti, J.T., 'Familiar Objects: Sculptural Types in the Collections of the Early Medici' in S. Blake McHam (ed.), *Looking at Italian Renaissance Sculpture*, Cambridge: Cambridge University Press, 1998, pp. 79–110

Passavant, J.D., *Tour of a German Artist in England, with Notices of Private Galleries, and Remarks on the State of Art*, 2 Vols., 1836

Pears, I., *The Discovery of Painting: The Growth of Interest in the Arts in England 1680–1768*, New Haven and London: Yale University Press, 1988

Pembroke, Lord, 'Introduction' in *A Catalogue of the Paintings and Drawings in the Collection at Wilton House*, New York and London: Phaidon, 1968, pp. 1–9

Penny, N., 'An Ambitious Man: The Career and Achievements of Sir Joshua Reynolds' in N. Penny (ed.) with contributions by D. Donald, D. Mannings, J. Newman, N. Penny, A. Ribeiro, R. Rosenblum and M. Kirby Talley Jr., *Reynolds*, London: Royal Academy of Arts and Weidenfeld & Nicolson, 1986, pp. 17–42

Penny, N., with the assistance of S. Avery-Quash, *A Guide to Longford Castle*, 2012

Penny, N. (ed.), with contributions by D. Donald, D. Mannings, J. Newman, N. Penny, A. Ribeiro, R. Rosenblum and M. Kirby Talley Jr., *Reynolds*, London: Royal Academy of Arts and Weidenfeld & Nicolson, 1986

Perry, G., Retford, K., and Vibert, J., 'Introduction' in G. Perry, K. Retford and J. Vibert (eds), *Placing Faces: The Portrait and the English Country House in the Long Eighteenth Century*, Manchester: Manchester University Press, 2013, pp. 1–36

Pevsner, N., *The Buildings of England 26: Wiltshire*, Harmondsworth: Penguin, 1963

Pincus, D., 'Introduction' in D. Pincus (ed.), *Small Bronzes in the Renaissance*, New Haven and London: Yale University Press, 2001, pp. 9–13

Pointon, M., *Hanging the Head: Portraiture and Social Formation in Eighteenth-Century England*, New Haven and London: Yale University Press for the Paul Mellon Centre for Studies in British Art, 1993

Powys Marks, S., 'The Journals of Mrs Philip Lybbe Powys (1738–1817) A Half Century of Visits to Bath' in *Bath History*, Vol. IX, 2002, pp. 28–63, https://www.bathspa.ac.uk/Media/CHC%20Images/Vol%2009%20-%2002.%20Marks%20-%20The%20Journals%20of%20Mrs%20Philip%20Lybbe%20Powys%20(1738-1817),%20A%20Half%20Century%20of%20Visits%20to%20Bath.pdf (accessed 25 June 2015)

Radnor, H.M., *From a Great Grandmother's Armchair*, London: Marshall Press, 1927

Radnor, H.M., and Barclay Squire, W., with a preface by Jacob, 6th Earl of Radnor, *Catalogue of the Pictures in the Collection of the Earl of Radnor*, 2 parts, London: privately printed at the Chiswick Press, 1909

Radnor, H.M., *Catalogue of the Pictures in the Collection of the Earl of Radnor*, third edn, ed. and revised by W. Barclay Squire, London: privately printed at the Chiswick Press, 1916

Radnor, J., *A Huguenot Family*, Winchester: Foxbury Press, 2001

Reaney, P.H., *A Dictionary of English Surnames*, revised third edn with corrections and additions by R.M. Wilson, Oxford: Oxford University Press, 1995

Retford, K., *The Art of Domestic Life: Family Portraiture in Eighteenth-Century England*, New Haven and London: Yale University Press, 2006

Reynolds, G., 'Late Eighteenth-Century Miniatures by Richard Cosway and Andrew Plimer' in G. Sutherland (ed.), *British Art 1740–1820: Essays in Honour of Robert R. Wark*, San Marino,

California: Huntington Library and Art Gallery, 1992, pp. 115–24

Richardson, J., *The Works of Jonathan Richardson*, London: T. Davies, 1773

Rijksmuseum, 'Winter Landscape with Ice Skaters, Hendrick Avercamp, *c.* 1608', 2016, https://www.rijksmuseum.nl/en/collection/SK-A-1718 (accessed 16 November 2016)

Roelofs, P., 'The Paintings: The Dutch on Ice', in P. Roelofs (ed.), *Hendrick Avercamp: Master of the Ice Scene*, 2009, pp. 32–5

Roethlisberger, M., *Claude Lorrain: The Paintings*, 2 vols., London: Zwemmer, 1961

Rosenthal, M., *The Art of Thomas Gainsborough: 'A Little Business for the Eye'*, New Haven & London: Yale University Press for the Paul Mellon Centre for Studies in British Art, 1999

Rowlands, J., *Holbein: The Paintings of Hans Holbein the Younger*, complete edn, Phaidon: Oxford, 1985

Schama, S., 'Perishable Commodities: Dutch Still-Life Painting and the "Empire of Things"' in J. Brewer and R. Porter (eds), *Consumption and the World of Goods*, London and New York: Routledge, 1993, pp. 478–88

Sebag-Montefiore, C., with J.I. Armstrong-Totten, *A Dynasty of Dealers: John Smith and his Successors, 1801–1924: A Study of the Art Market of Nineteenth-Century London*, London: Roxburghe Club, distributed by Maggs Bros., 2013

Sheppard, F.H.W. (ed.), 'Cork Street and Savile Row Area: Table of notable inhabitants on the Burlington Estate' in *Survey of London: St James Westminster, Part 2*, 47 vols., London: London County Council, 1963, Vols. XXXI and XXXII, pp. 566–72, *British History Online*, http://www.british-history.ac.uk/survey-london/vols31-2/pt2/pp566-572 (accessed 28 June 2016)

Sicca, C., and Yarrington, A., 'Introduction' in C. Sicca and A. Yarrington (eds), *The Lustrous Trade: Material Culture and the History of Sculpture in England and Italy, c. 1700–c. 1860*, London and New York: Leicester University Press, 2000, pp. 1–25

Silver, L., *The Paintings of Quinten Massys with Catalogue Raisonné*, Phaidon: Oxford, 1984

Sloan, K., '"Picture-mad in virtu-land", Sir William Hamilton's Collections of Paintings' in I. Jenkins and K. Sloan, *Vases and Volcanoes: Sir William Hamilton and his Collection*, London: British Museum Press, 1996, pp. 75–92

Smith, A., '"The Adoration of the Shepherds" in the Radnor Art Collection' in *Art Italies*, No. 21, September 2016a, pp. 67–73

Smith, A., 'Lord Folkestone and the Society of Arts: Picturing the First President', *William Shipley Group for RSA History Occasional Paper*, No. 29, April 2016b

Smith, R., 'Carpenter, Margaret (Sarah)' in *Concise Dictionary of Women Artists*, ed. D. Graze, London: Fitzroy Dearborn, 2001, pp. 223–25

Smith, R., 'Carpenter, Margaret Sarah (1793–1872)' in *Oxford Dictionary of National Biography*, Oxford University Press, 2004, http://www.oxforddnb.com/view/article/4732 (accessed 3 March 2016)

Spiker, S.H., *Travels through England, Wales and Scotland in the Year 1816*, 2 vols., 1820

Spring, E., *Law, Land, & Family: Aristocratic Inheritance in England, 1300 to 1800*, Chapel Hill and London: The University of North Carolina Press, 1994

Steward, J.C., *The New Child: British Art and the Origins of Modern Childhood, 1730–1830*, Berkeley, California: University Art Museum and Pacific Film Archive, University of California in association with the University of Washington Press, 1995

Stewart, R., *The Town House in Georgian London*, New Haven and London: Yale University Press, 2009

Stone, L., and Stone, J.C.F., *An Open Elite? England 1540–1880*, Oxford: Clarendon Press, 1984

Stourton, J., and Sebag-Montefiore, C., *The British as Art Collectors: From the Tudors to the Present*, London: Scala, 2012

Strong, R., *The Artist and the Garden*, New Haven and London: Yale University Press, 2000

Strong, R., 'Eworth, Hans (*d.* 1574)' rev. in *Oxford Dictionary of National Biography*, Oxford University Press, 2004, http://www.oxforddnb.com/view/article/37404 (accessed 9 February 2017)

Strong, R., 'The Radnor Miniatures' in J. Herbert (ed.), *Christie's Review of the Season 1974*, Hutchinson of London/Harry N. Abrams, Inc., New York, 1974, pp. 254–57

Strong, R., *The Renaissance Garden in England*, London: Thames and Hudson, 1998

Sullivan, R.J., *A Tour Through Parts of England, Scotland, and Wales, in 1778. In a Series of Letters*, 2 vols., London, 1785

Summerson, J., *Architecture in Britain 1530 to 1830*, New Haven and London: Yale University Press, first published 1953 by Penguin Books Ltd, ninth edn published by Yale University Press, 1993

Summerson, J., 'The Book of Architecture of John Thorpe in Sir John Soane's Museum, with biographical and analytical studies' in *The Walpole Society*, Vol. XL, Glasgow: Walpole Society, 1966

Sweet, R., *Antiquaries: The Discovery of the Past in Eighteenth-Century Britain*, London and New York: Hambledon and London, 2004

Tadmor, N., *Family and Friends in Eighteenth-Century England: Household, Kinship, and Patronage*, Cambridge: Cambridge University Press, 2001

Tate, 'Samuel Scott, A View of London Bridge before the Late Alterations', 2004a, http://www.tate.org.uk/art/artworks/scott-a-view-of-london-bridge-before-the-late-alterations-n00313 (accessed 18 July 2016)

Tate, 'Samuel Scott, A View of Westminster Bridge and Parts Adjacent', 2004b, http://www.tate.org.uk/art/artworks/scott-a-view-of-westminster-bridge-and-parts-adjacent-n00314 (accessed 18 July 2016)

Thomson, W.G., *A History of Tapestry from the Earliest Times until the Present Day*, third edn, with revisions ed. F.P. & E.S. Thomson, EP Publishing Limited, 1973

Thornton, P., *Authentic Décor: The Domestic Interior 1620–1920*, Weidenfeld & Nicolson: London, 1984

Tinniswood, A., *A History of Country House Visiting: Five Centuries of Tourism and Taste*, Oxford: Basil Blackwell in association with the National Trust, 1989

Turner, N., 'John Bouverie as a Collector of Drawings' in *The Burlington Magazine*, Vol. 136, No. 1091, February 1994, pp. 90–99

Turner, R., *Capability Brown and the Eighteenth-Century English Landscape*, London: Weidenfeld & Nicolson, 1985

Vertue, G., 'The Note Books of George Vertue Relating to Artists and Collections in England' in *The Walpole Society*, Vol. V, Oxford: Walpole Society, 1938

Vickery, A., *Behind Closed Doors: At Home in Georgian England*, New Haven and London: Yale University Press, 2010

Victoria and Albert Museum, 'Norfolk House Music Room', 2016, http://www.vam.ac.uk/content/galleries/level-2/room-52nh-norfolk-house-music-room/ (accessed 12 January 2016)

Victoria and Albert Museum, 'Longford Table', http://collections.vam.ac.uk/item/O55196/longford-table-side-table-goodison-benjamin/ (accessed 4 November 2016)

Waagen, G.F., *Galleries and Cabinets of Art in Great Britain: Being an Account of More than Forty Collections of Paintings, Drawings, Sculptures, Mss., &c. &c. Visited in 1854 and 1856, and now for the first time described*, A Supplemental Volume to the Treasures of Art in Great Britain, 3 vols., London: Albemarle Street, 1857, facsimile reprint published by Cornmarket Press, London, 1970

Waagen, G.F., *Works of Art and Artists in England*, 3 vols., London: John Murray, Albemarle Street, 1838, facsimile reprint published by Cornmarket Press, London, 1970

Walpole, H., *Aedes Walpolianae: or, a Description of the Collection of Pictures at Houghton-Hall in Norfolk, the Seat of the Right Honourable Sir Robert Walpole, Earl of Orford*, third edn, London, 1767

Walpole, H., *Anecdotes of Painting in England; with Some Account of the Principal Artists*, new edn revised by R.N. Wornum, 3 vols., London: Swan Sonnenschein, Lowrey & Co., 1888

Ward, G.W.R., *The Grove Encyclopedia of Materials and Techniques in Art*, Oxford: Oxford University Press, 2008

Ware, I., *A Complete Body of Architecture, Adorned with Plans and Elevations from Original Designs, Etc.*, London: T. Osborne and J. Shipton, 1768

Waterfield, G. (ed.), *Palaces of Art: Art Galleries in Britain 1790–1990*, London: Dulwich Picture Gallery, 1991a

Waterfield, G., 'Picture Hanging and Gallery Decoration' in G. Waterfield (ed.), *Palaces of Art: Art Galleries in Britain 1790–1990*, London: Dulwich Picture Gallery, 1991b, pp. 49–65

Waterfield, G., 'The Origins of the Early Picture Gallery Catalogue in Europe, and its Manifestation in Victorian Britain' in S. Pearce (ed.), *Art in Museums*, London: Athlone, 1995a, pp. 42–73

Waterfield, G., 'The Town House as Gallery of Art' in *The London Journal*, Vol. 20, No. 1, 1995b, pp. 47–66

Waterhouse, E.K., *Reynolds*, London: Kegan Paul, Trench Trubner & Co., 1941

Webb, M.I., *Michael Rysbrack, Sculptor*, London: Country Life Ltd, 1954

West, S., 'Framing Hegemony: Economics, Luxury and Family Continuity in the Country House Portrait' in P. Duro (ed.), *The Rhetoric of the Frame: Essays on the Boundaries of the Artwork*, Cambridge: Cambridge University Press, 1996, pp. 63–78

Weyer, F.W., 'Foreword' in Iveagh Bequest, Kenwood, *Thomas Hudson 1701–1779: Portrait Painter and Collector: A Bicentenary Exhibition*, London: Greater London Council, 1979

Whitehead, C., *The Public Art Museum in Nineteenth Century Britain: The Development of the National Gallery*, Aldershot: Ashgate, 2005

Whitelock, A., *Elizabeth's Bedfellows: An Intimate History of the Queen's Court*, London: Bloomsbury, 2013

Williamson, T., *Polite Landscapes: Gardens and Society in Eighteenth-Century England*, Stroud: Sutton, 1995

Wine, H., *National Gallery Catalogues: The Seventeenth Century French Paintings*, London: Yale University Press and the National Gallery Company, 2001

Wood, A., *A History of the Levant Company*, London: Frank Cass & Co Ltd, 1964

Woolfe, J., and Gandon, J., *Vitruvius Britannicus, or the British Architect; containing Plans, Elevations and Sections; of the Regular Buildings both Public and Private in Great Britain, comprised in one hundred folio plates, engrav'd by the best hands; taken from the buildings, or original designs*, 5 vols., 1771

Conference and seminar papers

Marschner, J., 'Becoming British: Queen Caroline and Collecting', paper given at *Enlightened Monarchs: Art at Court in the Eighteenth Century* study day organised by The Wallace Collection, Royal Collection Trust and Centre for Court Studies, 7 May 2014b

ACKNOWLEDGEMENTS

This book is based on the PhD thesis I completed between 2013 and 2017 as part of a Collaborative Doctoral Partnership between Birkbeck, University of London, and the National Gallery, which was funded by support received from the Arts and Humanities Research Council.

I would first like to thank the Earl and Countess of Radnor for their kindness and generosity in facilitating my research, by welcoming me into their home and allowing me access to their art collection, and for making the publication of this book a possibility.

I would also like to thank the following individuals who assisted in the supervision and examination of my doctorate: Kate Retford, Susanna Avery-Quash, Sir Nicholas Penny, Lynda Nead, Alison Yarrington and John Bonehill. Many others have provided advice and insights during the research that led to this book, and I would like to thank them for their time, especially Jocelyn Anderson, Philip Attwood, the late David Allan, Susan Bennett, Susannah Brooke, Michael Burden, Oliver Cox, Robin Darwall-Smith, John Goodall, Peter Humfrey, Adrian James, John Kitching, Catherine Loisel, Harriet O'Neill, Alexandra Ormerod, Philippa Martin, Tessa Murdoch, Peter Schade, Charles Sebag-Montefiore and Richard Stephens.

Thanks are also due to the archivists and staff at institutions where I have undertaken research on Longford Castle and its art collection, especially Claire Skinner, Steven Hobbs and the late Robert Pearson at the Wiltshire and Swindon History Centre, and Peter Durrant at the Berkshire Record Office.

Thanks also to those who have assisted me at the British Library; the British Museum Prints and Drawings Room; Cambridge University Library; the Heinz Archive at the National Portrait Gallery; the Fitzwilliam Museum Reference Library; the National Archives; the National Gallery Research Centre; the Paul Mellon Centre for Studies in British Art; the Royal Academy Archive; the Research Library and Archive at Sir John Soane's Museum; the Royal Society of Arts Archive; Senate House Library; the Prints and Drawings Room, Blythe House Reading Room and the National Art Library at the Victoria and Albert Museum; and the Witt Library at the Courtauld Institute of Art.

I would also like to thank Ian Strathcarron, Lucy Duckworth, Elisabeth Ingles and Michael Mitchell, with whom I have worked on this book. Finally, I would like to mention my family, who have provided support, encouragement and inspiration over the years: especially Richard Phillips, Emma and Dave Smith, and Andrew and Marianne Routh.

Amelia Smith

INDEX

Page numbers in *italics* refer to the figures (paintings, illustrations and photographs).
The names of the owners of Longford are indexed by surname as used in the text (des Bouverie, Bouverie, Pleydell-Bouverie); their wives are indexed by their maiden names, as shown in the text.